Crime and Social Change in Middle England

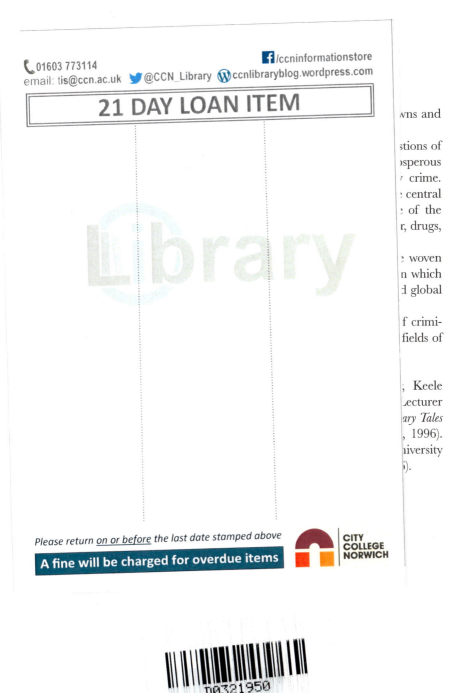

vns and

stions of
)sperous
r crime.
: central
: of the
r, drugs,

: woven
n which
d global

f crimi-
fields of

; Keele
Lecturer
ary Tales
, 1996).
hiversity
).

ID321950

Crime and Social Change in Middle England

Questions of Order in an English Town

Evi Girling, Ian Loader and Richard Sparks

London and New York

First published 2000
by Routledge
11 New Fetter Lane, London EC4P 4EE

Simultaneously published in the USA and Canada
by Routledge
29 West 35th Street, New York, NY 10001

Routledge is an imprint of the Taylor & Francis Group

© 2000 Evi Girling, Ian Loader and Richard Sparks

Typeset in Baskerville by Taylor & Francis Books Ltd
Printed and bound in Great Britain by St Edmundsbury Press, St
Edmundsbury, Suffolk

British Library Cataloguing in Publication Data
A catalogue record for this book is available from the British Library

Library of Congress Cataloging in Publication Data
Girling, Evi,
Crime and social change in Middle England: questions of order in an
English town/Evi Girling, Ian Loader, and Richard Sparks
Includes bibliographical references and index.
1. Crime – England – Macclesfield. 2. Crime prevention – England
–Macclesfield. 3. Police – England – Macclesfield. 4. Social change –
England – Macclesfield. 5. Macclesfield (England) – Social conditions –
20th Century. I. Loader, Ian. II. Sparks, Richard. III. Title
HV6950.M23G57   1999
364.9427'16–dc21   99-16452
CIP

ISBN 0–415–18335–9 (hbk)
ISBN 0–415–18336–7 (pbk)

In memory of Mike Collison, criminologist and biker, 1950–1996

Because I know that time is always time
And place is always and only place
And what is actual is actual only for one time
And only for one place
(T.S. Eliot, 'Ash Wednesday', 1930)

Contents

Preface and acknowledgements

In one of its advertising campaigns Barclaycard (a leading brand of credit card in Britain) deployed the following slogan:

> For instant cash around the world (including Macclesfield) all you need is your Barclaycard.

In the ads two Englishmen abroad (they are comic sub-Graham Greene types of middle-class Anglos) try to obtain money and services in a variety of exotic foreign locations. The comic hook of each vignette is the refusal of one of them (the pompous all-knowing one) to believe that credit cards work in such remote places. He therefore attempts various arcane and always disastrous forms of barter and bribe, while his junior colleague sorts it all out with his Barclaycard.

Of more pressing interest here than the use (part satirical, part complicit) of assumed English attitudes to all things foreign is the introduction of the name of Macclesfield into this scenario, since it is where the work reported in this book has been conducted. 'Macclesfield' seems to work in the ads as an ironic counterpoint to 'foreign parts' – if they are comically and excessively alien, it is comically and excessively English. By extension it is also *parochially* English: the expression 'around the world (including London)' would be baffling. So some degree of surprise (and amusement) must also attach to the idea that Barclaycard works *in Macclesfield*; that is, to the fact that this seemingly obscure English town (tucked away in the Cheshire countryside some 180 miles north of London and 15 miles from the nearest metropolis, Manchester) is part of the global system of financial services.[1]

Between 1994 and 1996, we conducted an intensive study of public concerns about, and responses to, crime as we encountered them in this unremarkable, relatively untroubled, moderately prosperous English town (and its neighbouring affluent village-suburb of Prestbury). We spent two years studying official documents and statistics, observing meetings, travelling in police cars and, above all, talking to people – residents, 'opinion-formers', criminal justice and other professionals – who live or work there. We spoke with them, individually and in groups, sometimes formally with a tape recorder running, sometimes much more casually, often at great length, about 'their town', their sense of its conflicts, problems and divisions, their memories of its past and their hopes and fears for its future, and about how this particular place was entangled (or not) with their own individual biographies. They also talked about the crimes that worried them, who they thought was committing them and why, what they thought ought to done about them and by whom, and about the steps they take – or might take – to provide themselves with a sense of security. This book – in large measure – is a record of these activities and conversations.

Yet, concerned as we have been to document the experiences, anxieties and aspirations of people living in this one small corner of 'Middle England', we also hope this book can make some small contribution to debates that stretch far beyond the boundaries of Macclesfield as such. There are two ways in which we think this is so. We have, first of all, endeavoured to take up and develop some of the *theoretical* issues that processes of 'globalization' raise for the study of 'local' places. In the world that we inhabit, the fortunes and prospects of any particular place are dependent on flows of capital and culture that lie beyond local (perhaps any) control, and on decisions taken quite elsewhere. We have set out to interpret and make sense of the sensibilities towards crime found among the people of Macclesfield in light of this aspect of contemporary social relations and social change. Yet, at the same time, we have sought to temper some of the more sweeping and speculative assertions of contemporary social commentary through close and detailed observation and interpretation in a local setting. Even in a mobile, wired interconnected world people continue to develop important material and emotional attachments to 'place', and crime and order can figure centrally in how these places are experienced, imagined and defended.

There are, second, various *substantive* aspects of the account that follows that resonate far beyond Macclesfield's borders. At its most mundane, this flows from our respondents' concerns with matters – such as burglary, drugs, conflicts about teenage disorder, experiences and demands of the police, the proliferation of alternative modes of protection, such as CCTV and private security – that arouse acute passions and political controversies in many different places. It stems also from the fact that, in speaking about these matters, people's crime-talk touches upon questions – to do with justice and welfare, inclusion and exclusion, the respective roles of citizen, state and market – that lie at the heart of contemporary debates about, and reconfigurations of, crime control. And it has to do with the fact that the responses to crime we document in this book – who people blame, the boundaries and distinctions they draw, the kinds of justice they seek, the forms of order they wish to preserve (or recreate) – reveal much about the place that crime occupies, not only within people's everyday lives and consciousness, but within contemporary social relations more generally.

This then is a book about how people in one English town think, feel and talk about crime and social order. But it also, in our view, testifies to some of the most pressing and tender concerns of our age, and in so doing demonstrates that our responses to crime cannot properly be disconnected from questions about the character and future prospects of our civic life and political institutions.

Since we commenced this study back in 1994, we have been fortunate to receive the encouragement and support of a great many people. First and foremost, we would like to offer our thanks to all those who assisted with or participated in our study, whether in a personal or professional capacity. Our special thanks go to all those Macclesfield and Prestbury residents who gave up their time to talk to us. Thanks are also due to the Hurdsfield, Moss Rose, Upton Priory, Weston and Victoria Park residents' associations; and to those staff of Macclesfield Police division, the Probation and Youth services, Macclesfield Crime Prevention Panel, Macclesfield Borough Council, Cheshire County Council, Prestbury Parish Council, Macclesfield Civic Society, Zeneca Pharmaceuticals PLC and a variety of other organizations who helped us in various ways. The assistance we received from many people went far beyond what we could reasonably have hoped to expect and we are grateful to all concerned – even if our promises of anonymity prevent us from acknowledging individuals by name.

Beyond Macclesfield, some thanks are also due. The research was funded by the Economic and Social Research Council as part of its 'Crime and Social Order' research programme, and we gratefully acknowledge their support (award no. L210252032). The Programme's Director, our colleague Tim Hope, was a source of continual help and encouragement; and we were also much stimulated and sustained by our interactions with other colleagues during the lifetime of the Programme. They included Tony Jefferson, Wendy Hollway, Betsy Stanko and Sandra Walklate. Pat Carlen helped us get the whole thing off the ground. She has never ceased to be a source of personal and intellectual support; so too was Ronnie Frankenberg in his role as 'project consultant'. Our thanks are also due to Leslie Bailey and Carole Maloney for transcribing the tapes and, in a similar vein, to Andrew Lawrence of the Department of Environmental Social Sciences at Keele for the maps, and Jon Sparks for the photograph that adorns the front cover. We also wish to thank all those who have at various points over the last several years proffered advice and suggestions on the various presentations and papers we have delivered or written, whether in the spirit of empathetic encouragement, or simply because they couldn't work out where the project was going or why an earth we were bothering to do it. They might not realize it, but Malin Åkeström, Tony Bottoms, Richard Ericson, Jack Katz, Sonia Livingstone, Vincenzo Ruggiero, Ian Taylor and Jock Young (among others) have contributed in one or other of these ways. Many thanks.

Finally, we want to place on record our appreciation of our colleagues (past and present) in the Department of Criminology at Keele, who, through the thick and thin of the last few years, have continued to make Keele the most convivial and intellectually stimulating of places in which to 'do' criminology (or should that be do 'criminology'?). During the course of this project, the department suffered the loss of Mike Collison, a much loved and respected colleague, and a stalwart of criminology at Keele. It is to his example and memory that we dedicate this book.

The authors and publisher would like to thank, respectively, Oxford University Press and Macmillan Press Ltd for permission to reproduce in

Chapter 4 and Chapters 6 and 7, material that appeared in an earlier form in the following places:

'Narratives of Decline: Youth, Dis/order and Community in an English "Middletown"', *British Journal of Criminology* 38, 3: 388–403, 1998.
'Landscapes of Protection: The Past, Present and Futures of Policing in an English Town', in P. Carlen and R. Morgan (eds) *Crime Unlimited: Questions for the Twenty-First Century*, Basingstoke: Macmillan, 1999.

1 Speaking of crime

Towards a sociology of public sensibilities

This is a book about people's responses to crime in an English town. For us both parts of this statement – that the book is about responses to crime and that it is about a town in England – are equally important. We begin from the view that people's responses to crime (the anxieties, fears and passions that it evokes in people, and the sorts of talk and action in which they may engage concerning it) are complex and variable matters. In that they are complex there may be numerous defensible ways of studying them, each of which may illuminate some different dimension of that complexity. The way that we have chosen seeks in particular to locate some of those public responses and dispositions within the social relations of one locality as we encountered them in the mid-1990s.

The place in question is Macclesfield, Cheshire in north-west England about fifteen miles south of Manchester. It is a place not wholly unlike many other small and medium-sized towns that dot the landscape of the English 'shires' – representative in some respects, unique in others (Hoggart 1993); and it bears in turn a more than passing resemblance to other more distant places elsewhere in Europe and North America. It is a place with a long history (here signified in the Old English resonances of its very name) and with its present portion of continuities and attachments, uncertainties, disruptions and discontents. It is not in essence an unusual or atypical place, falling as it perhaps does within what has in recent years come to be known, especially to journalists, as 'Middle England'.[1] Yet to much of criminology and urban sociology, by turns mesmerized and appalled by the drama, romance, glamour and degradation of the city, such places are still largely alien and unfamiliar.

Our decision to site our study in one place (and in such a place) arises from our conviction that some prior approaches to public responses to crime (commonly summarized under the deceptively simple yet contentious rubric 'fear of crime') have laboured under certain self-imposed theoretical and methodological restrictions. These traditions of research have generated much valuable information and given rise to no little amount of (sometimes heated and crabby) argument. They have also served to position 'the fear of crime' close to the heart of academic, media and political discussion of crime and crime control policy. Yet, we consider, they have also left much unsaid about the meanings-in-use of crime and its attendant concerns, anxieties and conflicts for people in the ordinary settings of their lives. We therefore set out to develop a way of investigating these topics that was both adequately sensitive to the nuance, detail and variety of things *that people may be saying when they speak about crime* and sufficiently alert to the particularities of the contexts in which they are said. In other words, we felt that at this point in the development of the subject there was something to be gained by studying public orientations towards crime *intensively* and *in situ*. The greater part of this book is thus devoted to a substantive account of what we think we discovered during two years of field research in the town and our subsequent efforts of analysis and interpretation. This introductory chapter elaborates and defends our views on why we think a detailed study of a single place remains a worthwhile activity to pursue in a global age (that is often said to be eroding the differences between places); outlines the reasons for our dissatisfaction with the current terms of what has come to be known as 'the fear of crime debate'; and proffers a brief summary of, and reflection upon, the research we actually undertook.

For the most part, we hope, this book wears its theoretical and strictly 'academic' concerns quite lightly. It is in the first place a report of empirical research rather than a novel contribution to social theory.[2] Nevertheless it should also be clear that there is intrinsically a rather expansive theoretical hinterland surrounding a research enterprise like this one. Were this not the case we would scarcely have been justified in persuading citizens of Macclesfield out of their houses to talk to us in draughty rooms on winter evenings – for we would be doing nothing beyond relaying back to them what they already know, however stimulating we, and we hope and believe they, may have found the experience. It is far from *self-evident* that bringing people together to talk about crime (and a relative handful of people at that, in a very restricted geographical location) is an important or useful thing to do – indeed no topic in the social sciences is its own automatic justification. Rather it is up to us to establish its relevance and interest – its little contribution to the self-understandings of our time and perhaps to the democratic deliberation of questions that trouble and vex us. This does mean, however, that some of the points in this chapter will unavoidably be a bit more dense and abstract than those that follow. We hope this will not tax the reader's patience overmuch.

Imagine four kinds of sceptical questioner, each uncertain about the relevance of a qualitative study of dispositions towards crime in a medium-sized English town. They are quite different from each other, so satisfying all of them within one text may prove taxing.

The first is an academic, perhaps one whom we greatly respect. He or she might say:

> Why have you knowingly gone to such an obscure location and only one, wilfully eschewing comparison? Surely you know that the action these days is in the arenas of serious and transnational crime and in crime control developments of international scale and reach? The world is whirling around our heads. Cities are in turmoil; prisons are full to overflowing;

billions of dollars' worth of illegal trade in arms, drugs, pornography are shifted daily. Meanwhile the entrepreneurs of crime control and 'security' never tire in their ingenuity with new gadgets, technologies and devices whose consequences we can hardly guess at; while populist politicians and media moguls are locked in a hideous embrace of exploitation and incitement. Democratic values, hard-won liberties, the sovereignty of the state itself are under threat from these and other sources. And here you are merrily trundling round the streets of Macclesfield, wherever that is! How can you justify such miniaturism now? *What can this tell me about any of the big questions – about globalization, about the emergence of a risk society, about the fates of modernity?*

The second is an administrator, or perhaps an 'administrative criminologist'. He or she says:

Why have you abandoned measurement in favour of interpretation when I have such beautiful and refined instruments for measuring fear these days? Of course our surveys used to be rather crude but we have worked long, hard and patiently to improve the questions, the sampling and the analysis. We can do time-series, we can do cross-sections and we can do international comparisons. We can break down the results by age, gender, class, race, residence, victimization experiences, political affiliation – you name it. We can do inputs, outputs, cross-tabs, regressions, factor analyses and multi-dimensional scaling. I'm sure your work is all very interesting, and no offence. *But what can you say that can inform policy in any way? What can I take into Ministers and sell?*

The third questioner is also a researcher, or at least a knowledge-worker of sorts. This one might be an opinion pollster, a focus-group investigator or perhaps a political adviser working for a political party, a pressure group or even (in these promotionalist times) a public sector agency. This distant cousin of ours is in her or his own fashion an activist, one who wants to anticipate and indeed to shape the public agenda on crime control and who therefore also seeks to 'take the pulse' of public feeling on crime but with distinct strategic aims in view. He or she might say to us:

I too am interested in finding out about public responses to crime and, like you, I know them to be replete with complications. Neither are my methods for doing so entirely dissimilar to yours. But I need to be able to translate this knowledge into recommendations, briefings and action plans. What can you tell me that I do not know already by my own means? What is there here that my think-tank or policy unit can use to convince hard-bitten politicians of left, right or 'third way' persuasion (who, incidentally, already believe that they know precisely what the public think and feel about crime) to take up this or that innovation in crime control policy? *In what ways does such a programme of research illuminate the contemporary political agenda on 'law and order'?*

Finally there is a more plural group of questioners. They are Macclesfield residents, or people living in another place which resembles it more or less closely. One is perhaps a pensioner living in a small house she bought from the Borough Council on an estate on the northern edge of the town. She says:

> It's not so bad round here but it isn't what it was. There are kids on the corner and they're not very polite. There are big steel shutters on all the shops. There are cars burning on the estate some nights. There's something bad in the paper every day and more mayhem on the telly. Even if I read your book would I be able to understand it? *Does any of this make any difference to someone like me?*

Next come a married couple of middle years – he is perhaps a self-employed skilled tradesman, she is working in a bank and they have children in local schools. They say:

> We're working all hours and we're doing ok. We have things our parents never had. But business is unpredictable and we have to think of the future. We think the children are all right but we're never completely free from worrying about them, especially when they are out in the evening. So we use the car a lot. You hear a lot of alarming things, and there are some funny people out on the street. Perhaps that's just the way things are now. Perhaps we're stuck with it. *Does any of this make any difference to people like us?*

Finally, for now, there is a local teenager. He's still in school, but not for much longer. He's had the odd run-in with the police but he has no record to speak of. He says:

> This place is getting to me. There's nothing to do and nowhere to go. Some pubs will serve you but the police are in and out. There's no decent clubs, no cinema any more and you need a car to get anywhere. So what if we hang out round the shops? Where else is there to be? I want to have a bit of a laugh. I want to be with my mates. But it gets a bit mean out sometimes. *Does any of this make any difference to someone like me?*

We take each of our imaginary questioners very seriously. We do not think that any of them is posing a merely facile or mistaken question. While they are composite figures of our own creation, we do not intend them to be 'straw' people. The questions they ask are ones that we carry around with us. The first puts questions about the intellectual sufficiency of a particular piece of empirical enquiry to its times. The second and third demand accountability both as to research design and method and as to application and relevance. The third group go straight to the issues of responsibility and political integrity. We hope that were they to read this book to its end each of our interrogators would know our response to their question – expressly or by implication – whether or not that response was one that pleased or placated them.

'Crime' and 'place': locating 'crime-talk'

One of the main contentions of this book is that when people talk about *crime* they are often also talking about *places*. This may seem obvious and rather innocuous. We think, to the contrary, that it is complicated and rather important. That we think this also helps to explain why we adopted the research strategy of studying people's responses to crime just in one town.

People often talk about 'the weather'; less frequently do they discuss 'climate'. Similarly, people often speak about 'the way things are these days' but only rarely about 'order'. This is not because they are not clever or knowledgeable – although most of us will often feel that, except perhaps on certain very restricted subjects, we lack the confidence, authority or facility with abstractions that belong to 'experts'. Rather it is because such questions arise *between* people in particular ways. They have differing degrees of urgency for us, different relations with our personal experiences, memories and aspirations, and arouse in us different kinds of involvement, passion, anger or worry depending on who we are and where and among whom we live.

Crime is, in our view, one of these ordinary, difficult topics, arguably one of the most difficult. The very term 'crime' notoriously evades definition, beyond the circularity of saying that it comprises acts prohibited by criminal law. For the most part when we talk about crime (at bus-stops, in pubs and workplaces, at school gates, in community centres, shops, living rooms) we are talking about events, happenings, stories (about what happened to me, you, your neighbour, on the street, round the corner, across town). Yet the open-textured and capacious nature of the category 'crime' also means that such conversations have no necessary stopping-off place. We deal with these proximate things also in the shadow of the knowledge that 'crime' does not only mean local nuisances, grievances and troubles but also things that are extreme, bizarre, arcane, menacing. We may also sense that what happens here is echoed elsewhere – or contrasts with what happens elsewhere – in ways that 'stretch' the problem across time and distance and demand explanation in more than just local and particular terms. Moreover, our understanding of these matters is not confined to personal experience, gossip or rumours; it also flows from newspaper reports, television coverage, magazines, movies, political campaigns and so on. In these respects crime figures at almost every point in our culture from the most general to the most intimate.

For reasons such as these, crime is a topic that never quite stays still and submits itself for dispassionate examination. Similarly, people's talk about crime (their 'discourse')[3] is dense and digressive. It slips from topic to topic, changes gear and direction. It talks in stories, instances and anecdotes but then moves to speculations, conjectures, theories. It roams from the present, to the remembered past to possible wished-for or threatening futures. It is heavy with experience and skips between abstractions. It makes sense of troubling and alarming events but also expresses confusion and uncertainty. It effects connections between people but also draws boundaries and distinctions and crystallizes hostilities, suspicions and conflicts. It invokes authority and demands order, yet voices criticism and mistrust of authorities and orders. In successive chapters of this book we demonstrate and elaborate upon some of these properties of people's responses to crime.[4] We do not do so idly but rather because we think that both much previous academic criminology and, still more, much of our contemporary political language has tended to flatten some of these complexities and to reduce 'the public' to the status of ciphers so far as their concerns, needs and desires in respect of crime are concerned. These are for us connected matters – the *theoretical deficit* in criminology's estimation of 'lay' responses to crime and the *legitimation deficit* in the ways that politicians and policy-makers have construed and addressed people's concerns – in that both are obstacles to democratic deliberation and institution-building. These are problems to which we return in our concluding chapter. For now though it is necessary to set out some of our views on the complexities of crime discourse – and in particular on the relations between 'crime' and 'place' – in a slightly more formal, and in this sense more obviously 'theoretical', way. We begin by assessing some of the implications for the study of 'localities' of what has come in a relatively brief period of time to be known as 'globalization'.

Globalization and the sense of place

In the view of much recent social theory, contemporary changes in the organization of economic activity (the advent of a genuinely global economic 'system') and the radical proliferation of communications networks (both for the movement of people, especially via air travel and for the movement of information, services and money by electronic media) have ushered in a new phase in the development of modern societies. Many of these dynamics are increasingly summarized (initially in technical debates and latterly in ordinary usage as well) under the term 'globalization'. The adequacy of many formulations of this issue, including the abruptness of its departure from earlier periods of 'modernity' can be questioned quite sharply (see, for example, Woodiwiss 1996). Even so it seems clear that some of our accustomed ways of thinking about aspects of economic, political and social affairs are in danger of becoming obsolete.

In the face of the increasing mobility of capital, information and culture we inhabit a world of 'networks' (Castells 1996) and of 'flows' (Lash and Urry 1994) rather than of fixed points and locations, and the practical significance that can be attributed to many entities whose solidity we have taken as given (whether they be actual 'places' or 'localities' or legal and political structures such as 'states') stands radically in question. The future of whole cities and regions (perhaps most obviously the great mono-industrial centres of manufacturing such as Detroit or the ship-building cities of the north-east of England) stands or falls on decisions taken quite elsewhere. When conurbations (such as Liverpool) enter a period of net loss of population one of the grand trajectories of nineteenth- and early twentieth-century capitalism is reversed. Conversely, when formerly marginal areas (the various 'valleys' and 'fens' of the computing industries for example) become globally important economic centres then something highly consequential, but perhaps in principle escaping prediction or control, is going on. What any of this means in human and political terms are among the most intricate and important questions that the social sciences now confront. Much of this debate exceeds our scope here (but see variously Featherstone *et al.* 1995; Appadurai 1996; Heelas *et al.* 1996; Gray 1997). However, to the extent that the fortunes of the single English town that has interested and concerned us are inescapably caught up in the whirlwind of these global transformations, a brief consideration of relevant issues cannot be avoided.

In a series of important books (and more recently – and accessibly – in his 1999 Reith Lectures entitled 'Runaway World'), Anthony Giddens (1990, 1991) argues that each of us is willy-nilly caught up in globalizing trends that we can neither control nor escape. The resulting awareness of powerlessness is dismaying, and can lead to a disabling sense of 'engulfment' for the individual. Yet the same developments make possible forms of experimentation, travel and lifestyle choice undreamed of by earlier generations. The world that is coming into being has many ambiguities, not least of which is the paradox between, on the one hand, the 'huge reduction in life-threatening risks' for most inhabitants of developed societies achieved by the development of 'abstract systems' (insurance, health screening, financial services and the rest), and on the other an accentuated level of risk-awareness. What underpins this quotient of everyday anxiety, in Giddens's view, is that it 'becomes less and less possible to protect any lifestyle, however pre-established, from the generalized risk climate' (1991: 126). In other words the complete 'immersion' of self in place is no longer feasible – the traditional bond between intimacy and proximity has been broken. We are closer to our distant friends and relations with whom we communicate by phone and e-mail than to our neighbours. We of course continue to seek security (provided in part by the studied uneventfulness of much of everyday life) and we invest trust in the reliability of our routines and expectancies – what Giddens terms our 'protective cocoon'. Among the aspects of experience which have to be reconsidered under such conditions is the one at issue here, namely the relation between the individual's lifestyle, choices and constraints, the place in which they reside (or, to put it another way, their 'home'; see Robertson 1995), and the kinds of concern and anxiety that may press in upon them about crime, security and order.[5]

The connections that Giddens identifies between the 'out-there' dynamics of globalization and the 'in-here' effects on our worries and sensitivities seem to us to merit serious reflection (albeit that they should not be accepted unquestioningly).[6] They encourage us to think about our main topic – the nature of contemporary public responses to crime – primarily as instances of reactions to a certain kind of 'risk climate' in the context of the changes wrought in the habitats of our daily life by globalization. Certainly one can readily see how some features of crime discourse lend themselves to being read in this way – tendencies towards nostalgia for a more secure past, for example; fear of strangers and disreputable 'others'.

Zygmunt Bauman goes further in the same direction, and makes the connection with fear of crime more directly. To the extent that fear is a response to 'ambient insecurity', he argues, it is likely to be amenable to inflammatory and demagogic political uses; to focus on the private consumption of security hardware and the fortification of privileged locations (homes, malls, hotels, leisure complexes); and tolerate and endorse the surveillance and immobilization of threatening and alien others with whom we have no natural sympathy or connection. In Bauman's view, 'urban territory becomes the battlefield of continuous space-wars' (1998: 22) in an environment characterized by 'the new fragmentation of the city space, the shrinkage and disappearance of public space, the falling apart of urban community, separation and segregation – and above all the ex-territoriality of the new elite and the forced territoriality of the rest' (1998: 23).[7] The rapid and disruptive changes set in train by globalization give rise to the sense that 'no one is in charge' and that the world beyond one's own front door is unmasterable:

> In an ever more insecure and uncertain world the withdrawal into the safe-haven of territoriality is an intense temptation; and so the defence of the territory – the 'safe home' – becomes the pass-key to all doors which one feels must be locked to stave off the threat to spiritual and material comfort. … It is perhaps a happy coincidence for political operators and hopefuls that the genuine problems of insecurity and uncertainty have condensed into the anxiety about safety; politicians can be supposed to be doing something about the first two just because being seen to be vociferous and vigorous about the third.
>
> (Bauman 1998: 117)

Bauman here takes up a long-standing criminological concern, namely the association that has often been drawn between periods of heightened social anxiety and episodes of populist severity in 'law and order' and penal affairs (e.g. Hall *et al.* 1978; Melossi 1993); and he asserts that under conditions of globalization such tendencies become chronic and embedded (cf. Garland 1996; Pavarini 1997).

Let us now begin to take stock of some of these arguments and to set out some aspects of their relationship to our own research. We have begun here, with some views on the impacts of globalization on 'place', 'anxiety' and 'fear' (rather than, for example, with a more standard treatment of the 'fear of crime' literature), for several reasons.

First, insofar as these diagnoses are plausible and well-founded, the kinds of transformation of economy, communication and culture entailed by globalization will be registered *in some form* everywhere. There may be many reasons for continuing to investigate aspects of social existence at 'local' levels but not as if 'the local' were not itself subject to change and redefinition.

Second, however, it cannot be assumed that the impacts of such large-scale social changes are in any sense *the same* everywhere. Indeed, it is intrinsically the case that globalization holds out very different fates to people depending on who they are and where they live. Exactly how the relations between the local and global dimensions of existence will be experienced, interpreted and managed by people in the ordinary settings of their lives therefore remains an open, empirical question – much more open, we would argue, than much of the talk of global-ization in social theory (which so often appears already to know the answers to all its own questions) allows.

Third, because notions of order, security, risk and anxiety are so close to the heart of these developments, public responses to crime may indeed be a particu-larly eloquent and indicative way of discovering their traces in people's lives and outlooks. Bauman is in this respect quite correct in focusing on anxiety, 'fear' and the consumption of security, and perhaps also in detecting that a rather febrile politics of 'law and order' is an entrenched feature of modern societies in the present stage of their development. Others, most obviously Beck (1992), have followed related lines of argument about technological and environmental ques-tions.[8] Yet neither Bauman nor Giddens (nor yet Beck) are particularly sensitive to variations in these experiences *between places*, beyond the development of certain highly defended 'locales'. There would seem to be a tendency in some recent social theory to dramatize and to focus on the extreme poles of the argu-ment – as witness the imaginative grip on this debate of contemporary depictions of Los Angeles (M. Davis 1990) or São Paolo and the more or less routine use of Ridley Scott's *Blade Runner* as a cultural reference point.

Fourth, therefore, we take as a point of departure in this research the supposi-tion that much talk of crime in 'local' settings will also be talk about 'place', at least in the following special sense. We have attempted to locate the 'crime-talk' (Sasson 1995) of residents of one English town in terms of their larger sense of perspective – on the place in which they live, on their place within it, and on its place in a bigger national or societal set of stories. In other words we seek to grasp a variety of expressed feelings, aspirations and worries (which are commonly corralled together under the term 'fear of crime') as aspects of mundane culture, in something akin to Raymond Williams's (1981) sense of that term. Our working assumption has been that people talk about crime, place and time in ways that are quite complexly interwoven, but that this complexity is nevertheless researchable, provided that it is approached in a grounded and interpretatively sensitive fashion. 'Crime-talk' and 'place-talk' are unlikely to prove to be clearly separable and both are likely to bear in some way on the experiences of change – whether that be viewed as positive, negative or ambiguous in its effects – that confront people both in the immediate circum-stances of their daily routines and through the larger relays of media and political culture. Crime resonates in *both* terms of the local/global dialectic. Many of the distinctions that are placed in question by contemporary social change (here/there; us/others; continuity/disruption; progress/decline; liberty/regulation; order/entropy; contentment/unease) arise routinely in crime discourse. We take it as given, therefore, that crime is an issue that positions the individual citizen in relation to a wide and often dismaying world. What we cannot do is state with confidence what the nature of that relation is in advance of empirical enquiry.

Paradoxically, therefore, our decision to study citizen responses to crime in a single, moderately affluent English town derives quite directly from an encounter with the debates on globalization and with the need to integrate their implications into the disciplinary concerns of contemporary criminology (on this, see also Taylor 1995; Taylor *et al.* 1996). Conversely, we suggest, crime discourse is a particularly apt arena in which to discover some of the lived consequences of those generic forms of social change. To move beyond the speculative generalizations of the grander forms of social theory on these matters, however, it becomes expressly necessary to foreground the question of 'place'. The consequences of modernity for the security, identity and subjectivity of people anywhere can only be disclosed, grasped and rendered intelligible *somewhere*. It follows in our view that the attempt to trace the contours of public responses to crime in one particular place, however criminologically 'ordinary' and obscure, is *anything but* a parochial or peripheral concern. Let us then elaborate on this a little further, but this time with more specific reference to debates on public responses to crime.

Crime, place and late modernity

Current social theory, as we have seen, wrestles with the transformative consequences of modernity and produces ambivalent views on the fate of 'place' (Lash and Urry 1994). The question here is whether this means that place is simply of terminally declining importance. We think that for certain purposes, of which interpreting public anxieties about crime and disorder is one, this is not the case – at least not in any simple sense.[9]

Rather, as we will show, there is a dialectic in citizens' crime-talk between distance and proximity, abstractness and particularity, generic formats and localized stories, the known and the other which is, in our estimation, an important aspect of the diffusion and circulation of public knowledge about crime and social order in late modern societies. Indeed, much 'fear of crime' discourse is largely about the protection of certain places or territories (homes, streets, communities, nations) against incursion, usually seen as coming initially from elsewhere.[10] Thus, while criminologists have become in some degree used to the idea of 'crime as metaphor', and familiar with the deployment of crime and punishment as resources of significance and value in story-telling, we may not for the most part have understood very clearly how powerfully those metaphors and meanings are relayed through the representation of places[11] and the creation of 'place myths' (Shields 1991; Lash and Urry 1994) and with what consequences.

There is a strong emphasis in much recent discussion on the 'criminology of place' (Sherman *et al.* 1989; Eck and Weisburd 1995). 'Ecological' concerns have come to enjoy a renewed prominence in recent North American, British and Scandinavian criminology – perhaps especially in analyses of the concentration of poverty and/or social disorganization in the work of Sampson and Wilson (1995), Hagan (1994) and others. Moreover, place-specific anxiety and fear have an evident bearing in many such analyses insofar as they relate to issues of neighbourhood change, 'white flight', 'ghettoization' and 'disrepute' (see generally, Taub *et al.* 1984; Skogan 1990), and the socially skewed distributions of victimization risks (Hope 1997a).

The development of reputations and place-myths, it is now clear, is materially crucial to the declining or ascending paths of neighbourhoods and towns (a point made in differing ways by writers as various as Bottoms and Wiles 1986; Logan and Molotch 1987; and of course Mike Davis 1990) – processes of polarization which show every sign of having intensified in the United States and Britain in recent years. But more generally, we will argue, if we wish to understand the filtration of *generic* social representations of crime, law enforcement and punishment (and the hegemony which certain among them enjoy over others – cf. Melossi 1994: 208) into everyday sensibility we will also need to comprehend the *situated* character of their reception and appropriation by people in the practical and mundane contexts of their daily life. On the other hand, the omnipresence of mass media and the 'time-space compression' (Harvey 1989; Thompson 1996) that they engender forces upon us as receivers a *reflexive* awareness of place – an assessment of our own place in relation to (and sometimes expressly in defence from) others. In other words, place-awareness nowadays tends to be relational and comparative.

One form that such awareness can assume – the one that particularly interests us here – may be a fretful awareness of the fragility of the relative peace and order of one's own place and hence the (sometimes literal) patrolling of its boundaries. As Doreen Massey (1994) points out there is an element almost of wishful thinking in the cosmopolitanism of some of those branches of social theory which seek to argue that place is necessarily of diminishing importance. Insofar as they interpret attachments to and identifications with places as wilfully nostalgic and politically reactionary they have an interest in contending that the future lies 'elsewhere'. On the contrary, Massey argues, the fact that places have become complicated, plural and replete with cultural contradictions does not mean that they have ceased to matter or that they are about to do so. Rather: 'If it is now recognized that people have multiple identities then the same point can be made in relation to places. Moreover, such multiple identities can be a source of richness, or a source of conflict, or both' (1994: 153).

In terms of the historical lineages of criminology, Macclesfield stands in deliberate and ironic contrast to the likes of Chicago and Los Angeles, Glasgow and the east end of London. It is a somewhat ordinary and, criminologically speaking, obscure location. To study crime-related worries in the discourse of citizens of a place that is neither metropolitan, nor especially poor, nor burdened by unusually high crime rates is to change lenses. Not only is this to venture into the criminological *terra incognita* of life beyond the big city but it is also to extend and in some degree to subvert the boundaries of criminology as a discipline. How have the economic and technological restructuring of late modern societies intruded upon the lived sense of security of citizens away from the capitals and 'headquarter cities' of those societies? Has the sense of continuity or 'community' of those more obscure places been disrupted or not? How, if at all, do the much discussed cultural transformations of late modernity appear from the vantage point of the relatively affluent yet relatively peripheral 'Middletown'? What inter-generational or inter-communal tensions and hostilities lie within the tangled social relations and reputations that compose any particular place? What does it mean, in late modern Britain, to have property, position, children to protect? What, conversely, is the experience of being poorer within an environment of comparative affluence and high consumption? Adequate answers to these questions require us to reconsider what has come since the early 1980s to be known as 'the fear of crime debate'.

From 'fear' to sensibilities

It should by now be apparent that the 'fear of crime', as this has conventionally been conceived and measured, is by no means our primary concern here. Rather, we have been attempting to develop a place-sensitive sociology of public sensibilities towards crime of somewhat broader intent. However, we do propose that some of the more perplexing and seemingly anomalous discoveries of the 'fear of crime' literature (especially those that have given rise to the extended and in the main unhelpful debate on the rationality or otherwise of public responses to the perceived risks of crime) become substantially more intelligible in the light of a thicker contextual understanding of place.

We make no attempt here to summarize the voluminous academic literature on fear of crime. Such an undertaking would consume the greater part of the space of this book and distract us from the primary task of presenting our research. Numerous informative overviews already exist (see, for example, Lewis and Salem 1986; Hale 1992); and at least one of the present authors has been round that track before (Sparks 1992a, 1992b). Nevertheless, since the work reported here owes its origins in part to our encounters with existing traditions of work on 'fear' and records our attempt (in common with others) to shift discussion in a somewhat different direction, some preliminary remarks are necessary by way of orientation.

At least since the late 1960s (the publication in the United States of the President's Commission on Law Enforcement and the Administration of Justice and its associated volumes of research in 1967 is often taken as a defining *point d'origine* here) much effort has been devoted to assessing the scale and impacts of crime from the points of view of public safety and 'quality of life' (both notoriously inexact and difficult terms) and in terms of the differing contributions and effectiveness of aspects of policing, punishment and social policies to prevention and control. A key development was the almost simultaneous 'discovery' by researchers of both mainstream (or as they later came to termed 'administrative') and radical or critical orientations of the intrinsic inadequacy of official statistics on recorded crime to provide the basis for such assessments. It is in retrospect easy to see why these developments should have generated continuous controversy. The refocusing of attention on the unilluminated 'dark figure' of crime by definition discloses a volume of 'crime' greater than that known through the official channels, and hence provides open-ended opportunities for investigation, manipulation, hype, diagnosis, commentary and critique. Moreover, the further implication that official agencies act as filters and definers for crime (processing and sanctioning some potentially crime-worthy events and not others) necessarily renders their decisions potentially politically contentious. Which crimes and whose victimizations receive what kinds of attention? Are the practices of definition and control that ensue systematically skewed to recognize primarily some categories of offending, by some people, against some others, in some places? And do those practices routinely act to the detriment of certain actors: youth, minorities, women?

The germ of much of the recent disputatious history of criminology and crime policy is contained in this thumbnail depiction. More immediately to the point, the creation of 'the fear of crime' as a specific object for investigation and intervention also derives in large measure from the same dialectic. If crime control is a politics *of* definition and *for* recognition, then criminology is the specialized arena in which certain struggles are played out on the level of categorizations, topics, models of explanation and claims to knowledge. One response on the part of government research agencies (both directly and through their sponsorship of others' work) to the arrival in earnest of such contingency within their fields of expertise and responsibility has been to institute regular surveys of victimization, starting in the early 1980s with the first British Crime Survey (Hough and Mayhew 1983). These have increasingly also taken measures of public concern, worry and perceived risk. In sum, the routine collection of two kinds of data (on experiences of victimization and on perceptions of risk) promotes the prospect of systematic comparison between them; and to the extent that they appear to diverge, or at least not to map neatly onto one another, an explanatory enigma arises. If public expressions of fear or concern appear to exceed measured risks, or to be unevenly distributed in relation to them, they present a puzzle – one that can moreover come to be regarded as a 'problem in its own right' (Hale 1992). It is in this space that the 'fear of crime' came to be constituted as a topic for enquiry and a bone of contention in theoretical and political dispute.

It is something of a common feature of the development of such techniques of risk accounting across a number of fields that they discover a lack of 'fit' between expert knowledge and 'lay' opinion. The development of a 'fear of crime' problematic bears many points of comparison with the literatures of nuclear safety, toxic waste disposal and other environmental and health hazards, not to mention some of the debates that now surround such topics as cloning and genetic modification (see further Douglas 1986; Krimsky and Golding 1992). Quite often in the early development of such debates expert views are propounded with great confidence, and public perceptions at variance with these may correspondingly be castigated as ill-founded, even irrational in origin. Research therefore follows on the nature and sources of lay perceptions – for example, on the aspects of public communication that tend to 'amplify' the sense of threat (Kasperson 1992), or the 'psychometric' mapping of which threats are selected for attention. Such research efforts may be connected with an explicit or hidden curriculum of public education for the purposes of managing, calming or correcting 'excessive' anxiety, or in order to advise the public on sensible and appropriate precautionary measures. Yet as research on public perception proceeds it may also discover that lay perceptions are more diverse, more nuanced and perhaps more situationally intelligible than at first supposed – for example, that they indicate an erosion of trust in the capacity of the system to manage the risks concerned, or that they embody a counter-knowledge based in practical experience (e.g. Wynne 1992, 1996). Moreover, certain forms of opposi-tional activism may enter the fray – re-analysing the official data or presenting alternative research suggesting that the fears were well-founded all along, at least for certain groups.

Debate on 'fear of crime' exhibits many of these dynamics, although this is not the place to set them out in detail. Like debates on nuclear safety or environ-mental degradation, crime is an arena of risk politics in which questions of the trust and credibility of official agencies are placed in question, where many voices contend for attention, and which cannot secure its boundaries against becoming involved in intractable debates about the nature and direction of social change. At times emphasis has fallen upon the social influences that may exaggerate and distort public perception for political or commercial advantage (as in arguments about 'deviancy amplification' (Cohen and Young 1973), 'moral panic' (Cohen 1972) or the 'cultivation' of public perceptions of a 'mean world' by mass media (Gerbner and Gross 1976; see generally, Sparks 1992a)). On occasion this initially critical perspective has found echoes in official discourse, as when the literature stimulated by the early sweeps of the British Crime Survey laid pronounced emphasis on the apparently heightened levels of fear expressed by ostensibly low-risk groups such as women and the elderly (Maxfield 1984). Such positions have met with angry criticism from 'left realist' criminologists, arguing that 'left idealist' and 'administrative' criminologists had colluded to produce a 'great denial' of the severity of crime victimization (see, for example, Young 1987). Feminists have demonstrated that disclosure by alternative programmes of research (including ethnographic and life-history research, or surveys of women conducted by women) of hidden victimizations tends to abolish, or at least to reduce and make intelligible, many alleged disparities between risk and fear (Hamner and Saunders 1984; Stanko 1990b).

One response of 'fear of crime' research in the face of the arguments and uncertainties thus generated has been to pursue ever more refined empirical research, carefully introducing more and more definitional distinctions and categories (e.g. Hough 1995). Alongside this, however, there goes the recognition that the initial conceptual solidity and apparent clarity of the construct 'fear' has tended to disperse. Researchers have begun to own up to diminishing confidence that they know precisely what it is that is being measured or that they are all capturing indices of 'the same thing'. Whatever 'it' might be 'fear' turns out to involve multiple dimensions (Ferraro and LaGrange 1987; Killias 1990), vicarious as well as direct experiences (Skogan and Maxfield 1981; Smith 1986) and to be open to varying conceptualizations as 'an expression of uneasiness' (Donnelly 1988), a 'judgement' of government competence to deliver collective security (Taylor *et al.* 1986) and an 'expression of powerlessness and uncertainty' (Smith 1989). In other words it involves 'abstractions' (or inferences) from experience – and hence by definition their *meanings* and *attributions* (Garofalo and Laub 1978) as well as the immediate impact of victimization as such (Walklate 1997). Yet, for some, such extensions of the notion of 'fear' run the risk of 'stretching the concept so far as to be in danger of losing its focus and explanatory power' (Hale 1992: 15).

Our response is that the study of public responses to crime does indeed require to be so 'stretched' but perhaps in such a way that 'fear' ceases to be its primary organizing idea. But this is not in any sense a problem; neither does it render those responses unresearchable (the search for 'focus' and 'explanatory power' under the unifying notion of 'fear' always was somewhat dubious). Rather, the attempt to open out discussion of citizens' discourses on crime to include a more various sense of the moral commitments, concerns, attachments and identifications that they might comprise is to make two important theoretical 'moves'. First, it is to return to the forefront of discussion a fuller appreciation of the political and moral resonances of the category 'crime' and of its implication in experiences of social change. Second, it is to insist upon the intelligibility of those ordinary public responses once they are *situated* against a proper understanding of the contexts and settings in which they are voiced (the very point at which 'fear of crime' research commonly holds up its hands in defeat is the point of entry, as C. Wright Mills long ago affirmed, of sociological craft).

As Mary Douglas has commented, against those objectivist tendencies in research on risk (which bears so many points of comparison with mainstream discussion of 'fear of crime'):

> There is no way of proceeding with analysing risk perception without typifying kinds of communities according to the support their members give to authority, commitment, boundaries and structure.
>
> (Douglas 1992: 47)

However, this is not to suppose (as Douglas on occasion appears to do) that the kinds of commitments we discover will be open to neat categorization, let alone disclose unanimities. Neither, as our foregoing discussion of 'globalization' indicates, can we now suppose that 'communities' straightforwardly exhibit 'boundaries' and 'structure', still less that these will map onto their territorial limits.

Rather, it means exploring, within the dense thicket of historical and cultural particularities that go into the constitution of any given place, the bearing upon it (filtered in however specific a form) of aspects of contemporary social organization and disorganization that may be quite general in scope, if not indeed pervasive. The little town whose fortunes matter so much to our respondents, the ins and outs of which provide the substance of this book, is indeed caught up willy-nilly in the global flows of capital and culture (cf. Lash and Urry 1994). What remains to be shown is that this has any bearing on the bundle of sensibilities and anxieties known conventionally as the 'fear of crime'. Our aim in this book is to flesh out in some detail how we think the fears of crime of Macclesfield residents connect with their sense of their place in the wider world.

To pose the matter in this way does not suggest any lack of interest in the distribution of crime risks or their relation to the traditionally studied axes of social stratification. Neither is it to impute irrationality or gullibility to those citizens for whom the danger of crime has become a besetting worry. As Douglas (1992: 29) comments, an interest in the cultural analysis of risk perception is not an assertion of agnosticism about the reality of risks. It does, however, mean exploring the social and personal consequences of people's feelings about crime and justice and their connections with other dimensions of social life. As Douglas further suggests, a risk is anyway not a 'thing' but a way of thinking – not just the probability of an event 'but also the probable magnitude of its outcome, and everything depends on the value that is set on the outcome' (1992: 31). In other words, crime is not just something that bashes us over the head out of ill-luck, like a falling branch. It is something for which we seek explanation and accountability – and how we explain it and who we blame may be highly symptomatic of who we are and how we organize our relations with others (1992: 6–7). In this respect crime may be one of those forms of 'danger on the borders' which gives form to a community's sense of itself and its distinctiveness from others. But it may also provoke anxieties that turn inwards, towards a sense of division from others who are socially and geographically close.

We are by no means alone in seeking to enlarge the scope of discussion of 'lay' responses to crime. Rather we share with others whose earlier work has in some degree influenced our own (especially Merry 1981; but also Baumgartner 1988) or whose contemporary efforts go in some part in tandem with ours (Stanko 1990b; Sasson 1995; Taylor 1995; Evans *et al.* 1996; Hollway and Jefferson 1997, 2000; Walklate 1998) the ambition of exploring some of the range of experiences, dispositions, passions, worries and, indeed, outright fears, that lay discourse on crime discloses. Our particular task in this book will be to investigate the diversity of those responses as we encountered them among the residents of one particular place at a certain point in its contemporary history. We will show how, in their discussions of crime, and of other matters of concern to them, those people develop their accounts of the past, present and possible futures of that place. Such accounts inevitably inhabit different registers of language and kinds of diction. They move from intimate, personal and particular stories and histories to larger observations and speculations, thereby dipping into those more generically available cultural resources that seem in some way to frame or lend sense to their own experiences – or on occasion to assert the dismaying feeling that such experiences *lack* sense, direction or hope of betterment. In such ways, we argue, people's responses to crime (in its association with other matters of concern to them) are both informed by, and in turn inform, their *sense of place*; their sense, that is, of both *the place* they inhabit (its histories, divisions, trajectories and so forth), and of *their place* within a wider world of hierarchies, troubles, opportunities and insecurities. While it has long been asserted that talk of crime is dense with metaphorical association and pregnant with political imagery, such perspectives have too rarely been informed by patient empirical enquiry. Here we indicate how crime figures in people's efforts to render an account of their own and their town's journey through modernity.

We went to an unremarkable place in order better to understand the involvement of crime in the larger processes of contemporary social change. As our responses to earlier debates on 'fear of crime' indicate we wanted to take account of people's talk about crime in ways that went beyond the estimation or measurement of their fears. Our point of departure was that people's ways of telling us about crime would intrinsically exceed the kinds of risk perceptions that 'fear' research commonly identifies and would instead open out into a wider domain of moral judgements, attachments and arguments about blaming, explaining and diagnosing diverse questions of order and insecurity as these arose for them in the particular settings of their daily life. In other words, those diffuse and difficult matters that 'fear' research has seen as lying in the obscure penumbra of its concerns became our primary topic. We wanted to explore some aspects of those broad dispositions and frameworks of understanding that David Garland, in a slightly different context, calls 'sensibilities' (Garland 1990). These we understood not as sets of abstract propositional statements (of the kind garnered, for example, in responses to public opinion surveys), but rather as topics in talk, arguments, anecdotes, pleas for understanding and so on – heavy with experience, and dense with local allusion and concrete points of reference.[12]

What we did in Macclesfield (and why we did it there)

Various methodological choices seemed to us to flow from the concerns that we have outlined above, both in terms of selecting a location in which to carry out our study, and in determining what modes of enquiry to adopt. We opted for Macclesfield – and, later, its neighbouring village-suburb of Prestbury (the subject of Chapter 5) – not only because of their proximity to our place of work, and because we needed a locality whose component neighbourhoods and 'communities' a small research team could come to know fairly well. It was chosen, more importantly, because we wanted to study somewhere that would enable us to extend the scope of research on public responses to crime outside the (inner-city) metropolis and into the less well-trodden settings of the shire counties and smaller towns; places that criminology's 'social problems' orientation (or what

Robert Merton might, more forthrightly, have called its 'slum-encouraged provincialism') have led it in relative terms to neglect.[13] We wanted, in other words, to identify a location that was – in criminological terms – obscure, ordinary, off the beaten track; and we outline in the next chapter the features of Macclesfield that made it appear to us to fit this particular bill. For now, let us confine ourselves to a brief reflection upon, and summary of, the research activities we undertook in this place.

Given our research aims it seemed apparent that our approach would in some respects resemble those of the tradition of British 'community studies' and of urban (and latterly suburban) ethnography. These allusions indicate both the first-hand nature of the research (both Evi Girling and Ian Loader lived in the town during the period of the study; Richard Sparks continued to live nearby) and the effort of interpretation involved in grasping the import of our data (principally people's talk) against a detailed understanding of the town's recent historical and cultural development (its economic fortunes, its changing demography, crime and policing information, and so on). Considerable space might be devoted here (but not necessarily well employed) in discussing the extent to which our work was 'ethnographic' in any strict sense of that term.[14] In that we lived in the town, and spent leisure as well as working time in it, we came to know it as *habitués* rather than simply as external observers. When we discussed aspects of its crime problems with residents they were able to make allusions to places, events and people in the knowledge that we already knew *something* about them – we were not in this respect mere visitors either in their eyes or our own.

It was never our intention, however, to advance an understanding of the town only through the kinds of immersion, cultivation of key informants and detailed (participant) observation that have characterized the 'classics' of modern urban sociology and criminology (see, for example, Whyte 1943; Gill 1977; Bourgois 1995). We did, to be sure, spend varying amounts of time immersed in the town's places – its streets, its pubs, shops and restaurants, its leisure amenities, its community centres and the like. Indeed, we did many of the same things that people living there would in any case do. But we also devoted numerous hours to observing the activities of police officers, youth workers and community (and crime prevention) activists, and to attending crime-related meetings of various kinds. And we benefited greatly from the assistance of residents and professionals who – among other things – shared with us their 'local knowledge', offered us key materials, suggested certain lines of enquiry, and provided introductions to people they (or we) thought we should speak to.

Thus it was clear from the outset that those forms of urban ethnography oriented to 'fixing' the researcher as a well-known figure *in one place* would be insufficient as a means of making sense of social relations in a town of nearly 50,000 inhabitants (not to mention a nearby 'village' – Prestbury – of a further 5,000). Our style of work was somewhat constrained (or at least focused) in subject matter, but stretched by the size of the territory we sought to cover. Hence, as fieldworkers, we were roving, free-floating ones, who consciously endeavoured to roam across the town's neighbourhoods, groupings, and lines of affiliation and division, seeking by multiple means (of which familiarization and observation were but one) to access the experiences, troubles and aspirations of the various constituencies (young/old, working-class/middle-class, indigenous/ incomer and the like) who reside and/or work in the town. This, of course, gave us access *as outsiders* to a form of local knowledge that *was not* generally possessed by Macclesfield and Prestbury residents themselves, in that our research effort engaged us in speaking to (and learning about the concerns of) individuals and groups who did not, for the most part, communicate with one another, or visit the areas of the town (such as 'the estates') that the others inhabited. Indeed, people would often speak to us knowing that this was the case, and would thus ask us either to tell them about what 'the other side' (such as local youths) had told us, or to pass on to others (such as adult residents, or the local police) their concerns and anxieties about crime.

In short, we made a very deliberate effort to employ *a range of complementary methods* each of which was intended to tap into some aspect of the relationship between crime, place and insecurity within the locality. They can be sub-divided as follows:

1 An analysis of publicly available statistical and documentary information on economic, social and demographic change within the town, and on patterns of crime and demands for policing. This has included information from the 1981 and 1991 Census (small area and local base statistics); economic and demographic data, local plans, and (publicity) materials produced by Macclesfield Borough, Cheshire County and Prestbury Parish Councils; official crime statistics; magistrates' court records and information on calls for police assistance (covering April and May 1995). We have also been able to make beneficial use of an extensive 'Quality of Life' survey conducted recently by Cheshire County Council (1996a, 1996b, 1996c), much of which touches directly on our concerns with drugs, youth, attachment to place and 'fear of crime'.

2 Familiarity with various local representations of crime-related matters as are contained in the local press and crime prevention literature. These include the general crime coverage in the established, weekly *Macclesfield Express Advertiser* and the *Macclesfield Messenger* freesheet, and the detailed examination of particular crime stories (notably, a local 'vigilante' incident which received prominent local and national media coverage – see further Girling *et al.* 1998). We have also collated information, for example, on the history, spread and duration of local home watch schemes and publicity/ information materials produced by the police and crime prevention agencies.

3 Centrally, a total of twenty-six focus group discussions with different sections of the local populace. In Macclesfield these comprised the following: (i) ten groups with middle-class residents – one each with managers, clerical staff and young men employed at Zeneca Pharmaceuticals; one with home watch coordinators living in Tytherington, and discussions with residents from the old High Street area (two), the area around Kennedy Avenue (two), Broken

Cross (one), and a new, walled housing development known as 'The Villas' (one); (ii) one group from each of the town's five council-built estates – Moss Rose, Hurdsfield, Weston, Upton Priory and Victoria Park flats; and (iii) four groups with teenagers – one with sixth formers at a local independent school, one with secondary school pupils from Moss Rose/High Street, one arranged through the detached youth work project on Hurdsfield, and one with male offenders on probation. In Prestbury, we conducted discussions with five groups of adult residents (retired businessmen, members of the Women's Institute, home watch coordinators, managers working at Zeneca, and parents with children at the local primary school), and with two groups of teenagers attending the local youth club.

4   A small number of in-depth biographical interviews with long-standing local residents, six in Macclesfield and two in Prestbury.

5   Individual interviews (nine) and group discussions (six) with criminal justice professionals and other local interest groups and 'opinion formers'. These included police officers (including the then divisional superintendent), probation officers, magistrates, youth workers, Borough Council officials, Prestbury Parish councillors, head-teachers, publicans and members of Macclesfield Civic Society.

6   Numerous hours devoted to informal conversations, observation and attendance at meetings. At its most structured, this entailed a period of observational research at Macclesfield police station (by Evi Girling); the active participation by one member of the research team (Evi Girling) in the local crime prevention panel; and a period of voluntary work/observation by another (Ian Loader) at Prestbury youth club. It also included a host of conversations with local residents and professionals (some of whom became important confidants and gatekeepers); attending meetings of tenants' associations, senior citizens' groups and other voluntary organizations; observing police–community consultative committees and two (well-attended) public meetings convened specifically to address problems of crime; and periods of observation in the magistrates' court and police vehicles.

We have generated by these methods a rich, multi-perspectival series of accounts which we have sought to understand both semantically (in terms of their form as transcribed texts, their characteristic vocabulary, their use of metaphor and so on) and contextually (in relation to their presuppositions of local knowledge, narration of events and *englobement* within other registers of discourse).[15] In so doing, our aim has been to construct a detailed and nuanced account of the varying sensibilities towards crime and insecurity present within this fairly typical English community. At this point, therefore, we will desist from further prefatory discussion and turn instead to our main topic, namely the record of our engagement with this town, its people and the place that questions of crime and social order occupy in their lives and consciousness.

2 About Macclesfield

Social change and a sense of place

It's a very mixed town. It's very old. And then there's the very new. There's a mixture of people living here. There's the new shopping, the old shopping, the new houses, the old houses. It's certainly got a history. You've got the silk history. I don't know whether it's still going, but it goes back a long way. It's unusual in that respect. Parts of it are very cramped, and others are open, and country as well. It's unusual in that. It's quite a varied town.

(male resident, The Villas)

Macclesfield is a town of some 49,000 inhabitants tucked away in the corner of north-east Cheshire at the point where the Pennine foothills to the east meet the Cheshire plain, which stretches away to the west. Once a single-industry silk-weaving town, Macclesfield has from the 1960s onwards experienced a period of pronounced economic and social restructuring which has seen the town become host to a number of multinational companies, especially the pharmaceutical giants Zeneca and CIBA-Geigy, together inevitably with their professional work-forces. It thus embarked on a period of hitherto unknown prosperity, and has retained relatively high employment and comparatively high property values even through the recession of the late 1980s and early 1990s. It increasingly represents itself, for example in the promotional literature produced by its moderately entrepreneurial local authority, as a comfortable place with an 'envi-able life-style'. It claims to combine the lifestyle attractions of modern amenities and transport (a mainline railway link with London, proximity to an interna-tional airport) with the 'heritage' orientation of a former mill-town on the edge of some beautiful open spaces. It is not – as we shall see – without its pockets of poverty and deprivation. But the influential Henley Centre for Forecasting recently numbered Macclesfield among the thirty British towns with the brightest econo-mic prospects.

In the course of the last three decades Macclesfield has both spread geographically and become more socially diverse. In brief and summary terms it is possible to identify three primary groupings: (i) 'old', 'born-and-bred', working-class families of two or more generations' standing (known locally as 'Maxonians'), a substantial proportion of whom either live in one of the town's five council-built housing estates or occupy the nineteenth-century terraced houses close to the town centre; (ii) an influx of working people who since the 1960s have arrived to take up jobs in the pharmaceutical industry or the burgeoning service sector; and (iii) incoming professionals working in the new industries or the administrative sector, or commuting to Manchester or elsewhere in Cheshire. For some of the latter group, moving to Macclesfield was merely a fact of occupational life and 'company moves'; for others it would have been a reflexive lifestyle decision – a flight from Manchester and towards the country-side. In these respects the town has grown by the twin processes of industrial regeneration and suburbanization.

These aspects of Macclesfield's contemporary history and current social composition – taken together with its relatively moderate crime levels (discussed more fully in Chapter 3) – made it for us an intriguing place in which to carry out the kind of criminological investigation we wanted to pursue. In outlining the backdrop to the more explicitly crime-focused chapters that follow, we want in this chapter, therefore, to proffer some details about the town that has occu-pied so much of our attention over the last several years. Three tasks, in particular, lie before us. Later, we want to narrate the story of the town's recent economic and social restructuring, provide an outline sketch of its current demography and divisions, and comment on official representations of Macclesfield as 'an affluent place'. We then consider the meanings attached to the town by the people who reside or work in it, exploring some of themes and motifs that go to make up our respondents' sense of place. Let us begin, however, with a descriptive introductory 'tour' of Macclesfield's constituent neighbour-hoods and 'communities', the places that will – in various and contrasting ways – figure prominently throughout this book.[1]

Macclesfield townscapes

Macclesfield lies some 15 miles south of its nearest metropolitan conurbation Manchester, on the southern fringes of the south Manchester and north Cheshire 'commuter belt' (see Figure 2.1); and Manchester provides both a place of employment for a good number of Macclesfield residents, and – as will become apparent – the source of many of their crime-related anxieties (Stoke-on-Trent, the nearest city to the south, seems far less economically and socially significant, and loomed not nearly as large on the mental maps of our respon-dents). Yet unlike many of the 'satellite' towns that line the road to Manchester – Bramhall, Poynton, Hazel Grove and, most clearly, Stockport – Macclesfield appears (or at least claims) to have escaped Manchester's influence. This may in part be a product of economic history, the town's silk industry equipping it with an independent *entrée* into the wider world. It may now be a function of land-scape and accessibility; travellers north being confronted with a choice between narrow, twisting minor roads, an often clogged trunk road up through Hazel Grove and Stockport, and a regular though expensive Virgin train service. Whatever the reason, Macclesfield remains – or at least feels – insulated from its metropolitan near neighbour, displaying proudly for the questioning visitor a sense of its own (non-metropolitan) 'distinctiveness'. As one member of the local Civic Society put it: 'I think it's a place that's kept its identity. It's not been swallowed up by either the Potteries or Manchester.'

Yet Macclesfield also retains a certain 'distance' from the assorted places that go to make up what Turner (1967) once called the 'swell-belt' of north Cheshire. For while the town stands as the eponymous focal point of a large and economically booming Borough, it is in certain respects the poor – or at least poorer – relation among its near neighbours. Encompassing the leafy and prosperous enclaves of Alderley Edge, Wilmslow, Knutsford and Prestbury (a place we consider at some length in Chapter 5), Macclesfield Borough contains some of the swankiest places (and largest houses) outside of England's 'Home Counties'. Staunchly Conservative (Macclesfield Borough Council remained under Tory control throughout the 1990s; the borough has long been the power-base of one of the more 'maverick' Conservative MPs, Nicholas Winterton), this is the place – as the editor of *Cheshire Life* put it – 'where posh northerners live':

Figure 2.1   Macclesfield and the south Manchester 'commuter belt'

There is a recognisable Cheshire Set: people who work in Manchester or Liverpool and live in the 'crescent of prosperity' – Macclesfield, Knutsford, Nantwich, Chester combined with landed people from south Cheshire. They move through the Chester races, the Chester Rowing Regatta, the return of the tall ships to Liverpool, and the events at the Cheshire Polo Club and charity balls.

(*The Times*, 31 May 1992)

Macclesfield stands in some – and in some respects stark – contrast to this extravagant, journalistic portrait of its near neighbours (were the constituency boundaries so arranged, the *town* of Macclesfield would in all likelihood return a Labour representative[2]). The town in the mid-1990s is – in terms of social class at least – a diverse place (it remains an overwhelmingly white town). In and around Macclesfield's borders poverty and affluence stand often cheek by jowl. The exclusive village-suburb of Prestbury (home to the highly rewarded success stories of commerce and the professions) lies but a mile from one of Macclesfield's council-built estates (Upton Priory). The terraced streets of nine-teenth-century weaver's cottages that encircle the town centre provide a home both to established working-class residents and to some young ('gentrifying') professional incomers. The middle-class 'commuter developments' of Tytherington, Kennedy Avenue and Broken Cross are interspersed among (and in some cases adjacent to) five council-built estates, which themselves range from the locally notorious, CCTV-protected Victoria Park flats in the town centre, to the seemingly more stable and integrated areas of Hurdsfield, Moss Rose, Upton Priory and Weston (see Figure 2.2). Macclesfield – as one long-standing middle-class resident put it: '[is] a perfect cross-section of social standing. You've got the deprivation. You've also got a lot of money and big houses.' Let us take a closer look.

The town centre and the 'old town'

What is perhaps most striking about Macclesfield's town centre and its imme-diate environs is their compactness. Today, the shopping district and the dense network of weaver's cottages that (at least partially) surround it, stand in sharp relief to the more 'suburban' housing of the post-war years. Architecturally at least, the contrasts are stark. This is for the casual visitor and resident alike a 'reminder' of what that much smaller Macclesfield was 'like' during the early and middle part of the twentieth century: a place (and this is certainly how many of our older respondents recalled it) characterized by a certain wholeness, know-ability and homeliness, one that was familiar, easily negotiated on foot, intimate even. As the post-war decades have passed by, it has become increasingly difficult to speak of the town in such terms.

The town centre has in the last twenty years or so come to be bounded by two major roads, which run north to south on either side. To the west runs Churchill Way, beginning at the prestigious King's School to the north and finishing at the

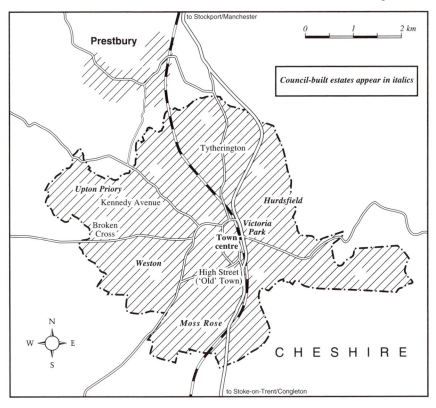

Figure 2.2 Macclesfield and Prestbury

top of Park Lane (and the road to Congleton and Stoke) to the south. The road is the product of some major 'slum-clearance' of the 1960s, during which whole streets (and their names) were wiped entirely from the map. The one building to survive the demolition (a small garage) stands stubbornly in the car park beside the new road, watching over the rush hour jams. To the east, runs the 'Silk Road', part of the main Stockport–Leek trunk road. Built in the early 1990s, and not much liked locally, it has the effect of dividing the town almost in two, with Victoria Park flats and Hurdsfield lying 'cut off' along the Buxton Road, as it heads out eastwards into the Peaks.

The town centre itself sits on two levels, hemmed in between these major thoroughfares. Along the lower level runs Sunderland Street, a rather neglected and forlorn looking part of town intermittently laced with a pet shop, snooker centre, DIY store, Cypriot restaurant/take-away, a tiny half-empty shopping arcade, and some renovated business units. At one end of it stands a war memorial, Park Green and the southern part of the town centre. At the other stands the bus and railway station. The former (as is so often the case with urban bus stations in Britain) is a littered, fume-ridden and altogether rather grotty place.

More surprisingly, the railway station fares little better. Housed in a modern building much in need of repair, residents would often remark what a poor (and misleading) impression it gives visitors and passing passengers of their town.

Immediately facing the station, and before the landscape rises steeply upwards, lies a large open space known as Water's Green. During the day, this is a pleasant enough if undistinguished location, the site of the odd market stall hoping to catch the passing pedestrian trade. However, encircled as it is by some five pubs, a chip shop and a kebab house, Water's Green has acquired local notoriety as a place where drunken youths congregate (and on occasions fight) following 'chucking out time' on Friday and Saturday nights (Macclesfield at the time of our research had no night clubs). To many local residents, Water's Green has come to symbolize the fact that the town centre is best avoided at night, especially at weekends. We will have cause to return to it in Chapter 3.

The main shopping area of the town stands behind and above Water's Green. It can be approached either through a steep, cobbled street (around which the bulk of Macclesfield's estate agents are to be found), or by one of two sets of solid, stone steps, one finishing behind the town's fourteenth-century church, the other behind the town hall. This is a fairly bustling commercial part of town which stretches north–south along Mill Street and east–west along Chestergate. The former (which has, subsequent to our research, been pedestrianized) runs like a main artery through the town centre starting in the south and winding its way upwards to the north. At its northern point it meets the robust, pillared town hall, and extends out into the old market place before falling steeply down into Jordangate where the library, police headquarters and multi-storey car park are located. The pedestrianized Chestergate runs off Mill Street at right angles from the town hall. Nestled between the two are the enclosed Grosvenor shopping centre and indoor market. Around almost every corner of Mill Street one obtains a clear view of the Peaks.

The shops themselves are in the main those that inhabit the high streets of most British towns and cities; though the Borough Council's desire to preserve the 'feel' of the town has prevented the arrival of any large department stores. Marks and Spencer, British Home Stores and T.J. Hughes (a department store selling 'seconds') are the only shops of any notable size. The town centre thus mostly comprises the standard household names (Boots, River Island, Body Shop, Next and so forth), as well as several of the sort of shops that characterize any typical high street, such as travel agents, film developers and sports shops (the latter, along with pet shops, seem especially common in the town). These, however, are interspersed with a more diverse range of retail outlets, each of which suggests something different about the town's past and its possible futures.

A number of outlets (the indoor market traders, greengrocers, fishmongers and a – town centre – Tesco) continue to sell food, though the bulk of local people now do their food shopping at the larger Tesco (by the Silk Road) or Sainsburys (located just beyond the town centre on the site of the old Infirmary). An assortment of timeless-looking hairdressers, clothes shops and other curiosities continue to evoke an older Macclesfield, while, in stark contrast, one also finds emerging signs of 'gentrification'. Two small 'up-market' arcades, some expensive shoe shops, two delicatessens (one, with its 'Established 1994' sign, seeking to create an instant aura of heritage), and some 'global crafts' shops, each seeks to cater for the town's young professionals. So too does the recently arrived 'Italian cafe' on Chestergate, the unusually snazzy 'Pizza Express' and two wine bars, all of which now compete with the more traditional and established collection of pubs and restaurants. At the other end of the social scale, a range of 'discount stores' serve as a reminder that Macclesfield is not all success and prosperity, while a number of empty units augur a perhaps less booming future for the commercial heart of the town.

Macclesfield's 'old town' lies immediately to the south and west of the central shopping area, and is, when not actually pressing up against it, certainly within easy walking distance. A casual glance at a Macclesfield map suggests that this part of town has been left 'un-named'. This of course is because this once *was* Macclesfield, and it is only in the post-war period that the 'old town' has come to appear as but one of the town's many 'suburbs'. Fleeting glances are thus deceiving. The 'old town' is in fact pivotal to many residents' sense of place, and it has in recent years been recognized as such, having been designated a 'preservation area' by the Borough Council.

The 'preservation area' comprises two compactly arranged sets of streets lying either side of Park Lane. One, to the south, centres around the old High Street and is laid out on a grid pattern between the picturesque South Park and Leek Road. The other, to the north, is formed in a more higgledy-piggledy fashion to the immediate west of the town centre. Both, however, consist of street after street of nineteenth-century terraced cottages, interspersed with *local* pubs and an assorted range of shops including grocers, a Chinese take-away, a butchers, ice cream parlour, pottery shop and designer furniture warehouse. The roomiest (and most eagerly sought after) of the houses are old three-storey weaver's cottages, many of which are now occupied by young middle-class professionals. The rest are compact, two-bedroom, street-facing cottages built around shared backyards. The old silk mills that used to provide work for the cottage dwellers have either been given over to new commercial uses, lie empty or have been converted into flats. This for the most part is 'first-time buyers' land and the streets of the area are littered with 'For Sale' boards. It is also, as mentioned, the part of the town that provides Macclesfield with much of its characteristic charm and cultural identity; something that matters both to the area's residents, and to those who live further out, but who can nevertheless invest in the fact that they live in an historic, old silk town. We return to this area – and some of its contemporary tensions and conflicts – in Chapter 4.

Around town: 'public' estates, private 'suburbs'

In the post-war years Macclesfield seems not so much to have grown, as have the outside world descend on its doorstep. There is, architecturally at least, a clear disconnection between the 'old' Macclesfield we have just described and the developments that have sprung up over the last few decades. In the latter half of the twentieth century, the amount of public and private development in the town has been extensive and, in respect of private building at least, it continues apace today (leading one Broken Cross woman to term Macclesfield 'a town run by builders'). The result has been that Macclesfield has expanded almost beyond recognition; not so much to the east, where development meets the natural obstacle of the hills; but certainly to the north, the south and especially to the west. Consider the following:

Public (or at least council-built) housing   The pre-war developments of Moss Rose to the south and Hurdsfield in the north-east have, since 1945, been joined by the Weston estate (1947) and Upton Priory (1960s) to the west, and, following the 'slum-clearance' of old terraces in the early 1960s, Victoria Park flats in the town centre.

Private housing   Major private developments include the (continuing) expansion of Tytherington to the north, and building around Ivy Lane, Kennedy Avenue and Longmoss in the west (thus bringing the once separate village of Broken Cross into the town, and now threatening outlying Henbury). Smaller developments continue to spring up across the town, prominent among them 'The Villas', built on two sites relinquished by Parkside Psychiatric Hospital.

Commercial and retail developments   Pride of place here must go to Hurdsfield Industrial Estate, built in the 1960s and currently housing, among others, Zeneca and CIBA-Geigy. The Lyme Green retail park – complete with car showroom, electrical stores and 'Superbowl' – continues to expand some 2 miles south of the town centre, and a second retail park has recently opened on the Silk Road to the north.[3]

One result of all this is that Macclesfield feels less and less like a 'small town', or at least no longer like a compact one. The more one now endeavours to get a sense of the place as some kind of whole, the more it appears to fragment into its diverse yet composite 'communities'. It is no longer an easy task to grasp the town in its entirety, to familiarize oneself with its nooks and crannies. Macclesfield has come to exhibit that defining feature of the urban condition: the existence of whole areas of the locality about which people possess little first-hand, unmediated knowledge.[4] This is perhaps especially so – as we shall see in Chapter 3 – of Macclesfield's council-built estates, most of which remain unvisited by, and largely unknown to, much of the town's (especially middle-class, incoming) population. Yet it is important to remember that these estates do not form a single entity. Hurdsfield, Victoria Park, Weston, Moss Rose and Upton Priory each possess a history, architecture and 'feel' of their own. They are also integrated into the town to greater or lesser extents and are understood and spoken about in contrasting ways by local residents. Let us therefore introduce each in turn.

Hurdsfield, one of the most long-established of the town's estates, lies on the north-east reaches of the town in the foothills of the Peak district. Situated just off the Buxton Road on one side, and separated from the Silk Road by its industrial estate on the other, Hurdsfield feels more socially and geographically integrated with the rest of Macclesfield than any of the other estates (it is not at all evident to the passing visitor, for example, when one has entered or left Hurdsfield). It comprises in the main three-bedroom, greyish stone, semi-detached housing with both front and back gardens, a large number of which have since 1980 been bought and then renovated by their former tenants. At its hub on Brocklehurst Avenue (named after a prominent nineteenth-century silk family) is a green open space surrounded by the local mini-market, a library and the Borough housing office. Opposite them stand Macclesfield's only two tower blocks. These, however, were neither a 'landscape of fear' (Tuan 1979) among local residents (in all probability because they are occupied by senior citizens); nor, in spite of their visible prominence, do they appear to be a major aesthetic talking point in the rest of the town. Among the people we spoke to, Hurdsfield was generally considered to be the 'quietest' of Macclesfield's estates.

Further down the hill, at the foot of Buxton Road, stands Victoria Park flats (known colloquially as 'Vicky Park' or just 'the flats'). Built in the late 1960s following the 'slum-clearance' of an area of old terraced cottages, Victoria Park consists of three blocks of grey concrete low-rise flats, broken up only by the red 'vandal proof' panelling that lines the walkways. The whole complex includes a pub (The Bull) and a sparse parade of shops (including a hairdresser and small grocer's). The flats are the most unpopular and 'difficult to let' of all the Borough Council's housing stock and have thus tended to house those in most desperate need of accommodation. Not one of the properties has been purchased under the 'Right to Buy' scheme introduced by the Conservative government in 1980; and, since 1992, the estate has been protected by a CCTV and concierge-controlled access system, for which the Council charges tenants an additional levy. We return to this in Chapter 3.

The flats sit in a triangle the other side of the Silk Road from the railway station. They are bounded on one side by Commercial Street, on the other by Buxton Road, and at the back by the park from which they take their name. Standing uncomfortably and incongruously between the flats and the Silk Road is Arighi Bianchi – one of the most exclusive furniture stores in the North of England. The contrast is stark, and one that seems to stand for a broader lack of fit between the flats and the town. For not only are Victoria Park flats architecturally odd in what is for the most part a town of houses (thus making them seem like some kind of imposition from the world beyond), they are also the only council-built estate that people routinely see – whether they be townsfolk, or merely passing motorists and railway passengers. It should thus come as little surprise to discover that – of all the town's estates – Victoria Park cropped up most often when Macclesfield residents spoke of crime or drugs. It is very much Macclesfield's Other.

The Moss (or Moss Rose as many of its residents prefer it to be called) is the oldest of Macclesfield's estates. It is also the most geographically isolated, located as it is about a mile south of the town centre, just off the Leek Road, behind Macclesfield Town's football stadium. Started in the 1920s to house people decanted from town centre slum properties, the Moss comprises mainly gardened semi-detached houses (many of which have again been bought and improved by their tenants), interspersed with a few streets of detached bungalows and some senior citizens' flats. It is bounded to the north by two streets of spacious private housing. In national terms this would by no means be considered a 'problem estate', though it shares with so many of Britain's public housing schemes a dearth of amenities. The Mayfield community centre aside, the area is served by two pubs and only one general store – the Late Shop on Leek Road. Children and young people hanging around the area have recently been a cause of concern among adult residents.

The Weston estate, built in 1947, lies on the western fringes of the town. Though clearly bounded on three sides by some large private housing, the Weston – much like Hurdsfield – seems somehow to merge into its immediate environs. With a more 'modern' feel than either Hurdsfield or Moss Rose, the Weston would also be considered 'good stock' in a 'good area' if transposed into, say, Salford or Manchester. The area comprises a mix of semi-detached houses and terraced bungalows, though some private housing is also currently being built on the estate. The area is served by a Post Office and Co-op on Ivy Lane, and a rather dilapidated parade of shops on Earlsway, the estate's main thoroughfare. These include a grocer's, video shop, chippie and off-licence, and stand next to the community centre and Ridgegate pub. The Weston has been the site in recent years of a fair degree of tension between young people hanging around the shops and older residents, tension which came to a head in June 1993 when a suspected teenage car thief was very publicly detained and 'humiliated' by a group of local 'vigilantes' (see, further, Girling *et al.* 1998).

Upton Priory was built in the 1960s to accommodate people from Scotland and Manchester looking for work in Macclesfield. Situated in the north-west of the town, it is nestled in a triangle between Prestbury Road, Priory Road and Kennedy Avenue. This gives the estate a rather isolated, self-enclosed feel and, apart from along Kennedy Avenue, one would not – indeed cannot – drive through it en route to anywhere else. At its northern point, Upton Priory borders the rugby club, the 'successful', grant-maintained Fallibroome secondary school (which many of the estate's children attend), and a small number of detached houses located within the confines of neighbouring Prestbury.[5] To the south (along Kennedy Avenue) it presses up against a modern development of large owner-occupied housing.

Upton Priory is internally sub-divided into three distinct areas. One, which by car can be entered and exited only by Priory Lane, consists mostly of good quality terraced housing with small gardens. The cul-de-sac roads are combined with a maze of pedestrian walkways connecting the various streets. A second, accessible by car only from Prestbury Road, comprises terraced housing and four grey, four-storey blocks of flats, and is again connected by a web of walkways (in 'designing out crime' terms, the whole area is a disaster). It also houses the infant and junior schools and is divided from the Priory Lane site by a small expanse of hollow woodland. The final part of the estate lies along the western end of Kennedy Avenue. It comprises terraced housing and some four-storey blocks of flats, coupled with a small amount of modest, recently completed housing on the market at £25,000. Marking the boundary between the area and the middle-class properties to the south of Kennedy Avenue, is a small parade of shops serving the whole estate (it's a good 10-minute walk to them from the northern end). These are housed in one block faced by an open green space and comprise a pub (The Oval – so-called because of its shape), a video shop, chemist, chippie, newsagent, off-licence and 'Select and Save' supermarket. Local youths in this area have again – as we shall see in Chapter 4 – been the cause of much concern to older residents.

The last of these estates was constructed by Macclesfield Borough Council in the 1960s, subsequent to which the bulk of the new housing in the town has been privately built. These five estates are thus now interspersed with, and some-times lie squarely adjacent to, the owner-occupied houses that now comprise the majority form of tenure in Macclesfield. Much of this has resulted in what one might call 'suburban' (or – with a touch of irony – 'greater') Macclesfield coming to possess a less 'distinctive' character, a rather more 'placeless' feel. To take a stroll around the streets of Tytherington, or those south of Kennedy Avenue, or through what is known locally as the 'Georgian Jungle' around Broken Cross, is to encounter mainly three- and four-bedroom, semi- and detached houses of the kind one finds across numerous English shire towns and metropolitan suburbs. These are places possessed of a spacious streetscape, fenceless front gardens that end when the lawn meets the pavement, and a dearth of shops, pubs and other public amenities (though Tytherington can lay claim to an original parade of shops, around which local teenagers have tended to gather; and the most recent wave of building has included a (membership only) golfing and leisure complex – the Tytherington Club). They are places largely 'abandoned' by their occupants during working hours. And in some instances (most visibly in the case of the two 'Villas' developments) they are encircled behind walls of the kind that increas-ingly appear to accompany new-build middle-class housing in Britain. These are ordinary, outwardly untroubled, comfortable, prosperous locations, very much bearing the mark of their mobile residents, very much integral to what Macclesfield has become. Richard Hoggart (1993: 45) captures something of all this in his portrait of middle-class Farnham in Surrey:

> For most of these executives their professional life could have landed them in any one of a thousand similar developments of similar housing. And tomorrow they may be required to move on, two hundred miles, to another similar estate. In such circumstances, you do not carry much idea of a collective memory; your history starts a short time back, is captured not in books, but in framed wedding and onwards photos on the mantelpiece and coffee table, is the history of your nuclear family.

Hoggart's account of Farnham in fact resonates closely with much that one finds in Macclesfield. The resemblances are striking: the 1960s architectural 'monstrosity' in the heart of the town, the shops, the old men outside Argos, the clothes, the bypass, the pubs, even down to the facade of the NatWest building – this could in so many senses be Macclesfield. The comparison also provides a reminder that, for all the local detail we have endeavoured to recover here, the global processes we set out in Chapter 1 are working to flatten the differences between places. As Hoggart (1993: xvii) remarks: 'So many characteristics of towns "like this" are bound to be shared that it may seem otiose to mention them; yes of course they do things in Farnham as they do all over the place; and yes the same winds of cultural change blow through all our streets; why bother to say so?'

Yet the place we have just introduced, and in which we spent two years speaking to people about their hopes, expectations and concerns, *is* Macclesfield. It is not Farnham. Nor is it anywhere else. And it is – as we shall see shortly – important to the residents of this town that this is – and continues to remain – so; albeit that they relate to the town, and feel 'connected' with it, in some greatly varying ways. Macclesfield – for many if not all of its residents – has particular social meanings; fits into their biographies in particular ways, is a place in respect of which they have particular material and often emotional attachments. 'Otiose' or not, we need to register and keep hold of this. People continue to lead 'local' lives (albeit through tokens of landscape and consumption that may be anything but 'local'); and we believe this has some important criminological concomitants and consequences. Before turning to these, however, there is more be said about Macclesfield, its recent fortunes, and the spatial and temporal idioms through which its residents talk about and make sense of 'their town'.

From silk to riches? The story of Macclesfield's 'success'

In 1945 Macclesfield was a fairly homogeneous working-class town where people lived *and* worked; where a man walked the streets with a long pole tapping people up for the day's toil, and where town would close for two 'Barnabas' weeks in June and residents would holiday *en masse*. As one female manager at Zeneca recalled: 'We all went off to Blackpool to sit on the beach with people we lived with at home. It's incredible.'

Contemporary Macclesfield could hardly be more different. Like so many other places in recent years, the town has experienced some profound economic and social changes; though unlike many it has been – in conventional economic terms at least – a net beneficiary of such changes. As its traditional industries (principally, and famously, silk) have declined and been superseded by a revised industrial and enhanced service sector, the town's indigenous working-class population has been joined by increasing numbers of largely managerial and professional incomers, and its national and global connections have been correspondingly accentuated. The most striking transformative 'moment' was provided by the pharmaceutical multinational Zeneca (formerly ICI), who moved their international headquarters to Macclesfield in the 1960s, thus 'saving' the town – it is said locally – from a 'Northern fate' (as one resident put it: 'We're lucky that Zeneca chose to make here their headquarters, otherwise I believe Macclesfield would have died'). Zeneca were subsequently joined by several other drugs companies (notably, CIBA-Geigy), thereby establishing Macclesfield and its immediate environs as a base for the pharmaceutical industry. The result of this, taken together with the boom of the late 1980s, and the continued migration of those in flight from Manchester, is that Macclesfield has become a moderately affluent, predominantly middle-class commuter town, though one, as we shall see, with both its pockets of deprivation and its fair share of insecurities and anxieties. We want in this section briefly to recount this story; describing first some of the (more significant) 'layers of investment' (Massey 1984) that contributed to this transformation (or – in more technical language – 'restructuring', see Bagguley *et al.* 1990), before going on to consider how this 'success' is marketed locally and who among the town's citizens are (in quantitative terms) its winners and losers.

Economic restructuring ...

Industrialization in Macclesfield was based almost solely around the silk industry. Following the establishment of Macclesfield as a country market town in the early seventeenth century, and the subsequent development of a reputation for the manufacture of silk buttons, the first sewing mill producing silk thread was opened by Charles Roe in 1743. The Macclesfield silk industry subsequently prospered and the town began to experience substantial growth: the population doubled between 1801 and 1821 and doubled again between 1831 and 1851. Thus it was that Macclesfield's fortunes came to be entwined with those of the silk industry – or, as local historical lore has it: 'Silk made Macclesfield and Macclesfield made silk.'

In the years between 1960 and the 1990s, however, the town's economic fortunes shifted dramatically. As the silk industry fell into a rapid long-term decline,[6] Macclesfield's economy developed a relatively stable and – according to Macclesfield Borough Council – 'enviable' diversification into new manufacturing, research and development, and service industries. On this (revised) foundation, the town has continued to prosper, to some extent bucking regional (the 'Northern fate') and in some instances national trends. This is a matter of some interest to local writers who generally attribute this success to a combination of three factors: the town's geographical location, the arrival and subsequent development of the pharmaceutical industry, and the significant growth of companies started and run by people living and working in the area, what one might call a 'small firms culture' (Jackson 1990).[7]

Macclesfield managed to translate its particular manufacturing tradition and culture into the latter part of the twentieth century through what the Borough Council describes as a very deliberate policy of supporting and enabling frameworks; an interpretation of success which largely takes the form of detailed accounts of how particular firms came to Macclesfield.[8] Chemical and pharmaceutical companies, in particular, have been very much responsible for Macclesfield's reputation as a desirable business location, as well as for much of its contemporary economic prosperity.

Zeneca (the pharmaceutical company) has maintained such a high profile in the commercial and social life of Macclesfield that it has become increasingly hard for people to envisage the kind of future Macclesfield would have had if the company had not chosen to move there in 1960.[9] When production started in April 1966, the firm employed 1,000 people and by 1967 there were 1,100 permanent staff and 40 part-time packing jobs. Subsequently, Macclesfield seems to have evaded cuts suffered by ICI employees elsewhere. For example when ICI nationally shed 8,000 jobs across the group in 1971–2, no jobs were lost in Macclesfield, and again, when between 1975–82 ICI cut its British workforce by 43 per cent, there were no significant cutbacks in Macclesfield. Instead of cutbacks there was significant investment in the Macclesfield sites and by the early 1990s the total Macclesfield (town) workforce had risen to 1,731, 80 per cent of them recruited from the local area (Jackson 1990).[10]

CIBA, a Swiss chemical company, began manufacturing in Macclesfield in the early 1960s. The directors of the company chose Macclesfield because it was in Cheshire, and in a more pragmatic vein than ICI, indicated that their decision was influenced by a set of enabling local authority frameworks which made readily available land with planning permission, and promised to house a substantial supply of labour in the area (Jackson 1990). Construction commenced in 1962 and production in 1964, with the company later moving its headquarters to the town in 1982. Explaining the decision to move to a local researcher (Jackson 1990), the managing director of the company drew explicit attention to the skills and social relations that he saw as the beneficial residue of Macclesfield's past:

> The high element of family relationships amongst the staff and the friendly helpfulness which have been a feature of life on the Macc site from the outset [and] the high manual dexterity of the Macclesfield employees, a remnant from the silk industry.

There is no doubt that the pharmaceutical industry – of which these two companies are the most prominent examples – has had a substantial impact on Macclesfield. These companies have – it is said – saved the town from the post-industrial decline that has afflicted so many other towns and cities across the North of England during the post-war period. They have contributed to a contemporary and revised sense of Macclesfield's 'distinctiveness' and a local aura of 'deserved good fortune'. Through the provision of funds and personnel, they play a large part in the town's life, Zeneca, in particular, being represented in a range of local schools, community groups and organizations (including the crime prevention panel).[11] And by bringing to the area a large number of highly skilled, highly remunerated managers and professionals, they have had a profound effect on Macclesfield's contemporary socio-demographic composition and social relations.

... its Marketing, its Winners and its Losers

Reading the (publicity) material produced by Macclesfield's urban managers and entrepreneurs – the Borough Council, Cheshire County Council, the local Chamber of Commerce – one obtains a clear sense of a town that has succeeded where other (ex-)manufacturing towns failed. Addressed mainly to potential investors and their staff (though also perhaps aimed at the local population[12]), this genre of 'local information' optimistically promotes the economic and cultural 'distinctiveness' of the town (and wider Borough). In respect of the former, it largely takes the form of a local 'folk story' of success. It speaks of a town that has successfully shrugged off its old industrial past; of a 'thriving economy'; local 'growth industries'; of Macclesfield's reputation for 'independence and self-sufficiency'; of its 'renowned small business sector and entrepreneurial spirit'. As one Borough Council publication put it:

> Today the borough has shrugged off the problems of declining industries and is a prosperous area with a thriving local economy and enviable lifestyle and environment.
>
> (Macclesfield Borough Council 1995: 39)

In respect of the latter, however, these 'declining industries' continue to play a part in cementing the town's reputation and future, now translated into a 'product' (the most visible signs of which are the Silk Heritage Centre and nearby 'working mill') that can attract visitors and help create a 'local niche' attractive to investors. This in turn forms part of what has become the marketing of Macclesfield as a desirable location with an 'enviable lifestyle'. The town clearly aims to attract 'high quality' developments, this adjective figuring prominently in both the Economic Development Strategy and the Borough's Draft Local Plan. The Borough Council (monitored and supported energetically by the local Civic Society) is also at great pains, in determining what does and doesn't get built, and to what specification, to protect the appearance and reputation of Macclesfield as an historic 'old silk town'.

All this of course is understandable enough. In an age when the fortunes of localities depend on attracting inward investment from across the globe, the 'place-marketing' of towns and cities (and their specific distinctiveness) has become an important task of local urban governance, especially outside of established 'headquarters cities' (Logan and Molotch 1987; Philo and Kearns 1993; Taylor *et al.* 1996).[13] But how does this promotionalism compare with what we might call Macclesfield's 'statistical reputation'; with what can be known about the town's contemporary social composition and demography, and the prosperity or otherwise of its residents? Let us turn briefly to some of these matters.

There are certainly many aspects of Macclesfield's socio-economic profile that support these 'official' representations of the town. The 1991 *Census* indicates that Macclesfield district had more residents employed in professional or managerial positions than any other in Cheshire (some 22.7 per cent of the district's adult citizens possessed diplomas, first or higher degrees). The picture at ward level, however, is somewhat more varied. Macclesfield's two northern-most and 'suburban' wards (covering areas such as Tytherington) had the highest proportions of people in managerial or professional occupations (Macclesfield north-east 44.4 per cent; Macclesfield north-west 42.4 per cent), while its two most southerly wards (which encompass the council-built estates of Weston and Moss Rose) recorded the lowest such levels (Macclesfield south 32.7 per cent; Macclesfield west 33.3 per cent).

A similar picture emerges in respect of unemployment. Throughout the recession of the early 1990s Macclesfield fared relatively well here. While levels of unemployment rose locally, the Macclesfield 'travel to work area' continued to record rates below both the national and regional (north-west) averages. In 1994 it had the lowest unemployment-to-vacancy ratio of anywhere in Cheshire, an indication of the relatively high number of vacancies in the area. Matters are again more uneven, however, when we look at the town itself. A breakdown of the 1991 *Census* by enumeration districts reveals the existence of pockets of high unemployment in certain parts of Macclesfield, with the rates of joblessness in parts of Victoria Park flats registering over 30 per cent. Across the town, levels of unemployment (as of April 1994) were as follows: Macclesfield central – 6.2 per cent; Macclesfield east – 10.5 per cent; Macclesfield north-east – 5.6 per cent; Macclesfield north-west – 4.6 per cent; Macclesfield south – 10.1 per cent and Macclesfield west – 6.7 per cent.

Three other measures warrant consideration here. In respect of housing tenure, Macclesfield (district) has by some distance the largest proportion of owner-occupied accommodation in Cheshire (76.8 per cent). In line with national trends, the provision of council housing in the town has declined since the 1960s. In 1969 there were 4,842 council-owned properties in Macclesfield, a number which had dropped to 3,839 by 1991 (though our interviews with Borough housing officers suggest that take-up under the 'Right to Buy' scheme introduced in 1980 has varied greatly, with most interest having come from Hurdsfield and Weston). The tenure situation in the different wards (as of 1991) is set out in Table 2.1.

In terms of car ownership, 78 per cent of Macclesfield households possess one or more cars, twice the current national average. According to the 1991 *Census*, 37.1 per cent of households in Macclesfield district owned two or more cars (compared to a Cheshire figure of 28.9 per cent), while 21.6 per cent of households possessed no car at all. Again the figures vary from ward to ward, as can be seen from Table 2.2.

Let us consider, finally, various measures of 'area stress'. In 1991, Cheshire County Council's Research and Intelligence Unit produced a report on areas of family stress using data from client records and the 1991 *Census*. Focusing on

Table 2.1 Housing tenure in Macclesfield (1991)

Ward	Owner-occupied (%)	Private-rented (%)	Council (%)	Housing Association (%)
Central	86.8	9.9	1.3	2
East	64.3	9.0	24.1	2.6
North-east	74.7	4.5	0.7	0.2
North-west	80.5	3.9	12.7	2.9
South	58.7	6.5	29.9	4.9
West	58.4	2.3	34.7	4.6

Source: 1991 *Census.*

Table 2.2 Car ownership in Macclesfield (1991)

Ward	Households with no car (%)	Households with two or more cars (%)
Central	26.9	25.4
East	35.8	20.9
North-east	27.3	29.6
North-west	19.8	35
South	38.3	18.8
West	32.3	26.5

Source: 1991 *Census.*

measures of stress for families with children and younger adults, a total of eight indicators were identified: free school meals, child protection, children and family referrals, children in care, community service orders, supervision orders, unemployment and lone parent households. The Council then combined the eight individual factors to produce a composite indicator of family stress, and ranked different areas according to this measure. While Macclesfield district had no wards which could be classed as 'stress wards' on the basis of *Census* variables, twenty-four enumeration districts (EDs) were classified as 'stress EDs' (encompassing 8 per cent of the Borough's population). Those for the town itself are documented in Table 2.3 below. As can be seen, the most predominant cluster of 'family stress' was identified in areas in the south and west of the town (encompassing Moss Rose and Weston estates), compared with much lower figures reported in the more prosperous, 'suburban' North. There is perhaps no better indicator of the way in which Macclesfield has been transformed in the post-war period into a place where poverty and affluence sit side by side.[14]

Table 2.3   'Stress EDs' in Macclesfield

Ward	No. of 'Stress EDs'	% of population in 'Stress EDs'
Central	1	1
East	2	17
North-east	1	7
North-west	2	13
South	4	28
West	4	23

Source: Cheshire County Council (1991).

A 'balanced' town?: the social meanings of Macclesfield

When asked in our focus groups about the town in which they lived – to consider what had attracted them to it, how it had changed, how they would characterize its social relations, what they liked or disliked about it – there was a widespread recognition among our respondents that the town's composition, prosperity and 'feel' had been greatly transformed in recent decades. This was often made sense of in terms of the impact of economic change on the town's inherited industrial reputation and 'way of life'. Some felt here that in the midst of these changes the town had managed to retain something of its 'northern feel'. In part this was a reference to Macclesfield's 'welcoming, very friendly, good-hearted people' (male resident, Kennedy Avenue), and to how it remained 'very easy to get to know people in the shops and pubs' (female resident, High Street). More generally, people pointed to the (residual) 'close-knit' quality of local social relations:

> There's a lot of people who have all their relatives living here. You talk to somebody and mum and dad live down the road, and cousin lives next door but one. It seems to be one of those towns that hasn't encouraged people to leave. Most of my family lives in Macclesfield. It's very much, just looking at this company, husband and wives work here, and brother and sisters, what have you. It's very much a family orientated town.
>
> (male clerical worker, Zeneca)

Many, however, felt the town was no longer 'like this'. This in part is a question of appearance: 'The image of Macclesfield, when I first came to live here was of a very old-fashioned mill town. It always looked a bit scruffy and run down. But that has gone now' (male resident, Kennedy Avenue). But it has also to do with the kinds of people that have been attracted to the town in recent decades, and their impact upon its architecture and lived social relations. As one Zeneca manager put it: '[There's been] an influx of wealth because of industry. They've moved people in, I guess fairly well-educated people that are getting good jobs. The demand for big detached houses has increased.' This recognition led many to speak Macclesfield as a town with 'above average wealth' and 'below average unemployment', and as having become 'an expensive place to live compared to other areas in the north-west' (home watch coordinator, Tytherington). In these respects, Macclesfield has come to seem somewhat out of place in the 'North of England', no longer what people expect:

> When people come to visit friends and colleagues in Macclesfield they're surprised at its location, at the town itself. People think of it, and there's the terminology, people often laugh at the name Macclesfield. I think it's had this downtrodden image, typical north. Particularly, like myself, coming up from the south in the last seven years. There's people in London who won't go further than north of the Watford Gap.[15] They think Macclesfield is something in the smoke-ridden north-west. I think people are very surprised. And I think when you compare the quality of life that people here have, I think it's very high.
>
> (male resident, The Villas)

Against this backdrop, let us conclude this chapter by considering further two aspects of local people's 'place-talk'; first, their sense of the qualities that the town offers its residents; and second, the assessments people make of the town's contemporary 'social mix'. As we shall see, they both seem to revolve around the question of whether Macclesfield in the mid-1990s can accurately be described as what one resident called a 'balanced' town.

'A lovely little town'

Despite the different places that Macclesfield's residents occupy in the wider world, it was striking during our discussions that people *from across the town* would (in certain respects at least) speak about the town using roughly similar vocabularies and motifs. Whether indigenous Maxonians or lately arrived incomers, inhabitants of weavers' cottages, council-built estates or middle-class 'suburbs', our (adult) discussants generally expressed feelings of (sometimes great) pride in 'their town'. For the most part, they believe Macclesfield to be a relatively benign, 'homely' entity, variously characterizing it as 'a lovely little town' (male resident, High Street), 'a very pleasant little town' (male resident, Upton Priory) or even as 'more of a village than a town' (female resident, Moss Rose). As one man, a resident of Broken Cross for some twenty-five years, remarked: 'Quite frankly, it would take an awful lot for me to move out of Macclesfield. ... We do complain about things. But I think that you would go a long way to find a better place.' As we shall see in the next chapter, sentiments such as this flow in part from the town being conceived of as a 'safe' place; or at least one characterized by a 'relative absence' of some of the more troubling and detrimental aspects of contemporary English society as these are experienced elsewhere – the pollution, drugs, racial tensions and associated evils of the big city. But they also seem to incorporate reference to Macclesfield's abundant positive attributes. For while various concerns about the town were voiced during our interviews and focus groups – mainly about ongoing expansion, the ensuing traffic problems and the risk posed to the town's character (as one High Street resident put it: 'I think it's a bit anonymous now; it reminds me of a lot of other places') – our respondents were in the main concerned to enthuse about Macclesfield and the high quality of life it was thought to offer.

In no small measure this has to do with various features of the town itself, with the availability 'on your doorstep' (home watch coordinator, Tytherington) of a range of 'excellent' facilities and amenities. The local hospital and shops were mentioned frequently in this regard, and were instrumental in persuading this Zeneca employee to move to the town: 'It had good facilities in the town, like the shops were good. You had most of the shops that you require without being too large, department stores which perhaps were not attracting too many people in from outside.' So too were the local schools, Macclesfield clearly being felt by many parents to be what one Upton Priory resident called 'a smashing place to bring up kids':

> It always seemed a nice place to bring children up. If you were in this area it was nice, let's be honest. The schools were good, the schools were good in this area. The job opportunities were good, and we've got relatively low unemployment in Macc, or relatively low compared to the rest of the country. But then it wasn't that far for children to go to Manchester, Stockport, there were other opportunities around if they wanted to get out.
>
> (female resident, Broken Cross)

Yet, as this account suggests, Macclesfield's attractiveness as a place also arises from its (spatial and social) location within the English landscape. Two aspects of this are of particular significance. On the one hand, Macclesfield appeals for being close to, yet distant from the metropolis; a separate place, yet one well-connected to other, bigger, more consequential places; a place that offers its residents the possibilities of the city, while insulating them from its most disquieting features. Hence this women's response to having moved to Macclesfield from London with her two young children:

> It was like heaven on earth coming here. This is fourteen years ago. The thing that struck me, you've got all the shops that you need. If you want the bigger shops, you've got 20 minutes on the train and you're in Manchester. You've got two hours to London. You've got the countryside on the doorstep.
>
> (female resident, Broken Cross)

On the other hand, Macclesfield can count as 'honorary countryside'. It offers both clear vistas of, and easy access to, the Peak District National Park ('a beautiful part of the country' (female resident, Upton Priory)), without being – as one

Zeneca clerical worker put it – 'in the back of beyond'. This is clearly apparent in the fondness for their 'adopted' town expressed by these 'incomers':

> We're surrounded by the most beautiful countryside. We've got Manchester on the doorstep, we've got Liverpool on the doorstep, we've got Warrington on the doorstep, if we want them. But we are surrounded by the most beautiful countryside.
>
> (male manager, Zeneca)

Sandra: I would say that is an attractive town.
RS: What about it?
Sandra: Both geographically, because of its setting on the edge of the hills and the plain, and because of its configuration, it's surrounded by a lot of attractive countryside and farming, and so it is a separate entity from, even though it's quite close to, somewhere like Wilmslow. It's still a very separate place. It's got its own feel and community spirit.[16]

(female resident, Kennedy Avenue)

Macclesfield then seems to appeal to its (adult) residents both for the distinctive identity and amenities it offers, and for its proximity to both the country and the city. This is encapsulated succinctly in the following description of the town proffered by a member of the local Civic Society. He also makes explicit the part played in this assessment by the town's position as a place of 'relative safety', a matter we return to in due course:

> To me it's a balanced town. It's just about the right size for a community to live in. It's got all the necessary shops, and if you want to nip for a bit of do-it-yourself you can. You've got everything here but without it having to be sprawling all over the place. Also I've always admired a place when you can stand in the centre and look out and see hills around. I thought I'd love to retire to a place like this, and we found it in Macclesfield. It's aesthetically attractive, and they haven't tried to destroy it too much. ... It's just the right size. It's got stable industry now, and I think this is reflected in its crime figures actually. Because the local paper, if anything happens it's highlighted. It isn't something of an everyday occurrence, it gets real media attention on the basis that it doesn't happen that often. It's got a good hospital, it's got good educational facilities. It's beautifully balanced, the whole place.

'A nice mix of people'?

This idea of 'balance' cannot, however, be so readily or uncontentiously employed to describe Macclesfield's current social composition and the relative prospects and insecurities of its residents. On this aspect of the town, the dispositions of our respondents varied much more widely, with some markedly different strands of thought and feeling emerging on the question of whether Macclesfield had come to be inhabited by what one Kennedy Avenue resident called 'a nice mix of people'.

Some among our discussants were clearly of this opinion, though it arose in one of two contrasting forms. One view recognizes that Macclesfield is now comprised of people from different class positions (with different income levels and prospects), but takes it as a matter of local pride that the town has successfully managed to accommodate such differences. Macclesfield here has (happily) become 'a cosmopolitan place' where one 'meets lot of people from different parts of the world' (male resident, Kennedy Avenue), a town with 'a real good cross-section of the social orders' (male resident, Broken Cross). For some – such as this Civic Society member – this clearly represents an appealing feature of contemporary Macclesfield: 'One of the things that attracted me about the town is the fact of having been brought up on a very large estate, a one-class estate, to come to a town where all classes live cheek-by-jowl, there's a real social mix. The town is still small enough for that to happen.'

Yet this 'nice mix' outlook on the town can also draw people to the opposite conclusion, one that elides the differences that might obtain between local residents. In our focus group with people living on The Villas, for example, one man asked his fellow residents to 'agree that Macclesfield "is predominantly upper-middle class"'. Earlier in the same focus group, another male resident had offered this account, characterizing contemporary Macclesfield as a 'single community':

> I think it's a very generalized town. The people are in it are not laid back, but content with life. If you compare it with a big city where you get communities that are different, there isn't in Macclesfield, it's one community. In general you can't say that is a poor area, or that's a rich area. There is a general economy throughout the town that is the same, give or take an inch. The people are also fairly content with life. Laid back, happy, they'll talk to you. You go to a big town and they won't. People will smile at you. It's a unified common denomination town.

It was in this vein that a number of our respondents commented on what one Tytherington home watch coordinator chose to describe as the 'very low percentage of foreigners in Macclesfield, considering that it was a textile area. One would expect to find a lot of Indians and Pakistanis.' It is certainly true that Macclesfield remains a predominantly 'white' town (though there are small Asian and Chinese communities). With some hesitation, a female member of the Civic Society wondered whether this – for some – might represent one of the town's attractions:

> Dare I say something else, this is being recorded and I'm more or less frightened to say this actually. One of the reasons that people like living in Macclesfield is that it's a white population, whereas if you go to Stockport, or Manchester, or the Midlands, a lot of immigrants came there. There was no work here for immigrants, therefore they didn't settle here, and that's one

of the things that makes it attractive to the white middle-classes who suddenly said: 'Right Macclesfield, you can go and work in Manchester.' That's one of the reasons they come here.[17]

These contrasting 'nice mix' assessments of the town's current social composition were generally voiced by our middle-class respondents (most of whom were 'incomers'), and are by no means universally shared. We encountered among others a more pronounced awareness of what one High Street resident called 'the two Macclesfields'; of the cleavages forged by recent economic transformations between largely professional 'incomers' and the indigenous working-class population (cf. Fielding 1995; Urry 1995). In registering this divide, some of the former spoke here in ways that tended to construct – or at least reinforce – a distinction between the 'cosmopolitanism of the elites' and 'the tribalism of local communities' (Castells 1993); with the latter being cast – by this Zeneca manager, for instance – as 'close-knit' and 'clannish', yet at the same time somewhat insular and parochial: 'They may well have pride in Macclesfield, but they haven't seen anywhere else. That's the sort of impression I get.' The following exchange illustrates much the same point and is worth quoting at length:

Jim: I think there are two tribes in Macclesfield actually. There are the people who are born-and-bred in Macclesfield. Then there's a lot of people, generally professional well-qualified people, who move here to work at Zeneca and the other large companies who are looking for skilled people. They stand out very clearly. When you walk down Macclesfield on a Saturday looking at the people on the main street, you can spot the ones from Macclesfield and spot the ones that have moved in, I'm sure.

RS: By their clothes?

Jim: Just the …

Tim: General bearing, isn't it?

Jim: General bearing, they [the incomers] seem more sophisticated.
        […]

RS: When you say two tribes, do you mean two groups of people that don't connect with each other at all?

Jim: I think there's a very tight infrastructure amongst the people who have always lived here. I see that particularly at work where there are large groups of them. They've got family connections which go back generations, which they're very proud of, and they have a lot of support from their families. Then generally people that have moved here have left their families behind. They have a different type of association with each other, it's more social and less family based. That means that they do different types of things. They go in different pubs, have a different way of life.

(home watch coordinators, Tytherington)

It was among those on the receiving end of this categorization, those who have done less well out of Macclesfield's recent resurgence, that we tended to find what one retired 'Maxonian' teacher described as 'resentment' towards contemporary social changes – towards people coming in who worked in Manchester 'on high salaries' and who were 'buying the bigger houses'. Some people here simply didn't share the 'official' depiction of the town as affluent. As one woman living in Victoria Park flats put it: 'Macclesfield isn't a rich town. It's mainly council estates, isn't it? You've got the Moss, the Priory. You've got this concrete jungle [the flats]. It's on the outskirts, Prestbury, Cheadle Hulme, Wilmslow, that's the rich, posh side.' Others evinced a much more pronounced sense either of Macclesfield in decline ('It used to be a thriving mill town, now it's going rapidly down hill', as one High Street resident put it); or of a 'boom town' that was not booming 'for the community as a whole' (male clerical worker, Zeneca). This point of view was expressed powerfully by this woman from Hurdsfield:

> Well I think from the town going into industry, it offered a lot of opportunities for people to be employed, but not everybody has that opportunity to do it. Are you with me? That's what I think. With the build up from the sixties of these big companies, without making any mention, because there's several of them, it has certainly brought the industry in and made it very, very prosperous, but not everybody is able to go and work for them. You have a sort of a split divide between those that are comfortable and those that really struggle, still working in the mills, still doing the mundane jobs. Not everybody is a whizz kid. Do you understand what I mean?

The above accounts notwithstanding, we encountered relatively little (overt) conflict between these 'two tribes' and, as we shall see shortly, little of the town's crime-talk is permeated by a divide between 'incomers' and 'estate-dwellers'. These dispositions towards contemporary Macclesfield and its residents nonetheless provide a clear illustration of some of the divides the town's changing fortunes in the wider world have opened up in recent years. At the very least, Macclesfield has come to be inhabited, sometimes – as in the High Street – side by side, by people who have very different histories behind them, very different futures ahead of them, and correspondingly divergent senses of their place. This exchange between three current inhabitants of the High Street – Margaret, a resident of over thirty years, and two of her younger, professional neighbours – illustrates this only too well. It seems a fitting note on which to bring this chapter to a close:

IL: Would you describe Macclesfield as a friendly place?
Jane: Yes.
Margaret: So so, it rather depends. It can be, but then again not necessarily. People I speak to I've spoken to for years. You get people in now and they just don't bother any more.

Fiona: I think it's a friendly place, it's one of the friendliest places I've lived, and I don't want to move. I've lived in Wales, southern England, middle England, northern England, and I think Macclesfield is great. It's small enough to get to know people. Yes, it's a friendly place.

Margaret: I think the people now keep themselves to themselves. Any trouble, people lock themselves in now and pretend it doesn't go on. They don't get involved, they don't get together to stop it. They pretend, hide behind their curtains. That didn't happen.

Fiona: Isn't that because it was a tighter close-knit community and you knew everybody along your street, and now you don't, because people have to move around for their jobs, and they have to go to Manchester for a job, they have to move if they're made redundant. We're in a society that moves around a lot more than we did thirty years ago.

3 The common places of crime
Crime in local talk

It is time to turn our attention more directly to questions of crime. We suggested in Chapter 1 that 'crime' and 'place' are in some complex, significant (and researchable) ways entangled; arguing that people's sensibilities towards crime depend on their sense of place, and that their orientation towards place is – in part at least – determined by considerations of crime and order. We now want to put some substantive flesh on the theoretical bones of this argument by examining the kinds of social commentary (about Macclesfield, its people and places, its relationship to the wider world) that is embedded within our respondents' crime-talk. In part this is a matter of exploring the felt impact of crime upon Macclesfield and the quality of life it offers. What offences do the people of this town most often speak (and worry) about? How in relative terms do they assess the scale of Macclesfield's 'crime problem'? But it is also about examining how crime operates as a means through which people make sense of the town's (and, again, the wider world's) 'moral architecture'. Whom do the citizens of Macclesfield blame for crime or think of as threatening their safety? From where are these threats alleged to come? Which parts of the town are considered safe? Which are best avoided? This chapter is concerned with these questions, with how, in other words, crime figures in the lived social relations of this particular English town.

In addressing them we take up the following substantive issues. We want first to examine the idea of Macclesfield as a relatively safe place, what one might term a 'bubble of security'; and to consider the respective threats to the town that are said to arise from internal and external sources. Having done this, and seen in the process how Macclesfield is imagined as a place subject principally to exogenous criminal dangers, we examine in some detail two sites *within* the town that are – albeit in contrasting ways and to varying degrees – construed as local 'landscapes of fear' (Tuan 1979). These two incongruous locations are the town centre (of a Friday and Saturday night) and Victoria Park flats.

A bubble of security? Local crime, travelling crime

In 1995 Cheshire Police recorded 4,150 offences for the six beats covering the town of Macclesfield. Broken down by beat, the totals ranged from 819 offences for

Beat 3 (covering Moss Rose/High Street) to 468 for Beat 5 (town centre east/Victoria Park flats). The number of recorded offences for the town's remaining four beats was in descending order as follows: Beat 4 (Broken Cross/Weston) 789; Beat 6 (town centre west/'old town') 769; Beat 1 (Kennedy Avenue/Upton Priory) 700 and Beat 3 (Hurdsfield/Tytherington) 605. The vast majority of these were property offences, the most prevalent of which are set out in greater detail in Table 3.1.[1]

It is not our purpose here to provide any kind of detailed analysis of these figures (though the number of thefts from cars in Broken Cross/Weston stands out, and it is worth noting the relatively low recorded crime levels for the beat covering Victoria Park flats). In national terms, however, it is clear that these figures remain low (some sixteen times lower, for instance, than those experienced by the not so geographically distant Salford, in Greater Manchester – see Evans *et al.* 1996). For the most part this was reflected in the assessments made by our respondents of Macclesfield's 'crime problem'. This was commonly reckoned – by people from across the town – mainly to take the form of 'petty thieving, sheds broken into, cars broken into' (male resident, The Villas); what one High Street resident described as 'a fair amount of minor crime'. These Hurdsfield residents summed up the situation in their area in the following terms:

IL: What about on Hurdsfield, what offences happen most often here do you think?
Bill: Car violence.
Joy: Petty ...
Harry: Petty things.

Table 3.1 Recorded property offences in Macclesfield (1995)

Area	Burglary (domestic)	Burglary (other)	Car theft	Theft from cars	Bicycle theft	Criminal damage
Upton Priory/ Kennedy Ave	82	70	34	174	28	109
Tytherington/ Hurdsfield	90	57	17	103	25	97
Moss Rose/ High Street	87	161	38	142	36	131
Broken Cross/ Weston	59	75	16	248	43	114
Town centre(east)/Victoria Park	13	108	6	33	12	69
Town centre(west)/ 'old town'	26	144	23	85	23	109
Total	357	615	134	785	167	629

Joy:	Like the trees on Nicholson Avenue, they've been snapped off. They were planted last year. I went down yesterday, and it's such a shame.
Don:	It's like petty break-ins, and breaking into cars and taking the odd car. We don't get many cars taken from this area. It might be, say, one a month, something like that. It might even be less than that. But you get a lot of break-ins [into cars], don't you?

'Opportunistic' burglary also figured prominently on many people's inventories of offences that afflict the town, while some thought that Macclesfield's reputation for affluence might attract burglars of a more 'professional' kind – an issue we return to below. But few among our (adult) respondents thought that the town faced problems whose seriousness or prevalence went much beyond that. As one High Street resident put it: 'It is not what you could class as a violent town, by any stretch of the imagination.' Summing up a discussion of Macclesfield's 'crime problem', one Villas resident put matters thus:

> My conclusion is this. I think that we're not a rich enough area to get high-tech organized burglary, because there isn't anything worth doing. It's going to be a youth who is bored, or a gang, who are just going to spray an aerosol across your window or your wall, just to be bloody minded, to put it bluntly. Or it's going to be the opportune bloke who's come, it might be from Macclesfield or come in, and is hard up and does it for a living and is going to break in on a soft target. He's not a professional, he's a semi-professional.

It was thus felt that while crime had become an endemic feature of contemporary life (and in this sense a problem *everywhere*), Macclesfield continued to be a place of relative safety – 'very friendly, very crime-free really', as one resident put it. This was certainly the predominant view of Macclesfield's 'crime problem' voiced by our middle-class discussants, such as this resident of Broken Cross: 'I don't think it's a massive one compared to a lot. But it's there.' It was also the view found among the local magistrates we spoke to: 'I feel that we've not only got a Vauxhall Conference football team; we've also got a Vauxhall Conference type crime rate, meaning we're at the bottom of the leagues.'[2] And it seemed to be the (current) assessment of these residents of the Moss Rose estate:

Peter:	The crime rate isn't too high, there's some places like …
Dot:	But it is rising, it's rising rapidly now Peter, isn't it? But on the whole we have been very lucky, we've lagged behind a lot of them. Even now I don't think we're as bad as some of the inner-cities and things like that.
Peter:	Oh, nowhere near as bad as them.
Dot:	For instance, we don't have people nipping out shooting each other, drug people, like that, we haven't as yet reached that stage when we have a lot of that going on.

Crime in Macclesfield, then, is for the most part considered to be 'not very great' (Civic Society member), and people often derived satisfaction from the idea that in this respect the town 'lagged behind' other places (a point we return to). Yet there remained a clear sense that in this town – as in every town – criminal threats to one's persons and property existed, and such threats were, among many, a cause for concern. Some expressed the view that crime in the town was getting worse, that Macclesfield was – as one Kennedy Avenue resident put it – 'creeping up' on the likes of Manchester. Others (as we shall see in Chapter 7) go to varying lengths to protect their homes and property from the threats they believe they face. So let us consider this matter further. How do people account for the 'crime problem' as it presents itself in Macclesfield?[3] Who do they believe poses a danger to them? To what extent are these threats seen as coming from within or without?

People not places: local estates, local rogues and local crime

The inner-city and peripheral 'council estates' of Britain's cities loom large in political, media and lay discourse, not only about crime, but also about the 'state of the nation' more generally. Throughout the 1980s and 1990s such places have received extensive coverage. Many have become 'household names' within their respective towns and cities; some – Broadwater Farm, Meadowell, Ordsall, Hulme, Blackbird Leys – have become nationally infamous as repositories of crime, drugs, violence and multiple deprivations. These are the symbolic crime locations of late modern Britain, urban 'badlands' set among areas of greater safety, wealth and repute. They have as such become the object of much reportage and analysis, whether of a journalistic, social scientific or governmental kind (Parker 1983; Barke and Turnbull 1992; Campbell 1993; Social Exclusion Unit 1998). And they have attracted a welter of criminological attention which has focused variously on such matters as the institutional production of 'problem estates' (Gill 1977); their 'criminal careers' (Bottoms and Wiles 1986; Bottoms and Xanthos 1989); the cultures and conflicts of their inhabitants (Foster 1990; Evans *et al.* 1996), and the histories, substance and effects of their vernacular reputations (Damer 1974). One way or another, these are the common places of contemporary crime-talk.

Macclesfield's five council-built estates were – albeit in divergent ways – the object of contemplation and concern among many of our respondents, both young and old, Maxonians and incomers, working- and middle-class. As one Broken Cross resident observed: 'There is a lot of isolation in Macclesfield, and an awful lot of deprived areas. You've got one or two areas in Macclesfield where the social deprivation is disgusting.' Much of this talk is concerned with the histories, problems and shifting reputations of *particular* estates, a tendency to compare and contrast being a feature of both lay and local professional reflection on this topic: 'When I originally came to Macclesfield thirteen years ago, the Moss estate was the problem estate. Since that time it has moved from there to the Weston estate, now it has moved onto the Upton Priory estate' (Borough

Council housing officer). But – as we noted in Chapter 2 – people's talk also focused on fate of 'the estates' as a whole, and how they have *collectively* fared in the midst of contemporary social and economic change. As one Weston resident said of the town's ongoing development:

> They're not thinking about the working-class or the lower-class, Weston estaters. They're not thinking about us, they're not thinking about the residents of the estates and things, as long as they've got their hands in that purse they don't give a sod. When I say they, I mean the hierarchy.

One born-and-bred Maxonian, now living around High Street, proffered a cognate observation about the plight of those 'stuck' on Moss Rose:

> I know, two, three generations of certain families in Macc, like on the Moss estate, who I've grown up with. And what they see is, with no disrespect to anyone else here, is people coming from outside, doing very well, going through Macc, who are not Macc people. Not taking jobs, I'm not saying that, but I'm sure they see that, all these people working for ICI, and they've nothing to do with Macc, and here's me stuck on my estate, and my dad's never had anything, and his dad has never had anything, and they live on the Moss, and they all live on the Moss, and they see nothing, and all they do is see these people from out of the corner of the window, they just see these … . They'll carry on, their kids will go like that. That's not disrespectful, there's some mates of mine. They think what are these people doing, I'd like to do that, I'd like to go to Tytherington Club. But these people from Macc, you try and get some of those youths and let them try and get into Tytherington Club. I'm sorry, you haven't got £20,000 or whatever for your BMW, go away, go back to your Weston estate.

As this account suggests, much of what people had to say about 'the estates' was in some way or other problem oriented, and much of it explicitly took the form of crime-talk. This was especially so among those – 'incomers' – who possessed little unmediated knowledge of the town's poorer places; some of whom – prompted perhaps by the threat of crime 'closing in' on their neighbourhood – appeared to keep a keen eye on the local estates and their 'troubles':

> We really enjoy it here, but there's been this problem of lawlessness and everything, the yobbos. I kept a record here, only the last week, of incidents that had happened. Like two coaches were torched across the town in the Hurdsfield area, and the Weston estate has been having problems, and so has Upton here. Oddly enough these are council estates.
>
> (male resident, Kennedy Avenue)

Thus it was that Macclesfield's estates were most often pointed to (either jointly or separately) by our respondents as the site(s) of Macclesfield's crime and drugs problems, or at least the parts of the town where such problems were most marked. The 'estates' (with Victoria Park flats far out in front in being actually named) were also identified as the areas of the town that (middle-class) people neither wanted to live in, nor visit, nor pass through. And crime seemed to serve generally as the means by which many (middle-class) Macclesfield residents speak about 'the estates' and make sense of the distinctions between them. In some instances, this has a grounding in local knowledge:

RS: Do they have different reputations as places to go?

Jimmy: Worst is Vicky Park flats. My daughter lives there, and we've had a lot of experience of it there. I think the next one is the Moss, and then over the last few months or so it's been the Weston, where there's been lots and lots of trouble, vigilante groups have sprung up. Then they've had occasional flare-ups here [Upton Priory]. It was quiet in Hurdsfield until last week when they burnt two coaches out. I lived there for a number of years.

(Kennedy Avenue resident)

In others, the town's press appear to be the richest source of information:

EG: Is there anything, any changes that you see, any direction that the town is taking, that you don't like?

Rob: I would say just from reading the local *Macclesfield Express* that there are beginning to be more problems, more problems with the council estates, particularly towards us at the back of the leisure centre. There's cars been burnt recently. It's basically out towards the Kennedy Avenue estate [Upton Priory]. The Kennedy Avenue estate has been set on fire at night.

(Villas resident)

These ways of speaking about 'estates' and 'crime' are familiar – and predictable – enough. Yet we must be careful here, for the dispositions of our respondents towards this issue also took what appear at first glance to be some surprising forms. Macclesfield's council estates were *not* for the most part seen as home to the town's burglars and car thieves (something that, for all its Otherness, holds even for Victoria Park flats). Nor did they figure in our discussions as places that were deemed to present a criminal threat to other – more affluent – parts of the town. In short, property crime was *not* construed as an intra-Macclesfield phenomenon. It is possible to discern at least three reasons for this, all of which serve to temper the discursive demonization of the town's council-built estates. Let us consider each in turn.

First, Macclesfield seems to be thought of as having what in various ways are regarded as 'good estates' ('I don't think we've really got a slum area at all', as one resident of Upton Priory put it), something that is reflected in their physical appearance:

You don't see much poverty and neither do you see a great deal of people rejecting their area. I mean you go down to one of the estates in Macc, the Moss estate. You don't see a lot of disbanded cars and cycle tyres and so on.

(local magistrate)

Some expressed this view comparatively, Macclesfield's estates being thought of as better – for the moment at least – than those that routinely feature in the urban nightmares of English cities:

Alright, these estates, or these areas, aren't like Manchester. Like you, I've been round and I've seen them, I've done it, they're not. It's not like Moss Side in Manchester, it's not like Salford. I've seen them, been through them. But slowly and surely they are becoming it.

(female resident, Broken Cross)

Others – such as these born-and-bred Maxonians now working as managers at Zeneca – possessed family connections that gave their assessments of the estates a nuanced and somewhat protective feel:

Sally: I think some of the council estates that were mentioned, the Moss, Weston, Hurdsfield, I think there is change there. I think a lot of people have either bought their properties, or are buying properties. I think it's the ownership thing. You can see, as you go down the road you can tell exactly which houses are owned by the people who are occupied in them, and you can tell the ones that aren't. But there is a change there, and if you look at the style of some of the houses, they're very, very … the workmanship is very good, and the gardens are absolutely wonderful. My youngest son has bought on Bostock Road, on the Weston estate, and his garden is the biggest garden I've ever seen. He must have nearly a acre of land. …

Andy: I think within the estates though, you mentioned Bostock Road, which is a nice area of the Weston. There are other nice areas, like Summerton Road and round there. In fact on the Weston you just think of Earlsway, places you like to avoid. And on Moss there are places like Belgrade Road, things like that, that you would want to avoid. In fact it's a very small area that you might want to avoid. In a way that's like a little town, a little town centre on the Weston, hanging round the flats on Earlsway. And on the Moss, if you're hanging maybe round the football ground. So in a way it's replica of a little town in itself.

It was felt, second, that while they might be the most crime-prone parts of Macclesfield, crime on the estates remains for the most part geographically contained, a problem whose impact falls mainly on the people who live there. As one local head teacher put it:

I can understand it. It wouldn't surprise me if a number of people, say on the Moss estate, got equally irritated by a minority of people who are determined to spoil everybody else's life and everybody's environment. I would have to say I would have a lot of sympathy with them.

The corollary of this, of course, is that 'estate crime' – the troubles that one traditionally, perhaps 'authentically', expects to find in such places – is not viewed as 'spilling over' into other, more prosperous parts of the town:

The same people are doing it. Some of the estates, there is more problems round there, the Weston, Hurdsfield. The kids on the estate, they rob their own or go to other estates.

(male resident, High Street)

There is, third, a sense that, despite the economic and social upheavals of recent decades, Macclesfield's estates remain woven into the texture of local social relations. In part this has to do with the way in which the town is imagined. Macclesfield's 'cheek-by-jowl' character, from which many draw such pride and satisfaction, is largely about the 'happy proximity' that is felt to exist between the town's estates and its more prosperous locations. On this view, the estates are very much integral to contemporary Macclesfield; they provide it with some of its 'character' (this, after all, is where the 'real Maxonians' live), and their 'integration' helps distinguish the town from conflict-ridden, segregated metropolises such as Manchester.[4] But it also flows from the presence of – now moderately affluent, middle-class – Maxonians who were brought up on one of the town's estates, and who retain friendships and kinship connections with them. Such people appear to have both a working knowledge of, and residual affinity with, Macclesfield's poorer, more troubled locations; something that (in a focus group setting) would often 'disrupt' the tendency of others to engage (from the 'outside') in what is viewed as misplaced, illegitimate 'naming':

IL: Are there particular areas of the town which you think are either safer or less safe than others?
Anne: Certainly from what you read in the paper, some of the estates.
Sarah: I don't think any of us would willingly move to the Weston estate.
Andy: I was born on the Weston estate. My parents still live there. Areas of the Weston estate are nice. Areas round the shops.

(Zeneca managers)

We found then that when our respondents spoke of *local* crime, about the threats to the town that emanate from *within*, they generally spoke not of places but of *people*. This is not to say that blame is always or even typically directed at particular, known individuals, for the relevant reference here was often – indeed most often – to categories of people. As we shall see in the next chapter, in so far

as our respondents attribute the town's (petty) crime to indigenous sources, they
do so principally in relation to 'local youth':

IL: What offences would you say happen most often round here?
Sue: Car thefts.
Helen: Car thefts. Break-ins. A good hiding now and again. Shop windows
               going in.
Sue: Shop windows.
Helen: These people are belting shop windows in as if they are going out of
               fashion. Do these people realize what they're doing to the people that
               own the shops?
IL: When you say 'these people' who would they be?
Sue: The youth.
Helen: Well the youth. It couldn't be people of our ages because they would
               know different.
IL: Are they local teenagers?
Helen: Well they must be.
Clive: The majority of them are local, but I think there's youth that come
               from other estates, Upton Priory, the Moss, and they do it as well.
                                                                     (Weston residents)

Among some, however, the town's 'crime problem' *was* felt to be the responsibility of a small number of individuals, sometimes known ones. As we shall see
in Chapter 4, this in a place such as Macclesfield can be a matter of some seriousness and consequence, both in terms of the impact such individuals are felt to
have on the town, and in terms of how local offenders can 'stand out' against the
backdrop of a place with a 'good' – but perhaps precarious – reputation to
protect (see, further, Girling *et al.* 1998). Aspects of this were touched on by one
of the youth workers we spoke to:

> The same names go over and over again, you know like each estate as far as
> I can see has got one or two young people on it and their names stick out as
> offenders, permanent offenders. They're not going to be anything other
> than that until they reach that period of maturation and just grow out of it
> you know. Like I say, you can go up to the Upton Priory, I know two names
> there which would leap out to you every time and then you go more onto
> the flats and Hurdsfield and the same ones will come up all the time. It's like
> it comes down to seven or eight young people, perhaps who are responsible
> for a whole week of the crime in Macclesfield.
>   (Local youth worker)

Yet this isn't the only or even dominant categorization that is made here. Others
situated the town's 'home-grown' criminals in an altogether more benign, even
light-hearted, order of discourse; one that is nicely illustrated by this member of
the Civic Society: 'There are folk in Macclesfield who do pinch things. We're not

quite as innocent as you think you know.' It would seem that the positive outlook people evince towards 'their town' is extended by some to encompass its offenders. Even they are a 'cut above' the kinds of criminals who inhabit other, more troubled spots on the English landscape:

> Most of the delinquents I would describe really as rogues rather than really nasty bad people that you tend to get in cities. For instance, we deal with people in court and you walk past then in the street a couple of days later, and they give you a big smile and say 'hello'. This is the kind of place it is.
>
> (local magistrate)

Places not people: travelling crime

Away Day Burglar is Jailed

> A 32-year-old man who burgled the home of a pensioner in Macclesfield was caught at the railway station as he was about to return to Liverpool. Police had been directed there after making enquiries in the town about strangers.
>
> (*Macclesfield Express Advertiser*, 27 September 1995)

This story captures succinctly the prevailing disposition among Macclesfield residents towards the town's (property) 'crime problem' and its sources. Pivotal to the local construction of Macclesfield as a 'safe place' in a 'troubled world' is the view the town's crime risks emanate largely from that world. It was the overwhelming impression of our respondents that property offences – burglary, car crime, shoplifting – are very much the responsibility of outsiders, principally those who hail from the nearby conurbations of Liverpool and Manchester. As one Civic Society member remarked:

> Sadly a lot of the burglaries that we have are actually people who come from the Liverpool area. So a lot of the crime, I'm not saying that there's no crime in Macclesfield itself, but a lot of it that does occur is people coming from outside.

The strength of feeling on this question is such that the threat posed by 'travelling crime' seems to have become an integral and indisputable part of local wisdom and story-telling (not one of our respondents actively sought to dispute this understanding of Macclesfield's crime problem). This is certainly the case among these residents of Hurdsfield:

Bill:	Most of the crime in this town is not from local, it's outsiders. I know that for a fact.
IL:	Outsiders from where?
Bill:	Manchester, Liverpool, anywhere.
IL:	What sort of crime are you talking about?

Bill:	Where they go breaking in, burglaries.
Joy:	In the shops and things like that, and shoplifting.

It was also the strongly expressed – and within the town, frequently trumpeted – view of the police officers we spoke to:

PC Jones:	You've got the travelling criminals because of the affluent area we're in. It doesn't take 5 minutes to come across now with the new roads that they've built right into Prestbury from the Manchester end and the motorway interchanges at Knutsford and Holmes Chapel. You know, we're an open target aren't we?
IL:	So do you think that Macclesfield attracts offenders from a fairly wide area?
PC Roberts:	It appears to, but why we don't know.
PC Smith:	Well it's a very affluent area and no matter where they go, they can guarantee they are going to get something. Like the area where I work, we haven't got what you would call any real resident burglars, all ours are travellers. They've come in because it's such an affluent area. No matter where they go they are going to get a video, colour TV, camera, whatever.[5]

This exchange touches upon two related aspects of contemporary Macclesfield – its situation and its reputation – that are commonly held to account for the prevalence of travelling crime. The first of these has to do with the network of motorways that connect the town to other places – notably Liverpool and Manchester to the north, and to a lesser extent the Midlands in the south. In this sense, travelling crime is the down-side of the town's 'good' communications; rendered possible by the very thing that makes Macclesfield a viable prospect for its commuting population:

> The nature of crime means that it moves faster. Shoplifting, people come in from elsewhere to shoplift in Macclesfield because it's an easy touch in comparison with Manchester, Liverpool. So they come and shoplift here and they get away very fast. They've got motorway networks and they're gone. Car theft, that moves a lot faster.
>
> (male Civic Society member)

Macclesfield is thought vulnerable, second, because of its reputation as an affluent town set in the midst of the generally more deprived North. For some – such as this local publican – the town suffers from being immediately surrounded by other even more prosperous and 'attractive' locations:

> The thing is round the Macclesfield Borough, you've got a lot of beautiful villages, gorgeous villages like Langley, Sutton. You've got Prestbury, you've got Alderley Edge, you've got Wilmslow, Gawsworth. You've got all these

beautiful places. People are coming along, they're in the boom times, they're making a few quid, now they buy a nice house, they buy a lovely house in Prestbury or whatever. There's a lot of money in those areas. It's an ideal target for somebody outside to come in and commit crimes.

Among others the town itself is spoken of the easy and appealing target; something that is apparent in this discussion of Macclesfield's felt susceptibility to criminal outsiders:

Jimmy:	I don't know enough about it to say really, but I should think the attraction in Macclesfield would be for the people to come in from places like Liverpool. Easy pickings in Macclesfield I should think.
Miriam:	On the motorways. From Manchester even.
Jimmy:	Easy pickings in Macclesfield I should think.
EG:	Why would they be easy pickings?
Jimmy:	Well, there's quite a good …
Miriam:	There's industry here, isn't there?
Jimmy:	They think people living in Macclesfield have a good income. This is what they're after.
Audrey:	A lot of rich people.
Jimmy:	This is what they're after.

(Kennedy Avenue residents)

To make these observations about local sensibilities towards travelling crime is not to deny that outsiders are responsible – at least in part – for the town's property crime (the home addresses of those appearing before Macclesfield's magistrates attest to this very fact). But it is to suggest that vernacular accounts of 'travelling crime' have in some significant ways to do with people's sense, both of Macclesfield as a place, and of the town's place in the wider world. They indicate, in particular, that Macclesfield is felt of as simultaneously *secure* and *fragile*. In respect of the former, travelling crime serves as one of the means by which the town is imagined as evading the worst aspects of the present as they are experienced elsewhere. The 'place-' and 'crime-' talk of residents entrenches a time warp in residents' regional and national 'maps of meaning' (Jackson 1989). Safe places such as Macclesfield are deemed not to be 'coeval' (Fabian 1983) with 'crime-exporting' locations such as Manchester and Liverpool. These places do not inhabit the same 'times'. Just as Macclesfield has 'forged ahead' in terms of economic prosperity and fortune, so it 'lags behind' in respect of crime and cognate social ills. Serious crime is thus something that happens elsewhere, in other times, in other places. It can only come to Macclesfield from the outside. Macclesfield's 'fragility' arises from the sense that the town can no longer insulate itself from the troubles that afflict the wider world; that it is somehow 'catching up' with 'the times'. In part, as we have seen, this is about Macclesfield being very directly threatened by its less fortunate but highly mobile 'neighbours':

Keith: I heard the Macclesfield police superintendent, I think it was about
            four or five years ago, say that the rate of increase of burglaries in
            Macclesfield was actually alarming. The actual rate of increase was
            higher than average. I think that has stabilized a bit.
Colin: We've caught up with the rest.
Keith: He was saying also that a lot of this was due to people coming from
            outside, being the cause of it.
Jane: Macclesfield was sort of targeted, people coming up from the
            Midlands.

(Civic Society members)

But it also gives rise to anxieties (of a more diffuse and less readily graspable
kind) about some of the most disquieting features of contemporary English
society 'seeping' into the town in ways that begin to undermine its quality of life
from within. Such worries about Macclesfield's 'porousness' were especially
apparent when the conversation turned to drugs:

Don: We seem to be about five years behind say Stockport, or somewhere
            like that. It's a bigger place, and it seems to take five years before it
            bleeds over into us and eventually we'll be taking up where they are. I
            know we've got drugs in this town, but it's not as big as it is in the
            Stockport area, or Manchester, or Salford.
Joy: We haven't got the same amount of people, have we?
Don: It takes us about five years.
Joy: Our lot seems to go to Manchester to get them, that's the impression
            that I get.
Mary: I think drugs is something that's very hidden, until you really go into
            depth.
Don: Well you can get them here now. Whereas one time you had to go to
            Manchester to get them, now you don't have to, there's people round
            here that supply them.

(Hurdsfield residents)

Travelling crime, then, presents both a clear and obvious threat to the homes
and property of Macclesfield's residents (people *do* come from outside to burgle
and steal), and a means by which the town and its relationship to the wider world
is registered and made sense of. The prominence this way of speaking occupies
in people's talk firmly indicates that crime is considered 'out of place' in this
town; something imported from beyond its borders, from *Other places*. It also
offers a powerful symbolic testament to people's sense of Macclesfield as occupying a fortunate place in a wider world of dangers and difficulties, to the fact
that it remains, as one resident put it: 'As good a place as anywhere else, and a lot
better than most.'

The town centre: the (troubled) heart of the town?

The future survival of town centres has in recent years come to occupy an increasing amount of policy concern and attention (Worpole 1992). Prompted by the explosion from the 1980s onwards of 'dry, warm and safe' out-of-town shopping centres, urban managers and 'local growth coalitions' (Logan and Molotch 1987) have become ever more attuned to the issue of how to create in the 'heart' of Britain's towns and cities a thriving and economically vibrant environment. Questions of crime (most especially alcohol-related violence) have featured prominently here, noted and acted upon as problems that threaten not only the use of the urban spaces and the quality of life they offer, but also the prospects of economic regeneration. As the manager of one fast food outlet said of Macclesfield's town centre:

> It [fear of crime] stops families coming in at night time. If it felt secure and was well-patrolled, they would come. But it's poorly lit, there are a lot of dingy corners, there's no security cameras, it doesn't give a feeling of security or safety. Okay, there's not gangs of kids roaming around. Often it's very quiet. But it feels unsafe.

We turn to the question of 'security cameras' in Chapter 7. For the moment we want to concentrate on the ways in which this particular town centre figures in the crime-talk of local residents. We saw in the previous chapter that the centre of Macclesfield remains pivotal to the town's aesthetic and historical consciousness. As such it serves as a focus for many local concerns about the town and its futures, whether in terms of traffic congestion, pedestrianization, building development, or the changing face of local shops. The town centre is also – by extension – a place that condenses many of the spatial and temporal metaphors that feature in our respondents' crime discourse; a site of some clear and obvious concerns about such things as travelling crime, the appropriate use of public spaces, violence and the 'problem of youth'.

Yet the town centre remains unusual as a common place of local crime-talk. Unlike 'the estates' – and most obviously Victoria Park flats – the centre of Macclesfield is a location that most of our respondents routinely use; one whose topography and leisure and shopping facilities people are – to greater or lesser extents – familiar with. It thus stands as a common reference point, a part of the townscape around which experiences can be discussed and shared. Only up to a point, however. For Macclesfield's town centre is felt locally to be two – rather distinct – locations; a safe 'pleasant place' during the day, a 'landscape of fear' (Tuan 1979) largely given over to the (unruly) young at night. Some expressed this distinction by referring to the town centre as a place familiar by day (Macclesfield's long-standing residents would still speak of 'town' as a place for chance encounters with known faces) but best avoided after dark. For others – such as these young managers working at Zeneca – the very opposite appears to hold; an anonymous place during daylight hours takes on for them a more 'intimate' feel at night:

I think Macclesfield attracts an awful lot of people for shopping. The population of Macclesfield is completely different on a Saturday afternoon.
When I go into town I know a few people, know them from work. But most
of them, 90 per cent, 95 per cent, I've never, ever seen their faces. I don't
know them. They come from Cheshire. It's a big catchment area, you've got
Congleton. Wilmslow used to be a lovely shopping area, it's dead. You'll get
a lot of people from Wilmslow coming to Macclesfield, from Congleton,
Prestbury, Alderley. Despite the fact that there's nowhere to park. [But] if
you go out at night in Macclesfield it's every other person [you know].

Of a day Macclesfield town centre was a location that many of our respondents
felt happy to use – some even made a point of shopping there rather than 'out of
town'. It was *not* a place that featured in the crime-talk of local adult residents –
though, as we shall see in Chapter 4, the same doesn't hold quite so strongly for the
young people we spoke to. In fact, the only crime discourse we encountered in
respect of the town centre during the day concerned shoplifting.[6] This offence –
while seeming to make little impact on local adult sensibilities towards crime –
generated considerable concern and activity among retailers and the police, with
'travelling crime' (again) appearing as the trope through which it was understood
and responded to. In October 1995 one police manager warned a town centre 'shop
watch' meeting of the threat posed by shoplifters from 'Manchester, Liverpool and
Stoke' in the run-up to Christmas; people who unlike (known) local 'offenders' – a
'rogue's gallery' of whom the police regularly presented to watch meetings – were
difficult to identify because of 'the lack of police intelligence'.[7] In the opinion of
one former police officer we interviewed, Macclesfield was a target for such
offenders because it was viewed as a 'soft touch':

> They classed us as country bumpkins. At one time the security at
> Macclesfield would not be as good as the Manchesters and the Liverpools,
> or the bigger cities or bigger towns. Macclesfield, Wilmslow as well, were
> just easy targets and not too far for them to come. In 20 to 30 minutes you
> could be from Liverpool to Macclesfield. And they would come around
> dinner time, causing a lot of problems milling with the shoppers, doing what
> they want to and disappear by about two o'clock and be on their way home.

It was in respect of Friday and Saturday nights, however, that the town centre
most often surfaced in people's crime-talk. Such talk focused principally on the
problem of alcohol-related violence between young males (what one Hurdsfield
teenager called 'beer monsters'); a problem that had come to be associated with
the gathering of large numbers of people at Park Green and (especially) Water's
Green following pub 'chucking out' time (the lack of a club in Macclesfield
means that the town's young drinkers are *all* thrown onto the streets shortly after
eleven o'clock – for those who still live with their parents 'hanging around' represents the only alternative to terminating the night by going home).[8] Some we
spoke to here intimated that this was something of a 'local sport'; part of a long

tradition of 'brawling and fighting' between people who are well known to one another and who build up a history of easily sparked off disputes and grievances. As one local probation officer put it: 'I think the problem with the town centre at the weekend is because it is such a small town, because so many people are known to each other, that trouble does occur because of old feuds.' Others, however, saw the problem in more global terms, as another instance of the troubles of the outside world permeating Macclesfield:

Tom: That [violence] can go on anywhere. That's not just Macclesfield, it's not peculiar to Macclesfield.
Margaret: No, but that's what you were saying, it used to be in Manchester, but now it's escalated. You wouldn't have got that.

(High Street residents)

Three kinds of responses can be discerned in relation to the (established) reputation of the town centre as a site of 'trouble'. Some clearly reckoned that it was not to be used of an evening, or at least could not safely be used by certain social groups within the town. As this female resident of Victoria Park flats put it: 'I wouldn't go up Macc town centre at night, unless I was with, say a couple of friends and their husbands as well, but there's no way that I could go up town with a bunch of women.'[9] Others felt – largely it seems on the basis of local stories and rumour – that certain parts of the town centre were prone to violence and thus best avoided:

There's probably a couple of pubs down the bottom end of Mill Street that you wouldn't go near at kicking out time. You might think twice at walking down the pedestrian part of Chestergate. But I mean saying that, I can't say that I'm actually in Macclesfield at eleven o'clock at night. You hear people talk about it, but that's it.

(male resident, Kennedy Avenue)

Others simply included the town centre on a longer inventory of places that were not to be visited after sundown:

EG: Do you know of any part of town which you would avoid using?
Dave: The town centre at eleven o'clock on Saturday night.
Tina: Any time anywhere near closing time.
Dave: It generally tends to be like Dodge City then.
Clive: There's an inordinate number of pubs in Macclesfield. At one point the number of pubs per person was the highest ratio per size of the town in England. It has a lot of pubs, and some of them you don't want to be anywhere near at a certain time of the night. They frequently get raided. But there are also areas, some of the council estates you don't want to be on at night either, the Moss.

(clerical workers, Zeneca)

A second response also speaks of the town centre as what one probation officer called 'a pretty scary place', but does so with reference to some direct experience of violence, threat or unease. Among some the victimization of close family members seem to have generated – or at least reinforced – a dim view of the town centre on a Friday and Saturday night:

> It can be very, very nasty. I mean our youngest son was involved in a serious road accident two years ago. He broke his leg in twenty odd places, broke his arm and both his feet, and he was attacked whilst on crutches, in the middle of town.
>
> (female resident, High Street)

Others clearly use the town centre, but do so with a certain wariness about its risks, about where one can safely go, and about whom one goes with. One female resident of Broken Cross expressed this sentiment thus:

> I don't think you'd feel safe walking through Macclesfield town centre on a Friday night or a Saturday. We went for a meal, four of us went for a meal at the Italian on the bottom of Mill Street, one Friday night I think it was. It could have been a Saturday. We actually walked back to pick the car up down Mill Street and down Chestergate. It was like full of, you felt a bit. … There were four of us, two couples, and I wouldn't like to walk through Macclesfield.

A third strand of thought and feeling on this issue holds more firmly to the opinion that locally circulating stories of town centre violence blow 'the problem' out of all reasonable proportion. People here generally acknowledged that there could at times be trouble in the town, but tended to attribute this to 'a specific minority'. As one clerical worker from Zeneca put it:

> There's a pub run. It starts off at the Amsterdam Bar, then it's the Bate Hall, out to the Bull, then it's down Mill Street, back up again. It's a sort of predetermined route, and that's where all the noise is. Ninety-nine per cent of it is harmless boisterousness, which occasionally leads to an act of violence. I think it's the noise and boisterousness which is intimidating more than anything. I think you tend to exaggerate what actually happens.

This view is echoed by two of the local head teachers we spoke to, who seemed keen to 'place' the problem on a broader canvas:

Isla: You go through the town and there seems to be an awful lot of rowdiness. But Macclesfield is my local town. I mean it could be ten times worse in the middle of Stockport, it might be a 1,000 times worse in the middle of Moss Side.

Mike: As a non-resident, I come here to concerts at the Heritage Centre and never think that I will park my car in town and so on. I never think about it. I feel as an outsider, that it doesn't strike me as a very threatening environment to come into.

Generally speaking this is also the understanding of violence in Macclesfield town centre held by the police. Few of the officers we spoke to thought that 'trouble' at Water's Green presented any serious or persistent policing problems. As one observed: 'The majority of them just stand around nattering but then you'll get the odd idiot that's got a point to prove.' Another officer generalized much the same point thus:

> I think you're quite safe to go for a night in the town. You'd pick the sort of pubs you went to anyway, wouldn't you? There's certain places that are younger but it's quite a safe at night in Macclesfield town without being accosted or assaulted or whatever. There are always going to be problems around food places at sort of half eleven or twelve o'clock where there is large groups of youths, but you wouldn't put yourself in that place, you wouldn't go to those places. This is where they've got nowhere else to go, they stand about. I think it's quite a safe town.

This had also come to be the view of one of the senior police officers we spoke to. On first arriving in Macclesfield he admitted to having been 'horrified' by the numbers that gathered around Park and Water's Green of a Friday and Saturday evening, and his first instinct had been – as he put it – 'to get them to bugger off home, to get them out the bloody way'. He then recounted the following experience:

> A few weeks afterwards I went up just in my civvies, that was like 11:30 p.m. when it was really heaving on a summer night. There was hundreds and hundreds of these kids and they didn't know who the hell I was, and I walked right the way through them, spoke to one or two, nobody was aggressive, you know, and I went about my way. But people's perception is to say, 'I wouldn't go out at night, it's terrible down there, they're all muggers and bloody rapists.' But it's a perception isn't it? They were all nice people, the lot of them. You obviously get some idiots don't you?

One – possible – outcome of this encounter is the following response to our enquiry about whether violence in Macclesfield town centre comes high on the list of local police priorities:

> No, it doesn't. We used to try and police a few extra in Poynton on Friday night and then move them back into Macclesfield later on for the idiots there. It could never be a high priority because, in fairness, there was never any major problem to it, as you probably found out yourself really.

The flats: a town's 'worst nightmare'?

Victoria Park flats – three blocks of four-storey, deck-access properties situated in the centre of Macclesfield – were opened in the late 1960s by the then Minister of Housing and Local Government who described them as 'an excellent scheme, imaginatively developed and pleasing to the eye'. Echoes of this view can still be heard today, over three decades later. A Borough Council housing official characterized Victoria Park as '543 units' of 'good family accommodation': 'We have several three-bedroomed, four-bedroomed and one five-bedroomed property at Victoria Park. The apartments themselves are extremely spacious.' A Hurdsfield resident described the properties as 'very, very nice inside'. One 35-year-old woman we spoke to recalled the following childhood memory of the flats going up: 'I can remember thinking they were great. They looked fantastic, I thought "wow!"' And this ex-resident (now employed as a concierge on the estate) proffered this account, both of his time living on Victoria Park in the late 1960s, and of what he saw as its subsequent decline:

> I came back [to Macclesfield] and wanted somewhere to live and they were available and they were very nice, they really were, they were beautiful and it was great, centre of town and no problem. I had almost a brand new open-topped sports car and I could park outside the flats and it wasn't touched and that was this area. And the majority of people, very genuine people lived here. Times have changed unfortunately, because if they hadn't changed I wouldn't be in a job, there wouldn't be a concierge system and no cameras. So there's been a massive change. An architect's dream has become a housing officer's nightmare.

How are we to account for this 'nightmare'? Why have 'the flats' come to be thought of as what the aforementioned official called 'the 'least desirable' of Macclesfield Borough Council's housing stock? A number of aspects can be identified here. In part this reputation has to do with the pre-history of Victoria Park (cf. Damer 1974). The flats were built on land cleared by the demolition in the early 1960s of what one High Street resident (who was *not* living in the town at the time) called 'very nice little cottages, *Coronation Street* types'. The fact that this culturally esteemed form of English housing (which made up in this case what one Weston resident remembered as 'a brilliant little neighbourhood') was superseded by deck-access building of the kind that has come to be widely condemned as an architectural 'dinosaur' (male manager, Zeneca) clearly rankles with many Macclesfield residents:

Brian: Where those flats are, there used to be a nice community there.
Peggy: Oh yes, I lived in that community.
Brian: There was loads of houses round that area.
IL: Weavers' cottages?
Brian: Yes.

Peggy: Outside toilets!

Brian: They demolished those in the early sixties. In the late sixties ['commu-nity architect'] Rod Hackney came along, and he started off in Macclesfield, up Black Road, doing little weavers' cottages up. He arranged for the people to get a mortgage and all this, then he gutted the houses and re-did them up. That's how he started off. If that philosophy had been taken when they were doing the flats. … They've lost more accommodation by knocking them down and putting the flats up. They'd have been better modernizing them all. Like some of those houses, they were massive. You could have turned them into small flats, only four storeys high. Then you had your two-up and two-down, but you could have extended them, put inside loos in, everything. It would have been a lot better. Plus there was its own little community down there.

(Hurdsfield residents)

Victoria Park suffers because it aesthetically disrupts what is felt by many to be the town's seamless continuity of architectural style. Standing as it does adjacent to the town centre (partly obscuring the view out over the Peaks), Victoria Park offers a constant visual irritation to Macclesfield's residents. The flats are a reminder of other 'times' (the 1960s) and other 'places' ('You could be in Birmingham, it's like part of the spaghetti junction', as one High Street resident put it); something that is out of keeping with the town's historical 'character' and contemporary 'affluence':

Paul: I think that the Victoria flats … I lived there for a very short time at the end of the sixties and they were put up and it was very much the brave new world, and now sadly they've become a place where the people … it's full of the people who are most deprived, who are ending there. That's just like everywhere else in the country, I know in many ways that a lot of poorer people have actually got worse off, but that really does rather stick out I think, the fact that when you drive through the middle of Macclesfield, that it sticks out physically, and one knows what the real position is of the people who live in there.

Mary: It's not just Victoria flats, the Weston, the Moss, are more deprived areas in terms of …

June: They're in a smaller area.

Paul: Victoria flats is so obvious.

(Civic Society members)

As this account intimates, Victoria Park has also acquired a local reputation as home to Macclesfield's most 'socially deprived' and 'morally depraved', those one police manager characterized as 'the least susceptible to standards'. It was a common refrain among adult residents and local professionals alike that the flats had become a 'dumping ground' (female resident, Broken Cross) for those in the direst need of accommodation, and that local housing policy had created what one youth worker called 'a mini ghetto' made up of a transient population of young single men and women, and lone parents (a problem the housing officials we spoke to were acutely aware of). This clerical worker from Zeneca clearly saw 'the flats' as having been 'created' by the Borough Council:

> They turned it into a home for waifs and strays, the Council. Anybody they thought wouldn't fit in anywhere else got bunged into Victoria Park. They created a whole sort of sub-culture within Victoria Park. Again, that was promoted, it didn't just happen.

So too did many of its current residents:

Mark: The problem with these flats, they bring people from outside in. And the first place they house them is in the flats. They're all coming in here, all the bad debt payers, they put them in these flats. They create trouble then.

Sharon: People who have been kicked out of houses.

Mark: People who have been kicked out of houses. They put them in these flats.

Thus it is that Victoria Park is set apart from the rest of Macclesfield (and its estates) on people's mental maps of the town, finding itself as the most 'visited' landmark in our respondents' crime-talk. During the course of our research the flats were variously described to us (by both residents and local professionals) as 'built for thieves', an 'Argentinean football stadium', a 'mini-Beirut', and as 'my worst nightmare'. They were frequently referenced as riddled with crime and drugs, and were most commonly named as the part of town in which people would least like to find themselves. This exchange between Zeneca managers is fairly typical of the kind of crime-talk 'the flats' prompted:

IL: Are there places that you wouldn't go in the town?

Tim: Victoria Park flats.

Joe: I think I would …

Anne: I think any of the estates. I would say that Victoria Park flats had to be the top of the list.

IL: Why do you say that?

Anne: Because when you read in the paper every week about people caught with drugs, people caught having fights, fires, or people that have been mugged, the chances are that the person who has committed the crime, or allegedly committed the crime, lived in Victoria Park flats.

Tim: Even the people who live in Victoria Park flats don't want to live in Victoria Park flats. It's skid row, they don't want to be there.

(Zeneca managers)

In the late 1980s Victoria Park's local reputation as Macclesfield's foremost place of danger – a reputation that has dogged the flats on and off throughout the period since they were opened – came to something of a head. Prompted by a story about a tenant who lay dead in his home for four weeks without being discovered, the flats were subjected to a flurry of local press coverage, mainly along the lines of 'thugs frightening tenants' and about the estate having become a 'rubbish tip'. And this in large measure is how residents and local professionals recall the flats during this period. Arson and vandalism were seen as rife, with the Council's repair bill 'running at £1,000 a week' (Borough housing official). Litter and 'dumping' were such that, 'there were areas where you couldn't see a blade of grass for debris' (Victoria Park concierge). Certain staircases were felt to be 'no-go areas' at night. And 'criminals and hooligans' were seen as making life a misery for residents:

> There were a large element of people that weren't going anywhere and had nowhere to go. You spoke to the kids, they'd got an air that going to prison was stripes on the sleeves. They never went to school, had no intention of going to school. Their outlook was what I considered negative, you couldn't talk to them. ...
>
> They would walk round, they knew who I was and many times there would be a bag of piss thrown at me off the balcony or a missile, you know, that was the way it was. The vandalism on a nightly basis was horrendous – balcony panels kicked in, there was domestic situations, the stairs were, every day were a mess. We found that they were transit people who'd sleep in chute rooms, they would sleep on alleyways, they would sleep in open staircases. ...
>
> The balconies on some nights were areas for football, skating, domestics, drinking, tramps, people pouring out of the pubs in the centre of town looking to get their head down somewhere. Doors were kicked, balcony panels were smashed, staircases were wrecked and that was the way it was.
>
> (Victoria Park concierge)

In 1992, following demands from the Residents' Association (RA), and a considerable period of consultation, Macclesfield Borough Council responded to these problems by introducing in the flats a concierge-controlled access system; a system whose specifications were formulated with the close collaboration of the RA and for which the association agreed to an additional levy of £7 per week on each tenant's rent:

> They [the residents] wanted a user-friendly person on a lodge, they wanted a communication system, they wanted a help system, they wanted somebody that they could go to on-site to have their problems sorted out, and their problems are wide and varied.
>
> (Victoria Park concierge)

The system comprises two main elements that combine to form a (potentially uneasy) mix of assistance, protection and control. Access to the blocks is controlled – for tenants and visitors alike – by a uniformed concierge, a total of twenty of whom are employed by the Borough Council (in order to emphasize the 'friendly face' element of the service, the Council took what one housing official called 'a conscious decision' to go for a 'soft uniformed approach rather than a peaked cap'). Each tenant has their own fob-key which provides them with access along the route to their flat, but not to other blocks or balconies (no keys are issued to residents under the age of 16). Moreover, each of the blocks is now subject to surveillance by a total of ninety-eight closed circuit television (CCTV) cameras mounted above balconies, entrances, staircases and lifts. These are monitored round-the-clock from one of three control rooms.[10] As one housing official said of this aspect of the arrangements: 'The basic aim is to control access onto the estate. That is their prime function.'

Yet the system is not exclusively oriented to control and exclusion. In addition to the upkeep and maintenance of the complex, the twenty concierges also have a range of what are basically pastoral responsibilities; something that led one concierge to describe their role in the following terms: 'They are Job's comforter, you know. They are a social worker, a provider, they're a friend, they do have a multi-task role, and it is sometimes quite thankless.' He went on the list the following services that the concierges provide for the tenants:

> We phone through all repairs for them, we also respond to their needs of emergency services, such as if they want an ambulance or a doctor we will make them that. If they have got some desperate messy situation between themselves and the family, subject to the nature of it, we will help them with that as well. If they wish to leave keys for tradesmen to go to their property we take their keys off them and we escort those tradesmen to their property – sometimes it's TV repair, sometimes it's carpet to be fitted, furniture to be delivered. We also aid them that when they come to the flats. Some people [he explicitly mentioned 'battered wives' in this context] haven't got a stick of furniture or any possessions at all and we actually find them furniture, which is a service we do free of charge and we help them along the way.

The most prevalent view of the concierge system – one found among both residents and local professionals – is that it has largely been a success (although one concierge spoke of 'an element that were unhappy' with the system, and reported a small number of tenants handing in their keys and leaving shortly after the scheme was installed; as one housing official put it: 'I'm sure we could all surmise why'.) In part this has to do with the enhanced physical appearance and feel of the estate (as one resident who returned to the estate having lived elsewhere put it: '[It] looks better now. They're lovely. They had all the windows done, and the security cameras done'); and with the sense of ownership that is said to come from residents having been given control over 'their' balconies: 'Immediately the system on each of the three phases became live, it was a case that mats appeared outside people's doors, hanging baskets appeared. That is something that just would not have happened before' (Borough housing official).

But success is also spoken of in terms of the impact 'cameras' have had upon crime, whether in terms of reducing burglary or vandalism, preventing town centre shoplifters from using the flats as a 'rabbit warren' to escape into, or confining youth nuisance and disorder to a few systemic 'blind spots'. Beyond Victoria Park, some clearly felt the system had – like CCTV everywhere (see Chapter 7) – instigated some great improvements: 'Look at Vicky Flats, the trouble they had there. They put a surveillance on there, there's no trouble there now' (female resident, High Street). This view was echoed by one of the senior police officers we spoke to: 'The crime reduced tremendously when that went in. I think it's gone exceptionally well. Crime has dropped by about 80 per cent on there you know since the bad old days.' And this group of officers provided the following enthusiastic assessment of the cameras and their effects:

PC Jones: The flats are virtually dead compared to what they used to be, aren't they?

PC Lambert: That's right, it's good policing that is [all laugh].

PC Hughes: That's right, fine officers, yes.

IL: How in particular has it helped down there, what effect has it had?

PC Lambert: Security-wise yes. We used to get a lot of flat burglaries there, doors kicked in, out, you know, in the house, out, gone. Now of course it all gets stored on tape, so you can even do it in retrospect.

PC Smith: It's an excellent facility for us. There's many times where we've used it and it's been great evidence.

IL: Has it actually cut crime on the flats or has it just made people feel safer?

PC Lambert: It's made people feel safer, but it has cut crime. But it's also helped an awful lot in the town centre crime. When all these lads who are brought in try telling us that they were elsewhere and all of a sudden you slide a tape in and say, 'Well isn't that you?'

Yet for all this the concierge system has clearly not offered Victoria Park any kind of panacea. The flats continue to be seen by many as the site of the town's most serious and endemic crime and (hard) drugs problems. One police officer we spoke to described the question of drugs in Macclesfield as: 'Sort of flats size. There is a problem down on Victoria Park, a heck of a problem.' One concierge cognately observed:

The drugs situation on this estate is prolific. We have had a lot of dealings with the police on drugs issues over the past two years, it has increased and increased and increased. They get it so cheaply. I think some of the drug dealers want to come here because it's a good market and as I say, you relate to the geography of the place, it's in the town, near the pubs, very useful.

It was widely recognized here that the surveillance system had done little to reduce the prevalence of drugs on the estate, although as one concierge noted: 'What is on camera is the trade, the traffic. You don't get forty people a day to one flat for a cup of tea.'

Nor does the concierge system seem greatly to have enhanced Victoria Park's reputation in the town. (There is even a curious way in which the CCTV system reinforces people's sense of the flats as dangerous location, *the kind of place where security cameras are needed.* The middle-class people we spoke to would consider the prospect of such close surveillance in *their* areas as both unnecessary and deeply inappropriate.) For all the recorded (and locally acknowledged) improvements in crime rates and the quality of life, Victoria Park remains Macclesfield's Other, the site of its most intractable problems, the town's single most common place of crime:

> They're like cardboard, you can hear everything that's going on, every squeal. You've got children running along corridors, you've got banging doors, lifts going up and down, it's a nightmare. It's a lot better since you've put your concierge system in, I will admit it, but it's still a nightmare.
>
> (female resident, Broken Cross)

In 1998 – two years after our research had ended – Macclesfield Borough Council decided that Victoria Park flats was to be pulled down.

4 Youth, disorder and inter-generational conflicts

It has in recent years become commonplace to assert that petty crime and low-level disorder are in the main activities of the young and that public anxiety about crime attaches itself in large measure – among adults at any rate – to these 'incivilities'. The gathering of male and female teenagers, unsupervised, in public spaces – on front walls, street-corners, in town centres, by the local shops – is said to prompt anxiety and unease among local residents and other (potential) users alike. Such a preoccupation with the activities of the young (and associated calls for somebody to take 'tough action') certainly comprises the staple diet of much party political and media discourse on 'law and order'.

These concerns echo loudly among many adult residents of Macclesfield. While the town may not be thought of as having a particularly exceptional 'crime problem', it was considered by many of our discussants to have what one resident described as a 'youth problem'. When asked in our focus groups about local crime, the talk of Macclesfield's adult residents would often turn – in a manner which suggested they took the crime and the youth question to be largely synonymous – to the problems and worries that they associate with young people's unsupervised occupancy of public places. One Kennedy Avenue resident voiced this concern thus:

> You don't get much in the way of crime from the more adult people in the town. There's undoubtedly a section of criminals in every town or city in the country. But the main bulk of aggravation comes from the young people, yobbos, schoolchildren, and they're very intimidating if you try to interfere in any way.

Together with cognate worries about drugs and children's safety, these concerns about teenage mis/behaviour impinge significantly upon adult residents' sense of Macclesfield as a 'liveable' place. Their talk also resonates closely with much contemporary political and media discourse about 'the youth of today', with parenting, joblessness, the dearth of youth facilities, and questions of authority, discipline and respect figuring routinely – to greater or lesser extents – in both. We will have more to say about these associations as this chapter unfolds, and will pay particular attention to how these rather placeless preoccupations (to do with youth and 'the condition of England') filter into people's sense of what is happening to *their* street, or neighbourhood, or town. But we also want to suggest that people's talk about, and responses to, teenage incivilities are more complex than is often assumed by editorialists, pundits and politicians, and that a focus on questions of place makes it possible to discern a tension between the sometimes rather punitive ways in which people talk about 'youth in general' and the obligations that people acknowledge to troublesome youth in their own specific localities.

We proceed as follows. Later in the chapter we document some of the worries about youth evinced by adult residents' crime-talk, and consider the contrasting ways in which differently situated Macclesfield citizens respond to the presence and behaviour of groups of teenagers. We then outline the various ways in which adult residents account for the 'problem of youth' and assess some of the competing sensibilities that are disclosed by their talk. We begin, though, with the objects of all this anxious discourse, young people themselves. How do they make sense of growing up in Macclesfield? How do questions of crime figure in the place-talk of the town's young?

Knowing your place: growing up in Macclesfield

Of all the residents of Macclesfield we spoke to, male and female teenagers were the least likely to be enamoured of the town's charms and the least disposed to describe it in positive terms – 'boring', 'rubbish' and 'poo' were among the epithets selected to describe the town to a notional outsider. Some in particular – such as these sixth-formers attending a 'prestigious' local school – were keen to distance themselves from the received impression of Macclesfield as an aesthetically pleasing place:

IL: What kind of place would you say it is?
Peter: Small town. Pretty basic amenities for a small town, shops, pedestrianized area.
Toby: Quite dirty.
Rachel: I don't think it's very nice, definitely not.
IL: Why do you say that?
Rachel: Because it's supposed to be one of the richest areas, and since I've lived in the area I've thought that this isn't that interesting.
James: Is that because you lived in New York?
Rachel: No, I'm serious, it's not that nice. If you go into town it doesn't look that nice, it doesn't look as good as it sounds.
          [...]
James: It's not a pretty town. I came from Harrogate, so that's quite a big town with lots of trees and pretty roads. Compared to that it's not ...
Toby: It's dirty.

Aesthetic matters are not, however, among the most pressing concerns of

Macclesfield's teenagers. More prominent in their place-talk is the felt sense that the town – despite its relative prosperity – does little to cater for the young, or even seem to care much about their plight: 'Macclesfield doesn't give out anything for the youth', as one 21-year-old male from Hurdsfield put it. Particular concern here was expressed by those not yet able to gain entry into pubs and clubs: 'When you're little it's okay because you've got parks, but when you get older you get bored with that sort of stuff. You want to do other stuff but there's nothing else. There's nothing for our age group.' (16-year-old male, Kennedy Avenue). Similar themes were expressed – albeit in more despairing tones – during our discussion with a group of older teenagers on probation:

IL: Is there enough to do you think?
Dave: No.
Mark: There's nothing to do.
IL: Nothing?
Mark: That's why you do crime, get into drugs.
IL: What do you generally do with your weeks or weekends? What places
           do you use in town?
Dave: I work at night, sleep most of the day, that's it. Do this and that, then
           go back to work.
IL: What kind of things would you like in the town? What would make it
           better for you?
Mark: Somewhere to go in the day where you could play pool, or snooker, or
           table tennis.
Dave: Instead of just pubs. That's all there is now, just pubs.

This is not to say that no provision for young people exists in Macclesfield. A number of County Council-run youth facilities are scattered throughout the town, though these rarely open beyond two nights per week and, as one local youth worker put it, 'only 6 or 7 per cent of our target age range use those centres'.[1] There is also a leisure centre and a bowling alley, though both lie on the outskirts of the town, and both – according to the aforementioned youth worker – operate 'mass exclusions of young people'. Some (under-age) teenagers reported making use of local pubs, it being fairly common knowledge among them which ones are lax about admitting and serving under-18s.[2] What Macclesfield lacks, however, is a club:

> The only problem in Macclesfield is that we need somewhere to go. If that club had opened and they had a under-16s night or something, then all they had to do was get a couple of bouncers and police and stuff on the front, and then they wouldn't have the vandalism there, would they? At Coco Savannah in Stockport, they're doing an under-18s night at the end of every month. That's alright.
>
> (17-year-old male, Hurdsfield)

The absence of such a club (and, for that matter, a 'big-screen' cinema) drives many of Macclesfield's young further afield in search of entertainment. For the most part – especially among younger teenagers – this extends no further than to nearby Stockport (some 10 miles north towards Manchester, and a 10-minute train journey away), where the Grand Central entertainment complex (complete with aforementioned club, multiplex cinema, amusement arcades and plenty of other teenagers to meet) provides the main attraction. Among those in their late teens and early twenties, trips to clubs in Manchester and Stoke (and even Wolverhampton and Birmingham) are more common. As a local youth worker commented:

> Eighteen, nineteen, twenty plus. Convoys of cars go up there [to Stoke] regularly on a weekend and we pick it up on a Monday afternoon when we open a Drop-In. They've basically blitzed their Giro [unemployment] cheque over the weekend.

One 21-year-old male from Hurdsfield – who spent most of the focus group publicizing his 'campaign' for a club – predicted great riches for anyone who could bring such attractions to Macclesfield:

> I tell you something, it would hit this town like a hurricane, you wouldn't see nobody on the bleeding street, that is for certain. Because things like that, you could have it open certain hours for the youngest, say 14 to 18, through the week, and all the elders in there over the weekend. Whoever opened it would be a millionaire within a month, I'll guarantee you that. That's all people spend their money for, we're going out of town all the time. Everyone is blowing everyone's wages just to get there, just for one night out.

Against this backdrop, several features of young people's talk about crime and place are noteworthy. Foremost among these are drugs, personal safety, and hanging around in public places – issues that are a potent source of conflict with, or, at the very least, of evident concern to, adult residents of the town. Let us take each in turn.

Drugs

The prevalence of drug-taking among Britain's youth has been documented in a number of recent surveys. A Home Office study published in 1995 found that, among 14- to 25-year-olds, 32 per cent of males and 17 per cent of females had taken a prescribed drug in the year preceding the survey (Graham and Bowling 1995: 26). A survey by Measham *et al.* (1994) of 14- to 15-year-olds in the north-west of England found that 36 per cent had taken an illicit drug over the course of their lifetime, with 20 per cent admitting to use in the past month. Almost one in three (32 per cent) admitted to having consumed cannabis; six in ten reported having been offered drugs. And in the 'Quality of Life' study recently conducted by Cheshire County Council (1996b), 55 per cent of respondents concurred with the proposition that 'drugs are easy to get in this area' (the figure rose to 60 per cent among 14- to 17-year-olds and 67 per cent among 18- to 24-year-olds). Some 68 per cent of teenagers and 70 per cent of young adults assented to the view that 'the majority of pupils at local secondary school have tried drugs'.

These figures find a resonant echo in the talk about drugs that prevailed among the young people we spoke to. Since what one 27-year-old (student and part-time local disc jockey) we spoke to called 'the boom of the mid-1980s', prior to which it had been necessary to travel to Manchester to purchase drugs, it is now generally agreed that it has become relatively easy to obtain drugs in Macclesfield – or at the very least, as one 15-year-old boy put it, to get hold of 'weed, trips, whiz and E'. Cannabis use in particular is considered to be widespread – a view that was shared by the youth and drugs workers we interviewed, one of whom spoke of cannabis having been 'normalized in Macclesfield'. The aforementioned disc jockey felt that cannabis use had moved in recent years from being secretive to overt, such that local (mainly 'small-time') dealers were now to be found operating in Macclesfield pubs (we were told repeatedly that proprietors of some town centre pubs turn a blind eye to cannabis smoking on their premises). The younger teenagers we spoke to cognately claimed that cannabis was, if not quite freely available, then at least easily obtainable within – even 'reputable' – local schools:

> You think of King's School as really nice, but half of the lads who I met last year smoke weed and everything, anything else they can get, they all deal and that, because they've got the money. They're at King's School and you think they're dead nice, but they're not.
>
> (15-year-old girl, Prestbury)

This particular instance of what Measham *et al.* (1994: 310) call 'the normalization of recreational drug use among English adolescents' (cf. Shiner and Newburn 1997) is evident in two further features of Macclesfield teenagers' talk about drugs, especially in respect of cannabis. It is apparent, first of all, in the rather measured, accepting and often knowing manner in which cannabis is spoken about. This contrasts starkly with the (far more sporadic) references that are made to cocaine or heroin, substances which – far from being considered a 'normal' part of growing up – remain closely associated in the minds of young people with the desperate world of the criminal Other:

IL: When you say drugs, what kind of stuff are they asking for?
Gary: Pot mostly, nothing more than pot.
Alan: All the major drugs in this town, there's pot, E's, trips, whiz, that's it. It's not that big in Macclesfield. There are few ragey dealers coming into this area.
Gary: I know someone who shifts a lot of brown [heroin] a week.

Alan: But I don't like smack heads for one. I've seen them round me and I just don't like it. They're scruffy, they're thieves, they'll pinch off you to score their own gear. That's horrible that is, I hate people who pinch off friends, it's well out of order.

(male teenagers, Hurdsfield)

It is evident, second, in the eagerness with which young people sought to discuss both the legalization of cannabis (which they generally supported), and in the desire of some of the users among our respondents to defend its use as against alcohol. As one 19-year-old male from Hurdsfield remarked:

I'll tell you something now, you'll see a guy smoking ganja and he's chilled, a lower level, he can't be arsed with none of it, you know what I mean. Then you get a beer monster that's got a microphone mouth, pot-belly, punching hell out of everybody, you know what I mean. Which would you prefer?

A place of safety?

A further significant feature of young people's (and especially, if not only, boys') crime-talk is that they resort far more readily and often than Macclesfield's adult residents to terms that denote violence, or trouble more generally. Though some among our teenage respondents spoke of Macclesfield as a 'safe place', others were keen to point out that, in terms of 'being hit and threatened' the victims are most likely to be – as one focus group of secondary school pupils responded in chorus – 'Our age'. Hence one 17-year-old boy's response to the following enquiry:

IL: Would you say Macclesfield is a friendly place?
Paul: It's a bit like New York.
IL: What do you mean by that?
Paul: Well a lot of people I've been talking to and that, I noticed when I was coming through Macc town centre that people are bumping into you and things like that. It's getting quite rough out there now.
RS: You mean all the time, not just Friday night?
Paul: No, no, this is shopping time, shopping time, Saturday afternoon. I'm not joking, people bump into you. It's getting quite a hostile town really.

This perception of the town may flow in part from young people's experiences as victims of crime and during our focus groups various such incidents were recounted (cf. Anderson *et al.* 1994: ch. 2; Hartless *et al.* 1995). These included allegations of having been stabbed (17-year-old male, on probation); assaulted by a local resident while hanging around (15-year-old boy, High Street); being beaten up in town (sixth-former at local school); having a coat stolen in the town centre (21-year-old male, Hurdsfield) and having one's room at a hostel broken into (17-year-old male, on probation). Concerns also attend, however, the more diffuse 'incivilities' of other teenagers, as in this discussion by sixth-formers at a local school of the problems caused by 'scallies':

Toby: A lot of crime does originate from them.

James: And they're all under-age.

Toby: I'm not putting them down in any way, but I do think that's where a lot of it does come from.

RS: From where, sorry?

Toby: Less well-off groups.

James: [Victoria Park] Flats.

RS: So where do scallies live then, do they all live in the flats?

James: Yes. Inner cities. They're all under-age.

Toby: It's a bit of an image thing really.

James: They're all under-age so they can't get into pubs and get drunk, so they've got nothing to do but walk around causing a bit of trouble. You see like big ones like us, and then you see little kids dressing like them.

RS: And what else do they do apart from asking for fags?

James: It depends how big they are.

Toby: If you don't, like, give them a fag or money for fags or something, then they'll start hassling you.

The teenagers we spoke to often exhibited both a keen sense of the different places that constitute Macclesfield and a particular way of understanding relations between them. These relations are principally spoken about in terms of the rivalries that obtain between different groupings (or, as adult residents more often called them, 'little tribes' or 'gangs') that hail from various parts of the town. Thus, asked to name the different areas that make up Macclesfield, our Hurdsfield focus group responded as follows: 'Weston, Moss Rats, Flat Rats – Priory, Weston, Moss and Hurdsfield – Bollingbrook, Broken Cross – Broken Cross! That's a neutral zone.'

These different groupings (as the description of middle-class Broken Cross as a 'neutral zone' suggests) attach mainly to Macclesfield's council-built estates and include not only the 'Moss Rats' and [Victoria Park] 'Flat Rats', but also the 'Weston Warriors', 'Hurdsfield Assault Team' (HAT) and Buxton Road Assault Team' (BRAT) (cf. Loader 1996: ch. 3; Watt and Stenson 1997). Their existence testifies not only to the significance some young people attach to belonging to an identifiable place (the names feature prominently on the graffiti that adorns the town); but also to the importance of knowing the relationship that exists between 'your place' and 'other places', and of being able to defend the former against the latter. As one participant in our Hurdsfield focus group put it:

If you go somewhere like Victoria Park, it's like rat race city, shitty nappies everywhere *[all laugh]*. There is, honestly. If you go to the Moss, the hedgerows have got like ten years of growth of crisp packets stuck on them. Hurdsfield, it's got a bit of pride, at least the road sweepers get on the footpath and clean the footpath as well.[3]

The result – according to this group of 15-year-olds from a local secondary school – is a social world comprising inevitable and inescapable inter-area tension:

Tina: We've had constant arguments between the flats and the Moss, the Weston, and Upton. You've always got that tension there, no matter where you live. You've always got that, always got some area that will hate you.

Josh: Me and him, we're out of the way a bit so we don't really get involved.

Tim: But if they wanted to come in from Macclesfield and hang around with some of the groups, then they'd get into it as well.

Sarah: You get labelled for where you live.

Tina: You know when you get one group that the other side hate, and other side hate them, you'll end up in the middle.

These tensions exist for the most part as forms of talk, a means of expressing one's attachment to, and pride in, the particular part of Macclesfield in which young people feel 'at home'. But – as the reflections of this 17-year-old boy testify – verbal conflicts do occasionally spill over into acts of violence: 'There'd been one big fight against the Moss Rats in South Park, and I ended up in hospital. I needed a stitch there, and a couple of stitches down here. It hurt a lot, so I decided enough's enough.' A local youth worker contextualized incidents of this kind thus:

IL: What about young people as victims of crime, what sort of things do you think they are at risk from?

Tom: Personal injury and attacks from other estates. I mean it's quiet now because it's winter and people tend not to be bothered about it; but in the summer when the fair's in town, I mean it really is, it's justice by geography. The amount of assault charges just go through the roof because estates meet in the same place and they hit each other. It may seem kind of petty and small but there has been some serious injuries to one or two young people.

Hanging around ...

A further – and not unrelated – aspect of young people's relationship to, and talk about, place, concerns the unsupervised use some of them make of Macclesfield's public spaces – street-corners, parks, local shopping parades and so forth. Across Macclesfield, we either observed or had reported to us a number of 'hot' – or, at the very least, warm – 'spots' (Sherman *et al.* 1989) where groups of young people routinely congregate, where local adult residents are worried and angered, and where the police are often called (14 per cent of calls to Macclesfield police station in April and May 1995 concerned youths causing a nuisance or acting suspiciously; see Chapter 6). These include some (though by no means all) of the town's council-built estates: at diffuse sites on the Moss Rose, and at the shops on Upton Priory and the Weston. But they also extend to the middle-class commuter development of Tytherington (where young people gathered in the woods, and at a parade of shops and a children's playground); and to the area of weavers' cottages around the old High Street. Here, a small local park (St George's) and a couple of shops were – according to one resident – attracting young people from Moss Rose, Weston and Victoria Park 'like flies to a jam pot'.

In the absence of what one 15-year-old girl called 'somewhere to go where we won't be bugging anyone', these various sites provide one of the few ways in which young people can associate away from the supervision of adult authority. They offer – as a member of our Hurdsfield focus group explained – a means of:

> Just having fun, you know what I mean, trying to make the most of the dump what we're in, standing on a car park, what else is there. Have a laugh, tease each other, get on, you know what I mean. Maybe get a little loud, but at least we're just stood in the middle of the pissing car park, we're not in the guy's pissing car pinching his stereo.

Yet the young people we spoke to were also well aware, or had been made well aware, of the worry and annoyance their presence – sometimes in large numbers – prompts among some local residents. As one 14-year-old girl from Moss Rose explained: 'If we go into St George's Park we always have people coming round complaining that we're making too much noise. ... You get that all the time, but we weren't doing anything wrong, it's just because we we're there.' The following discussion – between other members of a group of 14- and 15-year-olds who have taken to congregating in the old High Street area – provides a further indication of the inter-generational conflict that their (unwelcome) presence can generate. It is a conflict we will return to:

IL: Are there places that you regularly go to hang around with your mates?

All: Yes.

IL: Where would they be?

Josh: St George's.

Tina: Are you a policeman?

IL: No.

Debbie: Little parks. It all started off in [19]93, when everyone was in South Park, then it got closed. There was loads of trouble and police come and everything, and anyone who was there would just get thrown in, and everyone would just run, and that would be it. But if you run you'd get done for running, but if you stay you get taken in, so ...

IL: Did local residents complain about you?

Debbie: In the park, it's surrounded by houses and they will do. They have kids that are asleep.

Tina: We respect that. All they have to do is come out, but they don't, they ring the police and the police take it over the top and arrest us for making noise.

Locating adult worries about the young

We noted in Chapter 2 that one of the attractions Macclesfield holds for many of its citizens – one reason indeed why some were initially tempted to move there – is that it is considered a good place in which to 'bring up children'. This aspect of the town's perceived 'liveability' did not, however, prevent residents (whether parents or not) from expressing various kinds of worries about the safety and well-being of children and young people within the town. One such worry surrounds the question of drugs. A threat to the town's young that was viewed by many adult residents as having grown progressively worse in recent years, the 'advent' of drugs was often taken as a further instance of national (or in this case 'world-wide') problems (from which many thought Macclesfield had hitherto been relatively immune) coming to permeate the social relations of the town.

Though widespread among our adult respondents (one home watch coordinator referred to it as 'this tremendous problem'), worries about drugs were voiced most intensely in our discussions by parents of teenage children. Concern among parents focused mainly on the ever-present possibility that their offspring might be enticed into drugs by friends, other schoolchildren or by malign (adult) strangers; the anxiety here surrounding not only the potential harm that drugs may cause, but also the risk that their children might be excluded from school for possession. But parental worries also flow from the apparent dearth of reliable information about drugs and the resulting (sometimes 'engulfing') uncertainty about the scale of the problem; the 'tell-tale' signs of use to look out for; the harm caused by consuming different substances and how best parents might act to protect their children. These anxieties (and the inter-generational chasm that the question of drugs appears to be opening up[4]) occasioned among some of our respondents both sympathy for local parents, and an attempt to situate their difficulties in the recent history of the town:

> Going back a good few years when everybody knew everybody in Macclesfield, parents knew what their kids were up to because somebody was going to tell them, whereas now, families don't have that awareness. Kids can keep secrets more easily because there's a greater element of anonymity in the place by virtue of the fact that it's grown.
>
> (male resident, High Street)

Parental worries surfaced, second, around the issue of children's and teenagers' safety. In part, this amounted to a concern over the threats posed to the young by strangers or traffic – we came across very few parents who either didn't strictly delimit where their young children could play, or who didn't drop them (or arrange for them to be dropped) at school. But it also encompassed anxieties about teenage 'gangs' picking on their – especially male – offspring (one mother described how her 12-year-old son had been assaulted one Saturday afternoon 'because he was wearing something with a logo that these lads didn't like'), and concerns about the dangers faced by older teenagers who now wanted (or had been granted) permission to visit the town centre on Friday and Saturday nights. In these respects, many Macclesfield parents appear to embody what has in recent years become a national preoccupation with the threats posed – especially by strangers – to the young. As one parent reflected: 'I don't know whether anything has changed, but the media has brought such attention. You're frightened to death really.'

In the face of these perceived threats to the safety and well-being of children and young people our respondents often detailed the various efforts they made to protect their offspring. These ranged from one father who admitted having taught his 13-year-old son how to 'head-butt' as a means of self-defence (before immediately adding, 'That's terrible isn't it?'), to more common prescriptions about being in by a certain time. They also involved prohibitions on going to particular places (such as the woods in Tytherington – 'There's trouble round there and there's children who are out in the early hours'), and an insistence that children go only to their friends' houses or have their friends round – as one mother from Broken Cross put it: 'It's not unusual to have six in Tom's bedroom, playing music. But I know what they're up to.' The ambivalence this produces among young people is captured well in the following discussion between a group of 15-year-olds:

IL: Are your parents right to worry?
All: Yes.
Josh: They go a bit over the top sometimes. You explain you'll be alright.
Pete: If you was a parent you'd be the same.
IL: When you say they 'go over the top' what do you mean?
Sarah: Certain nights, 'Where are you going, what are you doing?' Once you've told them 'Make sure you're not doing … .' They trust me, but it's the people who I go out with who they don't know. Say I said I was going out: 'Who are they, where are they from?'
Tina: You have to give them their full life story.

This brings us to what is perhaps the principal source of adult concern about youth across various areas of Macclesfield: the unsupervised gathering of groups of male and female teenagers in public places. This again arose as a particular concern among parents, in part because 'hanging around' exposes young people to risks in respect of drugs and safety, and in part – as the above extract suggests – because it raises the troubling prospect that one's children might 'fall in' with 'bad company'. As one father living in Moss Rose put it: 'I don't like doing it, but you've got to keep a good eye on them. They've only got to get in with the wrong person and they're in trouble.'

In the main, however, our focus group participants appeared less explicitly concerned about the threats posed *to* young people while 'hanging around', than by the problems caused for others *by* the allegedly disorderly and intimidatory behaviour of young people themselves – something about which many spoke heatedly. These problems appear to impact significantly on the quality of life of many adult residents, and – when placed alongside young people's perceptions of the same issue – suggest that inter-generational conflict over the legitimate uses of public space is one of the principal cleavages that mark lived social relations within the town. We have already seen how the young people concerned view such conflicts; the response of many adult residents is encapsulated in the comments of these two women living in Upton Priory:

> They seem to feel that anything goes and people just do not count, these youngsters. Some of them, not all of them, seem to have a great disrespect for authority in general. They go about in these groups, and I know a lot of it is bravado, but they're a frightening sight sometimes.

> I like to see kids enjoying themselves, but the other day I had occasion to move two. They were teenagers. They were just sitting there shouting and carrying on. I opened the door and said, 'Would you like to go where you live, only there's people here with young children, they don't want them disturbing.' Now the filth that came out of one of them's mouth was … I was flabbergasted, really. I was thinking: 'Are they going to put a brick through my window?'

It is clear that people from across many diverse parts of Macclesfield face problems (of low-level disorder and petty crime) caused by groups of teenagers hanging around, albeit differentially so (the proportion of calls made to Macclesfield police station in April/May 1995 concerning 'nuisance or suspicious youths' ranged, for instance, from 20 per cent in Moss Rose/High Street to 9 per cent for the beat covering Victoria Park and the eastern side of the town centre). Yet it is also evident from our research that residents interpret the presence and behaviour of these teenagers in contrasting ways and invest it with varying degrees of significance; and these interpretations *cannot* simply be read off from actual levels of disorderly or criminal activity. They also appear to depend on which of Macclesfield's composite areas one is talking about (their respective histories, demographies, internal relations, trajectories and so on), and on the biographical relationship its inhabitants have to the place they reside in – how it fits into their past, present and possible futures. So how do local adult residents make sense of and respond to the congregations of 'disorderly youths' that hang around in different locations across Macclesfield? And how might we best interpret their different kinds and levels of response?

The people who tend to speak most emphatically about groups of teenagers hanging around (and in ways that connect their presence to some or other narrative of local decline) are those who possess the greatest levels of emotional and/or material investment in 'their area'. The former can stem from a number of sources. It may be the product of being 'tied' physically to the home or locality by reason of age or status. Or it may flow from long-standing residence and an ensuing sense that one's personal biography is deeply entwined with that of one's community. For such people – most often the senior citizens among our respondents – 'place matters'; and they often bring to issues of teenage mis/behaviour a sustained contact with and knowledge of the youths involved (and their families), their memories of that community (and in particular a reconstructed sense of its better past), and a heartfelt concern for the future prospects of what they regard as 'home'. The following exchange between established residents of Moss Rose captures well this sense of both 'community' and its decline:

Dot: We're having more trouble with youngsters now than we've ever had, than I can ever remember on the Moss.

Peter: Tonight was an example, wasn't it? *[A group of children had spent the early part of the focus group throwing stones at the building we were meeting in.]*

Dot: Yes. I mean it's all the time, non-stop, from morning right through to late at night, somewhere is being vandalized at all times.

IL: Is that a new thing do you think?

Dot: It hadn't used to be. I tell you, when I lived on the Moss before. When I was young and I lived on the Moss, alright, we had us cheeky devils, but that extended to nipping in somebody's garden and pinching their apples, or knocking on the doors and running off and hiding behind hedges. You didn't get the very bad. Occasionally, you'd get a bike pinched, but it were quite rare. It were the talk of the Moss if somebody had had their bike nicked. Can you remember that far back?

Moss Rose, Upton Priory and the Weston probably come closest within Macclesfield to communities where the presence and behaviour of groups of teenagers is viewed through the prism of such emotional attachment to place (in all three areas the tenants' associations – who do most to lobby around these issues – are run by older and, for the most part retired, residents). They also provide (along with Prestbury, albeit for very different reasons – see Chapter 5) instances of where such emotive attachment intersects with more material considerations. On Moss Rose, Upton Priory and the Weston, (ex-) tenants who have since 1980 purchased their houses from Macclesfield Borough Council now – as local estate agents will readily testify – find it difficult to sell their (often improved and lovingly cherished) properties. Against this backdrop, noisy congregations of teenagers not only impinge detrimentally on the quality of people's lives, they can also come to be seen as a threat to the value of newly-acquired assets.[5] It thus tends to be in these areas – on the fragile lower borderline of 'respectability' which is still worth defending, and where people neither wish nor easily feel able to leave – that one encounters the most power-fully felt expressions of concern towards teenage 'incivilities'; a concern that can on occasions – as was graphically illustrated by one 'vigilante' episode on the Weston in 1993 – engender among some the will to 'fight back', and more broadly a willingness to condone (or at least understand) the actions of those who do (see, further, Girling *et al.* 1998).

In some contrast stand those relatively affluent, often socially and geog-raphically mobile residents who are somewhat thinly attached to 'place' (cf. Gans 1995). In Macclesfield, this description perhaps best fits those young, child-free professionals who commute to work in Manchester or other parts of Cheshire; who are prone to spending long hours away from their place of residence (including, for some, evenings and weekends), and who thus have little reason to identify with the place they reside in. Notwithstanding that they have often chosen to live where they do (and are in certain respects concerned with the quality of life that it offers), such people have relatively few attachments to their community, and the greatest sources of identification (job, friends, family and so on) beyond it. They lack a history in the locality and, as people whose careers might at short notice demand that they move elsewhere, will in all probability lack a future in it.

It is these among Macclesfield's residents who – so long as the 'problem of youth' doesn't impact upon house prices, and in middle-class areas of Macclesfield it generally doesn't – seem most able to speak about the teenagers hanging around their area in abstract, dispassionate terms, to sever its connec-tion with wider meanings and chains of significance, and to generally downplay its importance. So it is that a resident of Kennedy Avenue can describe the youths at the local supermarket (an issue that deeply vexes the tenants' associa-tion on the adjacent Upton Priory estate) as a problem one learns to live with: 'There's not a great deal you can do about it personally. If you get the police involved, there's only so much they can do.' And so it is too that the coordinator of a Tytherington home watch scheme can sum up their 'youth problem' thus:

> It's not a regular problem, it seems to go through phases. Children will congregate either around shops near the off-licence, or in the woods, in large groups. They create litter, and they break branches off the trees, but we don't have any serious problems. I've not heard of anyone getting beaten up there, or any neighbour having a brick thrown through the window, or anything like that.

It appears then that the intensity with which individuals identify with 'fear of crime discourse' (Hollway and Jefferson 1997) does not merely arise from their direct or indirect experiences of victimization. It also intersects with people's personal biographies, the sense they have of their place within prevailing social hierarchies and their resulting relationship to a particular geographical commu-nity. To illustrate these connections further, let us take a closer look at how adult residents of one particular part of Macclesfield – the area around the old High Street – respond to the groups of youths who congregate in their 'community'.

Community, biography and the 'problem of youth': the case of 'low life' on the High Street

The area around the old High Street comprises – as we saw in Chapter 2 – a dense network of two- and three-storey nineteenth-century weavers' cottages (interspersed with old silk mills mostly now converted into 'designer' flats). Designated by Macclesfield Borough Council as a 'Preservation Area', this is the part of town from which much of Macclesfield's reputed charm and inherited self-representation as an historic silk town derives. This physical charm is not unrelated to the High Street area's recent fortunes. The area remains home to some long-standing elderly residents, many of whom live in rented accommodation; some equally established working- and lower middle-class residents, many of whom have been there for decades, and a scattering of young families with children. But in recent years these have been joined by a burgeoning number of young professionals, as the area has made at least a nod in the direction of gentrification (it is best characterized as an area altered yet not entirely colonized by mainly 'marginal gentrifiers'; see Rose 1984).

For these young professionals – mostly incoming first-time buyers who work in Cheshire or Manchester – the High Street seems an altogether pleasant place. As one such incomer – an emigré from the suburb of Didsbury in south Manchester – put it: 'I'm very much more aware of a sense of community here. [The neighbours] are not my best friends but they're good acquaintances. It's friendly.' For some of the more established residents, however, things do not appear so rosy. Following the property boom of the late 1980s, when house prices in the area soared, and many of the larger properties were bought by private landlords for conversion into bedsits, the area has also become home to a shifting population of what are seen as 'undesirable' incomers: 'the homeless', people released 'into the community' from Parkside Psychiatric Hospital, 'drug-takers', 'DSS [social security] cases' and former residents of Victoria Park flats. For some – such as Dawn Jones, proprietor with her husband Ray of a local shop – the neighbourhood has spiralled into decline:

> We have a transitional population round the corner. In the bigger [owner-occupied] houses here, things are more stable. But the ones that have been converted to bedsits they are a complete mish-mash of everything at the bottom end, the drones of Macclesfield. They are the people from Victoria Park who live very close to the legal line, and when they put the surveillance system into the flats they opted to move out. That is what we got down here.

The High Street has in recent years become an attractive meeting point for congregations of young people – mainly, according to residents, from one of what the Jones described as Macclesfield's 'three naughty areas' – Victoria Park, the Weston and nearby Moss Rose. As one established male resident put it:

> The Moss estate a lot of them live. Again, I'm not putting that down, because I used to live on the Moss, and there's a lot of nice people there. There's a lot from the Moss, there's nothing on the Moss estate, so they drift into town and that's sort of half way. It's a good sort of stopping off point.

Particularly during the summer, school holidays and in the weeks surrounding Guy Fawkes' Night, these teenagers are mainly to be found either in and around the local shops (the Jones claim that on occasions 'up to sixty youths' hang around in the street in front of their shop); or in (the aforementioned) St George's Park, a children's playground where the intended younger users are said to have been usurped:

Margaret: It's supposed to be for little ones, they're not allowed to go in it, the big ones are in it. The big ones are doing God knows what in it.

Tom: They dominate the play area to the exclusion of infants who are supposed to be using it. If you go in there Thursday, Friday, Saturday morning, and have a look at all the milk cartons that have been thrown about, I think you would be surprised what they do. They're putting tablets in the milk cartons.

Among these long-standing High Street residents the presence in the area of what they see as 'unruly' groups of teenagers (from elsewhere) is a source of considerable anger and disquiet – Tom and Margaret, both resident in the area for some thirty-one years, came to the focus group with the sole and express purpose of venting their frustrations. The disturbances the youths are reputed to cause ('They're either drunk, they're on drugs, or they're fighting', as Margaret put it), are clearly felt to have a detrimental impact upon the life of the local community. For some the combined effect of the teenagers and the 'undesirable' occupants of the bedsits is a desire to vacate the area entirely.

Yet these kinds of worries are rather less evident among the recently arrived young professionals who live in the High Street area. Tom and Margaret's immediate neighbour (a 25-year-old woman architect working in south Manchester) professed herself ignorant of the disorder that was alleged to be happening on her doorstep (much to the consternation of the former). Another local professional admitted to cognate surprise when the subject of teenage drug-use in the area arose:

> It's come as a revelation to me. I've been here five years and I work away from Macc, and I go away for weekends, so I'm only here for a relatively small amount of time. I'm in the house and out again. I'm quite surprised listening to your concerns and experiences.

Yet another (a chartered planning consultant working in Knutsford) managed to describe the 'incivilities' that so concern and anger her more established neighbours in the following dead-pan terms:

> When I've been to the shop I have seen a group hanging around on the opposite side to the shop. I don't go to the shop that often. When I was walking back along High Street a couple of days before bonfire night, the other week, I noticed that there were a lot of kids in the children's play area, and somebody had set off a rocket which had gone into the wall on the opposite side and narrowly missed a lady walking past. That's about it, the biggest incident that I have seen or heard.

We thus have starkly juxtaposed in this small Macclesfield neighbourhood social groupings with markedly different relationships to 'place' and divergent responses to the same group of teenagers. These teenagers appear to impact minimally on the lives and consciousness of residents for whom the area provides something of a (pleasant) retreat from a life lived largely – and rewardingly – elsewhere, and for whom residence is likely to be relatively short-lived. While for those whose lives derive much meaning from their local attachments (and whose past and future is closely bound up with the immediate locality), the presence of the youths (and the seeming reluctance of anyone to do anything about them) is seen as being deeply entangled with and implicated in the decline of the area and its 'community spirit'. As Patrick Wright (1985: 237) has observed, people can inhabit the same locality, but live in different worlds.

But this is not all. That people's sense of place (and concerns about teenage disorder) also depend upon matters of personal biography (that is, on one's past, present and anticipated future in the wider world) is also nicely illustrated by the case of the old High Street; and, in particular, by the recent life-history of the aforementioned shop owners, Ray and Dawn Jones. Encouraged by a government grant which supported people seeking to move from areas of high to low unemployment, the Jones' moved to Macclesfield from a village in the South of England in 1976 (he had just been made redundant). For Ray, a native of Cheshire, this was something of a return home; for Dawn, who hails from Devon, her first time in the North. They moved reluctantly and unhappily, forced by circumstances to leave their 'idyllic' rural home:

> It was quite a cultural change really, moving to Macclesfield. Suddenly it was a town, a northern town, which was quite different from southern towns, certainly there were a lot of derelict buildings and a lot of places taken down, a lot of the mills were gone. And it really wasn't very attractive.

They bought a 1950s three-bedroom semi just north of the Moss estate, and Ray took up the offer of a job at his uncle's transport firm. And they began to get connected: with neighbours (they helped organize the 1977 'Silver Jubilee' street party), with other parents through the Parent Teachers Association, and, in

Dawn's case, at the local college of further education. Things it seemed were 'going on quite well'. But his uncle's promise that Ray could take over the business failed to materialize and towards the end of the 1970s, when the business started faltering, a dispute ensued. Ray's uncle refused to relinquish control, and the business closed. Dawn for a while ran a small catering operation to make ends meet. In the meantime, she gained a degree from Salford University, and began work in Manchester as a financial consultant. In 1982, they bought the shop in the High Street – things were once again starting to look up: 'We thought we'd turned the corner. We'd had a rough six years one way or the other and the business hadn't worked. I was angry, worked for virtually nothing. Our financial position had deteriorated dramatically.'

For the first few years, while Dawn continued to work in Manchester, Ray built up the shop and it started making money. Then in 1985 the Borough Council closed the High Street to through traffic (it had been a short cut from the south into town). The effect on the shop was immediate and disastrous: 'It killed us. Instantaneous. We lost 80 per cent over nine months.' Since then the Jones' personal fortunes have – it appears – declined hand-in-hand with those of the area. Young people began gathering in the area and (as we have seen) in the late 1980s many of the houses were turned over to bedsits. The shop continued to struggle. In 1990 Dawn was made redundant. The shop was then dealt another – near fatal – blow by the outside world: 'Sunday opening absolutely decimated us. That was our best day. We were taking £1000 on a Sunday, we now take £320–£330.' Dawn and Ray Jones sum things up thus:

Dawn: Anyone looking at us from the outside, would say that materially we have done quite well. The fact that we have large mortgages hanging around our necks which we hadn't expected to have by now isn't what it looks like from the outside. Like a lot of people in their early fifties our expectations haven't been fulfilled. Normally by this time in life you would expect to ease off, to be more comfortable. Mainly because of the recession and other things our financial situation is very tight. We cannot afford to go out that much. We're tied by the shop. Because of the atmosphere in the area, because of the youths, the enthusiasm for running the shop has to some extent died and if we could off-load it we would. But you have to be realistic, the prices are no good.

IL: Why are you minded to close it?

Ray: Because I am working for about 38p an hour and there are not that many people in this country who are doing that. I've got bitter, a lot bitter. I feel that this [Conservative] government has let us down very, very badly. I considered myself middle class and I was quite happy to go along my middle-class road. Looking back to twelve, fifteen years ago, I thought, 'Well life doesn't look too bad looking down my road.' But that has been eroded now and I am in the bottom half, we are in the bottom half of the class strata and we are well, well into the bottom half. And the middle-class is gone, it is eroded.

Thus have the expectations of one middle-class Macclesfield couple been shattered. The certainties they recall their parents enjoying are gone. The things they believed would be the reward for hard work – security, stability, the opportunity to 'ease off' in later life – have not been forthcoming. They anticipate their futures with some trepidation. Against this backdrop, the presence of 'disorderly' teenagers in the local streets is not just in some material sense the last straw; it also powerfully exemplifies a world gone horribly wrong:

IL: How do you feel about the next ten years of your life?

Ray: Apprehension. We are living, not looking very far ahead, we can't, we daren't, it's bleak. We hoped we'd be semi-retired by now. I thought I'd be working twenty-five, thirty hours a week and enjoying it. I am working sixty-eight, seventy hours a week and I am not enjoying it.

Dawn: And if you have the problems with the youngsters we had last autumn that was the final straw. If everything else is okay you can cope with it, but when you are already in a situation of under stress, that stress affects people's attitudes, and the customers do not want to come in because of the kids outside, and you have to watch them because they are stealing and causing trouble. It's another pressure that you don't want.

Disorder and national decline: youth and the condition of England

In *Disorder and Decline* (1990) Wesley Skogan sets out what has in recent years become an influential thesis within criminology: that (unchecked) teenage 'incivilities' are read by residents as signs of neighbourhood decline and prompt responses (such as a desire to leave the area, or an unwillingness to regulate the behaviour of the young) whose effect is in fact to engender such decline (cf. Wilson and Kelling 1982; Lewis and Salem 1986). There is of course a cavernous gulf separating even the poorest parts of Macclesfield from the structurally disadvantaged neighbourhoods of North American cities that routinely figure in this literature. This though – as we have seen – does not prevent many of the town's adult residents from similarly viewing the mis/behaviour of the young as signalling some kind of decline in the spirit or – to use Lewis and Salem's (1986: 99) term – 'moral reliability' of their community.

Yet the 'environmental cues' provided by 'disorderly youths' are not merely taken as signs of neighbourhood decline. They are also read more broadly – and *politically* – as issues that are deeply entangled with other aspects of economic, social and moral change (or, more specifically, decline), and as matters that call up questions of authority and, ultimately, government (cf. Dowds and Ahrendt 1996). Although the problems created by 'disorderly youths' may seem pressingly local, adult residents often account for them in terms that stretch far beyond the boundaries of their community (or indeed Macclesfield) as such. Such problems speak, it seems, to the condition of both the wider 'national community' and the world beyond. But what meanings are invoked in this regard? What aspects of the wider world are young people's attitudes and behaviour thought to be entangled with? What (national and global) pressures are seen as acting upon the locality, in what ways, and with what effects?

Some among our respondents explicitly couched the 'problem of youth' in terms relating to the job market and, in particular, to dislocations in the kinds of opportunities that were once open to the working-class young men of post-war Britain. As one male Weston resident put it:

> When I left school, you left school and you went into an apprenticeship or whatever it was, some sort of job. You went through a process. You sort of met a girl, you got engaged, you got married and had children, and on it went. It was a sort of unbreakable cord, but it isn't any more.

Sometimes this position – which roughly corresponds to what Theodore Sasson (1995) terms the 'blocked opportunities' framework – takes on a more local idiom as a commentary upon some of the recent fortunes and possible futures of the town. Consider the following exchange between two established middle-class residents from Broken Cross:

Joan: These young people with perhaps not very many brains, let's face it, and not very well brought up, would go into hard physical labour when they were young. Those jobs don't exist now. They would be in foundries and mills, and they would be too tired to be so awkward. This is a lot of the problem, they haven't the brains to keep up with society, like your son going to Oxford. But there's nothing else for them to do. What else can they do, where can they go? So they're hanging about, they're getting into drugs, they're looking for trouble. They were too tired before. They were rotten jobs, I'll admit, but it gave them something to do, it gave them a wage packet, it gave them a community to belong to of these other people working there. They haven't got that now. What have they got? They've not got a lot have they really to look forward to.

Tony: That's generalizing Joan.

Joan: I'm not saying they weren't … but they had a purpose in those days.

Tony: A lot of these kids have got jobs and it's just something to do at night.

Tony's objections to Joan's couching of troublesome teenagers in terms of jobs flow from his attachment to a second, more prevalent, and often more forcefully expressed, mode of explanation: what one might call the 'crisis of the family'.[6] Under this umbrella, our focus group participants would – in terms that resonate closely with many current tropes of media and political discourse on 'law and order' – connect juvenile crime and disorder with a number of valued components of social life that had – as one participant in our Moss Rose focus group put it – 'gone by the board'. On occasions this would take on a sympathetic form, a reference to parents struggling to cope, or else quite innocently unaware of the problems their children cause. As one established male resident put it in respect of High Street: 'I'm very, very sure that most of the parents of the teenagers that congregate outside our house don't know what they're doing at all, they're oblivious to the fact that they're creating damage.'

More often, however, discourse on the family was invoked in a spirit of blame, as residents from across Macclesfield bemoaned variously: the decline of 'parental control', the inability of parents to 'chastise their children', the collapse of 'discipline', the disappearance of appropriate (male) 'role models', and a culture of questioning that has encouraged children to know of 'rights' but not 'responsibilities'. Tony interjects this line of argument into the above discussion thus:

> I think what we're coming round to, we're coming round to the main subject in a way. It's about upbringing, it's about parents. Nothing else, it's about parents. It's not where you live, what the house is like, it's about the attitude of parents. The word that is missing today is respect. That's what's missing today. Nobody has respect for anybody or anything else, apart from themselves. It shows up in all sorts of different areas.

In responding to teenage disorder using these terms, people were for the most part speaking at some remove from the particular problems of their locality. These discourses are however (as we have seen in the case of jobs) susceptible to local application, able to operate as a commentary on the strained social relations of particular communities. Thus it is that accounts couched in terms of the family often attach themselves to those (by definition 'bad') parents who seem content to let their kids roam unsupervised in the neighbourhood. Indeed, the frequency with which such charges were laid in our discussions suggests that the principal intra-community cleavage opened up by teenage disorder is not so much between young and old, but between 'good' and 'bad' parents; those who care about their children and their community, and those who allegedly don't. Such exasperation about – often known – parents was fairly commonly expressed across various areas of Macclesfield, in this case by residents of Weston and Upton Priory:

> I think it's lack of parents' control, to be honest. There's too much of where the parents have both got to go out to work and the kids left to fend. … I mean you've got the case outside, you've one youngster there. He's a great little lad, don't get me wrong. He lives on our street. But he is left to wander the streets. I have seen him when the heavens have opened and there's two or three of them sat on the curb, that kind of thing, because they don't bother going home.
>
> I opened my front door yesterday, and I won't mention whose children it was, but there were 8- and 9-year-olds, there was three of them sitting on my doorstep smoking. Where do they get the money from? How on earth do their parents not know?

A third means by which adult residents accounted for teenage mis/behaviour is one that brings into sharper relief the values and outlooks of young people themselves. Here attention focuses, not so much on jobs and family life (though these remain pertinent), but on some seemingly more diffuse and difficult to grasp mutations in the cultural and moral order (in fields such as education or the media for instance) that are felt to have impacted detrimentally on the dispositions of 'the youth of today'. The means by which people routinely 'condense' these changes and their effects into a readily graspable form is to speak of the young lacking 'respect': respect for parents, teachers, police officers, for their elders generally – in short, 'respect for authority'. As an established female resident of the High Street area put it (in response to a *general* question about how Macclesfield had changed):

> Children have got no respect for a start off. … Years ago, if children were causing disturbances or what not, you said something to them: 'Go away!'; they went, there was no moither. Now they won't. [They say] 'What are you going to do about it?'

Among elderly residents of the town questions of 'respect' were most often invoked using terms that suggested its steady erosion and loss. While such residents often conceded that neither they nor their own children had been angelic teenagers, they nonetheless reconstructed their pasts (and by extension the wider local and national past) as a time that was (more) ordered, socially harmonious and civil (cf. Pearson 1983). As the following discussion between middle-class residents of Kennedy Avenue illustrates, these powerfully felt 'social memories' (Fentress and Wickham 1992) draw upon both reconstructed personal experience (of past *and* present) and widely available, mass-mediated modes of talking about the fate of post-war England (and its youth):

Jimmy: Let's be honest the days have gone when … it's not parental authority these days, the police have no authority, and what authority they have got is insufficient to deal with the problem.
Audrey: Teachers have no authority.
Jimmy: No. Teachers have no authority.
Miriam: There's no deterrent.
Jimmy: In our day if we misbehaved the school master gave you a clip round the earhole, that was it, it did you a lot of good. There was no question of complaining to the police or the authorities about it because he was perfectly within his rights. It certainly helped, I think, to keep … Nowadays there's nothing.

These sentiments were not, however, confined to the elderly among our respondents; nor were they always obviously invoked in a spirit of wistful nostalgia. Among those who took a generally more benign (or even welcoming) view of the social and cultural changes of recent decades (and who certainly evinced little enthusiasm for 'getting back to how it used to be'), it was often still felt that such change had (for better *and* worse) made more complex and contested some hitherto taken-for-granted aspects of inter-generational relations. Some chose 'the pendulum' as the metaphorical device which best captured their ambivalence towards such alterations (as in 'the balance has swung too far to the other side'); others preferred to speak in terms of key turning points: 'Don't you think the trouble started in the sixties when the school teacher said call me Charlie instead of Sir?' In either case, an unspoken acceptance of the need for and benefits of change is coupled (uneasily) with the felt sense that the resulting 'question everything' culture has produced children and young people who know 'their rights, but not their responsibilities', have 'lost a healthy fear of doing wrong' and who seemingly lack the discipline in which the previous generation had been schooled. As one retired female resident of Broken Cross put it: 'Thirty years ago they had to be prepared to put more effort in. I grew up when if you hadn't got the qualifications you went to night school. They'd laugh at you now if you suggested that.' Ray Jones's response to hearing that teenagers have appropriated a term whose legitimacy for him depends on its association with government captures well the worries felt by many about the kind of world such changes might possibly be producing:

> We had a conversation in the shop this morning about the thieving that goes on in the town. A young adult in her early twenties said, 'You know they don't regard it as stealing, they don't call it nicking, pilfering, they call it "taxing".' Now, the word taxing, is taking something that you have a certain right to have. And this is the way these youngsters feel. That if you've got a nice stereo in your car they think it is their right. You have that and I will have that as well and they tax you; they take it and they don't see, the word theft is not in their vocabulary. That is the way they have grown up, they have a right to whatever they want.

These accounts demonstrate how locally occurring forms of teenage mis/behaviour prompt discourse that slips away from the locality (as both its referent and locus of explanation) and accounts for 'the problem' in terms of the economic or social or cultural or moral decline of 'the nation'. Thus posed, the youth question fairly readily prompts responses that fit snugly with, and borrow terminology from, dominant media discourse and political rhetoric on 'law and order'; with all its angry denunciations of 'permissive' child-rearing, 'ineffective' policing and 'soft' punishments, and its attendant calls for someone to take 'tough action'. It seems that when 'teenage disorder' comes to be framed and spoken about (in abstract terms) as a problem pervasive in and endemic to contemporary English society as such (not to mention one from which 'our town', or 'our area', or 'our street', or 'our kids' are no longer able to exempt themselves), the resulting feelings of what Giddens (1991: 193) calls 'engulfment' make 'firm measures' (taken at the national level) seem like the only viable solution.

Disorder and local decline: what's happening to *'our* kids'?

Yet these punitive, often criminal justice-centred, impulses have seemingly little to do with the concerns people voice about the condition and fate of *their own* community. When Macclesfield's adult residents speak about locally occurring teenage mis/behaviour, they rarely evince a desire to banish or exclude young people, to place them somehow beyond the boundaries of 'community' (though their 'social memories' do of course operate as exclusionary devices, distinguishing those who recall a 'better past' or who embody its values, from those who don't). Indeed, with the partial exception of the area around the old High Street, residents mostly acknowledge the young people occupying local public spaces as 'our kids', and as 'belonging' to 'our community'. Their demands are thus not for measures that risk accentuating difference and division still further; but for those which might 're-incorporate' the young, thereby restoring to local social life a lost cohesion, discipline and civility.

This is most clearly so among those whose response to teenage disorder is a seeming wish to strike up a dialogue with young people about what it is that causes them to hang around the streets and what might be done about it. The following exchange from one of our two High street focus groups is especially interesting in this regard, not only because the discussants are keen not to come across as 'soft' on youth crime (hence demonstrating the currently marginal status of the position they are voicing), but also because of the evident doubt as to whether received forms of youth provision are in fact what 'today's teenagers' really want:

Peter: Nobody is bothering to say, I'm not defending the kids, but say why they are doing it in the first place. There's nothing, there's just nowhere to go, nothing to do. I'm not saying it should be given to them on a plate, but there isn't anything at all, no facilities.
[...]

EG: What would you say that the younger people in Macclesfield would want?

David: It's a bit difficult because attitudes have completely changed from what it was ten years ago. They seem to grow faster, they seem to be doing a lot of the things that we used to do when we were eighteen. When they're twelve and thirteen, they seem to be smoking. I'm not saying we should give them what they want, but we should ask them what they want first.

(High Street residents)

It is also evident among those who bemoaned what they saw as the dearth of facilities available to young people in the town and who viewed this, not only as being causally implicated in teenage disorder, but as indicative of some widespread lack of concern for youth among townspeople and local decision-makers alike. Having noted how Macclesfield's young have been ignored during 'all this building and progress', one Weston resident continued thus:

Helen: They're just roaming the streets like lost souls until it's time to go in at night time. And when they go to school in the morning, 'What did you lot do last night?'. 'Oh we walked up and down so and so.' But saying that, on the other hand you get what we've had to put up with here.

IL: We'll come onto that soon.

Helen: I think basically what it is, it's very unfair that they're not … they're so busy about filling their own purses, the oldies, my generation, and they don't give a sod about the young ones. Do they care about the young ones? 'No'.

This confluence of irritation with and concern for young people was amply demonstrated at a public meeting on the Weston which took place one Friday evening in July 1995.[7] The meeting was called by the Tenants' Association (TA) following a story in the *Macclesfield Express Advertiser* suggesting that the TA were about to enlist the services of a private security firm to patrol the estate (it turned out that the association had no such intention). Some sixty residents (mainly aged over 35) packed the community centre for the start of the meeting, along with a couple of teenagers and an area social worker. The residents listened (impatiently, as if fearing they had been lured along under false pretences) to speakers from the TA, Borough Housing department, and the local police inspector, before finally launching into their questions. Incidents were recounted, and action demanded, about youths in people's gardens, noise and aggravation around the shops, and cars 'hurtling' up and down the main street. One woman argued ill-temperedly with the inspector about what the police counted as an 'emergency', while another loudly demanded that a private security firm *was* brought in (her request was heavily defeated on a show of hands, one resident proclaiming it would give the estate 'a bad name'). Two of the teenagers (and the social worker) attempted to defend themselves and then left. The chorus of complaint about teenage crime continued, though several speakers (including those from the TA and the police) were at pains to point out that this applied to only a minority of youths, and that most kids on the estate were 'all right'.

After about an hour a group of around six or seven male and female teenagers (who had previously been walking up and down outside, prompting some occasional accusatory pointing from those inside) entered the meeting. They sat down, lit up cigarettes and listened. After a while one of their number spoke up. He said they had nowhere to go, didn't cause all the trouble on the estate, and were often attacked themselves (either by teenagers from other estates, or by drunken men leaving the local pub). The mood of the meeting was transformed in an instant. Questioning shifted to what the 'local' youths wanted and to how they could be protected, and a constructive – albeit still tense – dialogue ensued. The residents' anger and frustration had evaporated in the face of 'real' teenagers.[8] A meeting between the TA committee and the young people was set up for the following day, and a 'follow-up' public meeting for six weeks hence; seven people turned up.

If this demonstrates that adult residents often want to do something *for* (rather than merely *to*) local teenagers as a response to disorder, it is also apparent that they wish to control the nature of that 'something'; to re-incorporate the young on terms laid down by the adult community. This for the most part means trying to 'contain them in institutions run by "respectable citizenry"' (Brown 1995: 23), something that has in recent years led to frequent confrontations between Macclesfield residents and the youth service over who controls local youth clubs (those on Moss Rose, Upton Priory and – as we shall see – Prestbury have for periods shut down at least in part as a result of such disputes). For while residents (and particularly tenants' associations) strongly support the idea of youth clubs, they are in practice unimpressed by the 'licence' such clubs appear to grant young people, and endeavour instead to run places where teenagers have regulated 'fun' under (non-negotiable) adult rules, and where respect for authority might be (re)instilled.

Much of the disquiet felt by residents concerns the qualities possessed (or lacked) by the professional youth workers appointed to run these clubs (it is a condition of County Council funding that such an appointment is made). At one meeting between the Tenants' Federation and local agencies (called to discuss 'anti-social behaviour' on Macclesfield's estates) a representative from Moss Rose accused local youth workers (in front of the team leader of Cheshire County Council youth service) of exhibiting 'a high-minded attitude', of 'thinking they're God Almighty!' and of being 'unwilling to take advice from local parents'. Others we spoke to commented on youth workers being 'too young' or as 'having university degrees but no experience'. Yet another claimed they were 'too familiar with [young people] to command their respect'. In short – as this Upton Priory resident put it – youth workers are seen as lacking the experience, skills and disposition that the 'required' task – that of exercising control – demands:

> It's like in the youth club for the 13- to 19-year-olds. You provide them with equipment, we've recently had two pool tables donated, decent pool tables. What do they do in front of the youth workers? They let the fire extinguisher off all over the pool tables, all over everywhere. The youth workers don't stop them. They say, 'Oh it was an accident.'[9]

Thus it is that young people are seen as seeking for themselves – either on the streets and other public places, or (with the apparent connivance of youth workers) in youth clubs – an autonomy from adult authority that many among our older respondents equate with unruliness, indiscipline and disrespect. These residents thus take great exception to, and stand stubbornly in the way of, the kinds of – loosely supervised – provision that many young people appear to want and that some local professionals see as offering a potentially lasting solution to the kinds of inter-generational conflict we have documented in this chapter.

5   Anxieties of affluence in Prestbury village

'This', he said, 'is a damn good place to live in. I'm sure the village is doomed, but I'm fighting as hard as I can to limit the doom.'
  (former chairman of Prestbury Parish Council, quoted in Turner 1967: 59)

It is time now for a slight detour. We want in this chapter to revisit some of the substantive themes covered previously (notably, travelling crime and teenage incivilities) and introduce an issue about which we will have more to say later on (namely, policing), by considering how crime and order feature in the lived social relations of Macclesfield's neighbouring 'village-suburb' of Prestbury. As we shall see, many of the worries Prestbury residents have about these matters form in particular ways, and are powerfully mediated by what they have invested – materially and emotionally – in the distinctive, 'haven'-like qualities of 'their village'. A focus on Prestbury should thus enable us – partly by means of comparison and contrast with Macclesfield – to refine our interpretation of how people's anxieties about crime and disorder are shaped by both their sense of the place in which they live, and by their place within the social hierarchies of the wider world.

Even the loosest journalistic deployment of the term 'middle England' would struggle to bring Prestbury within its ambit. An affluent enclave lying some 3 miles north-west of Macclesfield, in the midst of Cheshire's 'swell-belt' (Turner 1967), Prestbury houses some of that county's economic and social elite. Prestbury has long provided a home to the rich, famous and infamous, including over the years such luminaries as 1970s pop icon Noddy Holder, the convicted fraudster Peter Clowes, and ex-Manchester United footballer Eric Cantona. More commonly, this is a place for those who are 'climbing up', or who have prospered in, or retired from, the worlds of global finance, business and the professions; one that doesn't so much reproduce itself (the house prices lie beyond the reach of most first-time buyers), as constantly replenish itself from outside. The 1991 *Census* records that 33.4 per cent of the 5,272 residents possess degrees or professional qualifications and that 65.6 per cent occupy managerial or professional positions. As of 1991, 87.8 per cent of properties were owner-occupied and 63.2 per cent of households owned two or more cars. Unemployment stood at 3.6 per cent.

This is a place whose residents have for the most part actively sought to reside there; for whom Prestbury represents not merely somewhere to live, nor merely a significant financial investment, but also an act of positional consumption, a mark – in Bourdieu's (1984) terms – of 'distinction'. The physical signs of this are clearly evident. At one end of the village high street, a picturesque, tree-lined thoroughfare at the heart of which stands a grand thirteenth-century church, one finds – proudly displayed on its very own post – the latest (1995) of Prestbury's 'Best Kept Village' in Cheshire plaques (it triumphs repeatedly and plaques stretching back to the 1960s adorn the wall of the adjacent bank). Looking down the high street from here, one gets a clear and immediate sense of, not only the village's affluence, but also its exclusiveness. Prestbury doesn't seem to have run-of-the-mill 'high street' shops, but rather shops unique to Prestbury; something apparent not only in specialist outlets like the 'Ye Olde Chocolate Box', or the art gallery, or pottery shop; but also in the fact that the more mundane retailers are designated '*Prestbury* Flowers' or '*Prestbury* Travel'. Even so global an enterprise as the National Westminster Bank is housed in a topsy-turvy Tudor building (formerly the priest's house), suggesting that Prestbury's high street bank has something special to offer its customers.

Prestbury, then, is a place to which people generally resort while striving for, or having accomplished, 'success' (Pahl 1995). But what sorts of 'nourishment' (Matlass 1994: 80–1) do Prestbury's citizens derive from their residence? What kinds of identity, community and security infuse their sense of place? And how best are we to understand the worries and anxieties about crime and disorder felt by the prosperous middle classes who occupy this particular corner of the English social and spatial landscape? This chapter is concerned with these questions.

'A special place': the social meanings of Prestbury

In October 1995, a feature in the *Sunday Times Magazine* set out to advise an imaginary 'horde of barbarians' where in Britain to go in search of the best plunder. Having trotted through the usual list of candidates – Bond Street, Hampstead, the 'stockbroker suburbs' of Surrey – our invaders are told (at which point the reader is meant to feel surprise) to head 'north':

> The richest village in Britain is not in the spoilt self-satisfied south: it is near Manchester, in Cheshire, and its name is Prestbury. It is, per square mile, the home of more millionaires than any other place in Britain. Prestbury is an old-fashioned English village: after all, it still has a post office and a railway station. But it is not an American Golden Ghetto, such as Tuxedo Park in New York State, where a wall, anti-tank traps and a private armed police force protect the wealthy in their mock-Tudor palaces. No. This is a village of 5,000 jolly, welcoming people in the Byzantium of the North.

This article proved to be a major talking point – and irritant – in the village and was variously described during the course of our focus groups (it had appeared shortly before we began interviewing) as 'scurrilous', 'pretty dreadful', 'in bad taste' and 'totally unacceptable'. This was due in large part to residents having felt misrepresented (the feature went on to make reference to the prevalence of Mercedes Benz, foreign villas and servants, and had described the local 'ladies' as 'blonde, rich, thin as beanpoles'); but it arose also from a sense that the piece had reinforced the already dim view of the village held by outsiders. As one member of the local Women's Institute said of Prestbury: 'It has a reputation for being very snobby, millionaires all over the place, unfriendly, dreadful.'[1]

There are, however, aspects of the *Sunday Times'* account with which Prestbury's residents would heartily concur. The first of these concerns the imaginative placing of Prestbury in the 'South of England'. Our respondents – a number of whom had in fact moved up from the 'Home Counties'[2] – were fond of remarking just how 'out of place' Prestbury seems when set against prevailing cultural images of 'The North'.[3] The following are typical in this regard:

> It's a very affluent area, one of the nicest areas in the North I suppose. You could liken it to Esher in Surrey.
>
> (home watch coordinator)

> There are many villages that are just the same as Prestbury in the south-east, on the Kent/Essex border where we lived, they're ten a penny . When we came back to Cheshire and we looked around for something like a village with a school, a pub, a hotel, etc., the only one you could find was Prestbury.
>
> (primary school parent)

Prestbury residents would also take little exception to the *Sunday Times's* depiction of the place as 'an old-fashioned English village'. This particular 'key concept in English social life' (Strathern 1982: 249) was deployed time and again by our respondents as a means of condensing what it was they liked about the place. The term is used to convey Prestbury's aesthetic qualities – 'attractive', 'picturesque', 'well-kept', 'pretty' and 'quaint' being among the characteristic phraseology. It is also mobilized – as in the above account – in association with Prestbury's 'integrated facilities', the ready availability of post office, pubs, railway station, restaurants and good schools. And it is employed to say something about the character of local social relations, denoting both the scale and variety of activities, clubs and organizations,[4] and the 'friendly', 'close-knit' quality of relations between its inhabitants. This – according to the group of retired businessmen we spoke to – is a place where all-comers are able to get along:

Gilbert: You've got a very good mix of old Prestbury, people that have been here a lifetime, or a good many years, twenty, thirty odd years. And you've got, you might describe us as the incomers, people who have worked abroad, internationally, come in with the likes of Zeneca, ICI as it was, CIBA-Geigy, the major companies. We found that the mix works extremely well and it's one of the most pleasant places that we've ever lived.

[...]

Jim: One goes along with the dog and you say good morning to everybody and they say good morning back, how are you, and I say, 'Well draw up a chair if you've got twenty minutes', that sort of thing.

Gilbert: It's one of the most friendly places that I've ever lived in, and certainly in the United Kingdom.[5]

Such glowing praise was not, however, universally employed to characterize contemporary Prestbury. Some residents evidently found the village rather less hospitable than the terms used above might indicate; contending variously that 'lots of people think they're too good'; or, 'there's lots of cliques, you're either in or out'; or, as with this parent who has resided in Prestbury for some eleven years, that: 'the neighbours surrounding us are totally appalled that we have children. They go out of their way to be awkward.' Others appear resigned to Prestbury no longer being the distinctive village it once was, or at least no longer corresponding with their received expectations of the 'English village'. One home watch coordinator put the matter thus: 'It's a dormitory suburb. It doesn't have, for me, the atmosphere of a village because it's too transitory. Not many people live here very long.'[6]

There is little disputing that Prestbury is a cosmopolitan, evidently urban place of some 5,000 or so generally mobile people, akin in many ways to what urban sociologists call 'exurbia'. But, the foregoing reservations notwithstanding, there is equally little doubt that the *idea* of Prestbury as a village – and an archetypal 'English' one at that – is pivotal to many residents' sense of place; nor that this 'village-in-the-mind' (to use Pahl's (1970: 61) term) is a 'thing real, powerful, political and moral' (Matlass 1994: 8). With its evocative suggestion of scenic and social harmony, its rich and warm associations – long celebrated in literary renditions of the pastoral (Empson 1935; Williams 1973) – with order, tranquillity, meaning and security, and its corresponding distancing of the chaos, anonymity and violence of 'the city', the 'village' is a powerful and compelling icon of English culture. It is, as such, something that many of Prestbury's citizens have actively sought (and taken on large financial commitments for), hold dear, and are prepared to defend.

Thus it is that many of the worries of contemporary Prestbury residents concern what they perceive as threats to 'their village' and its attendant way of life. Two aspects are of initial interest here. The first centres upon the possibility of Prestbury being swallowed up (due to the growth of either) by Macclesfield – or, more remotely, if more troublingly, by Greater Manchester. Not that Prestbury residents felt ill-disposed towards Macclesfield. Many of them both routinely make use of the town (for shopping, eating out, the leisure centre and so forth) and spoke of it in mainly positive terms – describing it variously as a 'surprisingly rewarding town', 'a very, very nice place', 'up and coming', 'a market town with everything you want' and as having 'nice shops with proper service', 'a big Sainsburys' and 'a good train service to London'.[7] Prestbury's citizens are, however, keen to distinguish the two places, emphasizing the 'separate identities' of each and, in particular, 'the distinct, different character' of Prestbury. The attendant worry (much of which, among Parish councillors at least, is focused on the ongoing expansion of what one councillor called 'the Tytherington estate') is that Prestbury may become a suburb of 'Greater Macclesfield':[8]

Robert: Macclesfield is a mill town, and Prestbury grew up as a result of the church, and as an affluent place for people from Manchester. I would say that it is distinct.
James: It's distinct in the same way that Bollington is. There is a few of these places on the outskirts, and I think it should be relatively distinct. I don't particularly want to become part of big conurbation.
           [...]
Emily: I think you'll find that most people put their address as Prestbury, Cheshire. They don't mention Macclesfield at all.

                                                                    (Zeneca managers)

A second, more pressing, concern to residents is the question of traffic; an issue that was not only a central preoccupation of the Parish Council, but one which also figured highly (and certainly *more* often than crime) when people were asked to name items of troubling change, or to select 'the worst thing' about living in Prestbury (the growth of the number of houses and people in the village also featured prominently in this regard). Three problems in particular were identified: (i) the volume and speed of commuter and freight traffic passing through the village; (ii) congestion caused by parents dropping off and picking up their children from the local primary school;[9] and (iii) those occasioned by tourists 'consuming' the village and its amenities at weekends (something residents generally viewed with a mixture of pride and a sense of violation). In each case the 'problem' and its attendant dangers are felt by people to be exacerbated by the lack of pedestrian walkways on some roads, and by the absence in Prestbury of *any* street lights. One female resident summed the various issues up thus:

RS: Is there anything about Prestbury that you particularly dislike? Is there any worst feature?
Emily: The traffic. The traffic and the drivers. A feature perhaps of the area, not Prestbury itself, but all around the area, a lot of fast cars, very expensive cars, driving round very recklessly along the lanes that were never actually intended for the kind of traffic that they take, very narrow roads. There's actually nowhere to go if there are any problems.

Because the road through Prestbury is considered to be one of the main roads, it's an A route, it has a lot of heavy, wide traffic, like big coaches, and now they've deregulated the buses there are buses and huge coaches going up and down narrow roads. I just find that an increasing frustration. And it is dangerous.

(Zeneca manager)

People's powerfully-felt impression of Prestbury as what one resident called 'a special place' is, then, not solely organized around its positive qualities, central though these undoubtedly are. The idea that 'this place' (and 'our home') is being assailed by, and needs to be defended against, threats from the outside world, is also a constitutive part of what Prestbury means to its citizens. The sense of troubled times, of a place not quite being as it should be, of Prestbury being 'a postcard olde-worlde village full of English charm, until you get to know it more' (primary school parent), pervades not just residents' concerns about traffic or Greater Macclesfield swallowing them up; it similarly permeates their talk about travelling crime, the presence in the high street of what are felt to be disorderly, drug-consuming local teenagers and the apparent disappearance of the 'village bobby'. It is to these issues we now turn.

Travelling crime revisited: 'calculated criminals' and other intruders

Prominent among the crime-related worries of Prestbury residents is the threat of property crime, especially thefts of and from cars in the village's two car parks, and burglaries. Occupying – as many do – 'relatively secluded' houses which lack immediate neighbours and are left unoccupied for long periods of the day, the threat posed by burglary is of particular concern. Stories detailing the prevalence of housebreaking or the *modus operandi* of burglars arose commonly during our focus group discussions. The following exchange is typical:

Harold: I think the amount of burglary, housebreaking is pretty high. Even living in cottages, my neighbour has been burgled, my next door neighbour but two has been burgled, a neighbour probably about seven or eight cottages away has been burgled within the last two or three weeks. As far as the big houses are concerned, I'm sure Gilbert will be happy to fill you in.

Gilbert: Yes certainly, we've been broken into three times.

(retired businessmen)

In respect of property crime Prestbury residents, and for that matter the police, believe the village to be the target of both petty, opportunist offending and more organized forms of professional theft; what one retired businessman termed 'calculated criminals' in search of jewellery and antiques. Some of the responsibility for petty offending in the village was laid by adult residents at the door of (local) children and teenagers (and linked in many cases with drugs). But for the most part residents' concerns about property crime did not attach to people from either Prestbury or Macclesfield. (None of the town's estates, not even the adjacent Upton Priory, were constructed as preying on Prestbury, in the latter case perhaps because many Prestbury teenagers attend the same 'successful' state school as children from the council estate.) Rather, the criminal threat to Prestbury is seen as being posed by those travelling from further afield; with residents here sharing with those of Macclesfield worries about the following 'crime-exporting' locations:

Helen: You mentioning Liverpool does bring one point to mind. I think so far as burglary is concerned, it's the close proximity to Liverpool.

Max: It's very easy to get on the motorway.

[...]

Mark: I think the police would say they come from Manchester.

(home watch coordinators)

For many, Prestbury's vulnerability to travelling criminals – one Church official called it a 'burglar's paradise' – is viewed as the product both of a good system of road communications and the difficulties of conducting informal surveillance in such a unlit place. As one resident put it: 'One of the advantages, in my opinion, of street lights would be that these vehicles could be seen. The chances are that somebody would at least get a description of them, and might even get the number plates.' It is, however, Prestbury's reputation for wealth that residents deem to be the chief attraction for undesirable criminal outsiders (one of the things that irritated people about the *Sunday Times* feature was that it might attract such outsiders to the village; recall the journalist's use of the 'horde of barbarians' as a rhetorical device with which to introduce Prestbury). As one resident said of the frequent reference to Prestbury 'being the richest village in England': 'That's nice in its way, [but] that could attract the criminal fraternity. There are more millionaires per capita here than anywhere else.' The following extract – taken from our focus group with members of the Women's Institute – encapsulates the foregoing concerns especially well:

Jill: But I think the outsiders, they really do ... This wonderful place with motorways, they do use the motorways to get to us. Liverpool, Manchester, Macclesfield to a certain extent, Stockport. We're so handy.

Mary: I think that the reputation that there's a lot of money about, they think that the houses are good pickings. Such a lot of the houses are stood by themselves or up drives that they can get round. Particularly while they're away.

These anxieties of affluence are not, however, confined to burglary alone. Residents also believe they attract more than their fair share of 'pedlars'; people either hawking their wares from door to door around the village, or those 'who call on spec, always wanting to do the driveway, or do your guttering'. The presence of such traders is rarely framed in a manner that denotes positive 'initiative' or 'enterprise'. They are for the most part classified as suspicious intruders; at the very least 'forcing' unwanted goods and services on people in invasive and discomforting face-to-face encounters; at worst, potential burglars. As such, 'pedlars' are able to provoke a complex of emotions including not only suspicion, but also fear (especially among those who live alone; the calls, it seems, are often made after dark), engulfment and guilt:

Alice: Look at all the pedlars we have round the door. They come from Nottingham, Birmingham, Liverpool, and they come in by dormobile, and they saturate the place, don't they?
Max: On wet nights.
Alice: On wet nights when they look pathetic, and you feel really mean saying no.

(home watch coordinators)

In the midst of these various worries, residents remain divided over the extent to which the village has 'a crime problem'.[10] For some the criminal threats posed to their homes and property are clearly of concern and can impact in significant ways upon people's daily life and consciousness. One Prestbury parent spoke of expecting to have been burgled 'virtually every time' he returned home. Another described herself as 'very conscious' about burglary before proceeding to participate in the following exchange:

Laura: We lock our doors when we're gardening. We never used to.
Jill: I don't put the alarm on when I'm gardening, because the doors are locked. I don't leave downstairs windows open at the front when I'm not in the room.
EG: Do you think that Prestbury has a lot of burglar alarms compared to other areas?
Jill: Oh yes.
Kim: Absolutely.
EG: How would you compare then crime in Prestbury to crime in other places?
Kim: Oh, it's not so bad.
Liz: I think it's about the same.
Jill: I would think it's about the same.

(Women's Institute members)

This exchange ends with what is perhaps the prevailing feeling among Prestbury residents about the village's 'crime problem', a feeling that intersects often closely and explicitly with people's sense both of 'this' and 'other' places. For some here, it is important to keep the matter of crime in perspective and not let it overshadow the village's abundant positive attributes: 'Although we do have a lot of crime, I think one has to get it in proportion, that it is still a very pleasant part of the world.' Others – such as this home watch coordinator – are clearly keen to distance Prestbury from the kinds of places that readily and negatively surface in English popular and political discourse at mention of the word 'crime':

> The other part of the area that I know is Salford and that's a den of thieves if ever there was one. I suspect that we are probably more on a par with some-where like Henley, or Esher, where they're affluent. It's a different sort of crime.

But these sensibilities towards place can also operate in a reverse direction; to heighten and structure people's feelings about, and responses to, crime. For while many residents felt that crime levels in Prestbury were fairly moderate relative to other places, such offending as does occur can nonetheless jar with what they hope and expect to be the case in 'their village'. As one resident put it:

> I think it [the local crime problem] must be on a minor scale compared with other areas. It's just that it's more noticeable in Prestbury because you just don't think that things like that could happen in such a lovely place.

Worries about disorder: 'anarchy in the village'

Of all the residents we spoke to, young people were the least likely to share the prevailing view of Prestbury as 'a lovely place', or to feel that it 'belonged' to them. While teenagers readily concurred that Prestbury was 'one of the richest villages in Britain', they were also at pains to point out how little it has to offer them. As one 16-year-old boy put it: 'It is a traditional village where people like us have nothing to do. That's why it's shit.' They are also – as with this 16-year-old boy and 14-year-old girl – more likely than adult villagers to be made aware by their peers that Prestbury is considered 'snobby':

> They think we're all jumped up because we've all got money and stuff. I got asked today how much dinner money I got, and he said, 'I bet it's about 50,000 quid.'

At the time of our research, a group of male and female teenagers (roughly between the ages of 13 and 17) had taken to congregating routinely in centre of the village; either in the churchyard, or in the village high street by the off-licence and 'traditional' telephone box (dubbed 'the office' by the youths concerned). This had become the preferred site for hanging around since the old meeting place – the sports pavilion on the recreation ground – was burned down under suspicious circumstances a couple of years previously, and anything from five to twenty or so teenagers were to be found there of an evening. For the young people involved, such hanging around is both a response to having 'nothing else to do', and an assertion of their 'membership' of the village:

Josh:	What else are we supposed to do?
Vicky:	It's our village as well, not just theirs.
Josh:	When we ask them where they hang about and everything they say where, but when they ask us where we've got to hang about, what have we got?
Vicky:	We've got a youth club, yes, fair enough, but there's weekends. In the summer there's nothing to do.

(16- to 17-year-old teenagers)

Some among the adult residents we spoke to appeared largely untroubled by the presence of these youths, believing them either to occasion few problems, or else evincing some sympathy for the plight of the local young. Some felt these young people were neither 'hard nuts' nor 'violent', and did not find their 'exuberant showing off' especially frightening. Others pointed to the lack of youth facilities in Prestbury – 'it's got something for everybody, apart from maybe the teenagers', as one put it; or believed such young people – often on the basis of parental experience – were at what one resident called an 'awkward age'. Having recounted – during our focus group with home watch coordinators – her 'nightmare' trying to keep her daughter in the youth club and away from consuming alcohol with her friends in the village, Alice endeavours to understand rather than merely condemn:

> Yes, but they actually go through a period when they want something a little different. My daughter was in the choir for years, was head chorister, and she had swimming, horse riding, she had the vicar's horse for years that she looked after. We filled their lives, then they come to a point when, I suppose it's the old hormone business, and it's far more exciting to be out in the churchyard with a couple of your friends in the dark, when you should be in the youth club. It's far more exciting than anything mummy has written down as your hobby for tonight. I'm not making excuses, believe me.

The plea that ends this account indicates Alice's awareness that she is speaking, not only against the prevailing weight of 'law and order' discourse, but also counter to the dominant mood among Prestbury residents. This mood is one of anxious concern about the impact on the village and its quality of life of what Arthur Harris (a resident of over twenty-five years standing, with whom we conducted a life-history interview) called 'anarchy in the village among the village youth'. The *Parish Council Newsletter* of spring 1993 articulated these concerns in the following terms:

Crime

A pity to open on a sad note, but it has become increasingly evident that a section of our society does not share the values of the majority in relation to respect for the property of others. This has shown itself in two main areas –

apparently mindless vandalism and carefully targeted theft. In the former category one thinks of the arson and damage to the football pavilion at the Recreation Ground, the burning of the building at the rear of the Post Office and the general despoliation of the Churchyard and Village with litter and worse.

This 'litter and worse' is reckoned to be the responsibility of that 'small minority' of – it was generally felt – *local* teenagers who 'colonize' the centre of the village. As one resident put it, in an effort to distinguish the issue from that of travelling crime: 'If it's kicking in a door and making life hell for the chap who runs the bottle shop, or wrecking the telephone box, my impression is of the children of Prestbury.' These 'children' were a major talking point – and frequent subject of story-telling – in our interviews and focus groups. Among some, such talk focused on specific incidents of disorderly or criminal behaviour (sometimes observed, more often picked up third-hand) foremost among which were: vandalism to the church, telephone box and local shops; youths swearing at, harassing or obstructing passers-by; petty theft (in one instance, of the church collection); shoplifting, and the making of reverse-charge calls to friends from the phone box. Among others, the presence of young people was characterized as a problem in more diffuse terms; one spoke of the them as 'cheeky, but threat-ening'; another of having to 'push your way through them'; a third of 'a sense of oppression' and of 'feeling under pressure in certain areas of the village'.[11]

Worries about the presence of teenagers in the village are particularly power-fully felt by parents in Prestbury. Those whose children had grown up often expressed relief about not having to bring teenagers up in the village *now*; while, the father of two small children voiced worries about how he would compete with the 'lure of the village' in forthcoming years. Among current parents of teenage children two concerns predominate: preventing their offspring from falling in with what they saw as 'bad company' (not least in respect of drugs), and the possibility of their sons or daughters being 'picked on' by teenagers in the village. Having recounted how his two sons had had 'several youths jump on them and rough them up' at the church gate following choir practice, and explained how he does not now allow them into the village 'unless it is absolutely essential', one parent summed up these various 'troubles with kids' thus:

Terry: The concern to us as parents is that I don't like my son, who's 14 years of age, and is responsible, I don't like him walking through Prestbury, and there are occasions when he may have to walk through, because they are accosted by undesirables.

Geoff: Is this people coming from outside?

Terry: They grab hold of them and say 'Do you take drugs?'

RS: Are you talking about undesirable adults or . . ?

Terry: No, undesirable teenagers, who are sitting on the benches outside the church trying to cause trouble. Friday night especially, at quarter to ten, and elderly people are petrified to walk through the village because they're being taunted and being abused.

There is little doubt that these worries about youth and disorder are acutely felt by many of Prestbury's adult residents; that they can in part be accounted for by people's direct and indirect experience of threat; and that adult crime-talk represents an attempt to make sense of material practices (the youths *do* hang around, they *can* be 'cheeky') that appear to many as strange, unwelcome and without immediate precedent. It seems clear also that the worries expressed by parents of (teenage) children in Prestbury have as much if not more to do with their role and status as *parents*, as they have to do with their place of residence.

Yet the sheer intensity of these worries suggests that other things are felt to be at stake here, not the least of these being people's sense of the kind of place Prestbury ought to be, and the kinds of behaviour and social interaction that are expected to flow from this. This generates, first, a set of expectations about the tranquillity, orderliness and polite sociability that is supposed to attend village life and a set of cognate conventions as to the appropriate use of village spaces; conventions that don't extend to its unsupervised, noisy occupancy by groups of young people. But it also creates hopes about the kinds of children and young people who ought properly to inhabit such a place, something that the 'congregation' of teenagers who improperly hang around the churchyard fail to live up to. As Arthur Harris remarks: 'These are kids that are not involved with the church choir, they're not involved in the scouts, they're not involved in the cricket club, which they could be. They're not involved in any of these.' Here residents' sentiments towards teenage misbehaviour share much with their feelings about travelling crime. It is not, in relative terms, that Prestbury is seen as having an especially acute problem of teenage incivility. The issue, once again, is that it is bedevilled by such troubles at all. For the existence of such incivility not only runs counter to people's sense of what an 'English village' aesthetically and socially should be all about; it also undermines the cherished possibility that people have found – in the midst of an England in seeming moral decline – a safe and orderly place in which 'you know your children are going to mix with other decent children':

> It was a lovely looking place, [that's] why I wanted to come here as soon as I'd seen it; because I felt it looked like a village, and you could see that it was acting as a village, and that's the environment that I wanted my children to be brought up in.
>
> (home watch coordinator)

So what's gone wrong? Who or what is held by residents to account for the 'despoliation' of the village? Who has failed properly to regulate Prestbury's young? Two issues are paramount here. The first of these appears at first sight to be about parenting, but is perhaps best interpreted as a conflict between the (seemingly threatened) cultural norms of those established residents who invest time and effort in 'the village' and its 'character', and the values of those for whom Prestbury offers merely a (temporary) backdrop to their private lives (cf. Cloke *et al.* 1995; Taylor and Jamieson 1998: 166). Thus, it was often alleged (by the former) during our discussions that some among Prestbury's residents seem not to care about either their children's whereabouts, or the impact their behaviour might be having on the quality of village life. Such parents – we heard repeated time and again – are thought to provide their teenage children with 'money to go and do something in the evening so the parents can either have a party, or they can go out' (it was a common refrain among our respondents that Prestbury's young have too much money); let their offspring roam the village till all hours; or take the side of their 'innocent children' in the face of attempts by others to control their misdemeanours. The following account – a version of a tale we came across frequently – captures some of this well:

> A nice brand new Mercedes will drive through Prestbury at eight o'clock on a Saturday evening, or thereabouts, and drop a child, or two children off, and the parent leans out of the door and is actually seen passing a wad of notes, not a £10 note, but a wad of notes across to them. This goes on on a regular basis. It's not an isolated incident, there may be several sightings every Saturday night of this happening. Then they are seen to pick them up at half past twelve or one o'clock in the morning, whilst the parents go off doing whatever they are doing.
>
> (primary school parent)

A second set of causal attributions are levelled by residents at the youth club – something that we have already seen figure highly among adult concerns in Macclesfield. Having been closed for a period (in part due to allegations of ill-discipline) the senior youth club re-opened in September 1995 under a new part-time youth worker. The bulk of the teenagers who congregate around the church also attend the youth club (which opens on Wednesday and Sunday evenings), even if on club nights many are only intermittently present *inside* the club itself (the club and the church lie a short distance apart either side of the high street). Residents, the Church and the Parish Council are in the main (and certainly in principle) supportive of the youth club and wish it every success. It is, however, the subject of two main concerns. The first of these surrounded the fact that the youth worker was both a professional and an outsider. The worry about the former (this again echoes a refrain commonly expressed in Macclesfield) attaches to the suspicion that he is one of those 'well-meaning souls who don't really know what they're letting themselves in for … and do things that are really more identifying with the youth rather than being an adult looking after children'. The concern regarding the latter is that the youth worker lacks sufficient local knowledge – that he has 'very little interest in the village and doesn't know the children', as one put it. Suspicious rumours also attach to the incumbent's connections with the adjacent council estate:

We've got a housing estate on the outskirts of Prestbury where he used to have, at Upton Priory, where he used to have a youth club. That was closed down because of disruptive elements, and he's come down here and I feel sure that some of the children have come down here with him.

(Arthur Harris)

The other main concern centres around the operation of the youth club. This was most vocally expressed during a life-history interview we conducted with Arthur and Sybil Harris, both resident in Prestbury since 1971, and active and well-connected in the village. They both spoke with much nostalgic regret about the recent fate of the youth club. They evoked a time some years back when the club was run by two local professionals ('highly intelligent, both doing very interesting jobs, yet prepared to give their time') and had an organized programme that included 'drama', 'debates', 'holidays', 'climbing', 'potholing' and 'trips to the shows in Manchester'; and it was against this reference point that the youth club, and the incivilities in the village, were registered and assessed. The current club is, for the Harrises, but a shadow of its former self. The loud music, absence of 'organizational patterns and standards', lack of a 'proper membership scheme' and so forth amounted to an 'aimless exercise' that should proceed no further. Their proposed solution (which they had suggested to the local beat officer) was to start afresh with parental volunteers:

Now I think [the youth worker's] ever so nice and I haven't really got the measure of him. But I just think the Prestbury kids can run circles around him quite honestly, and I feel quite strongly that it should actually be closed down, the building cleaned up, swept up and cleaned up.

Our observations do little to bear out the Harrises interpretation of the youth club. The youth leader receives a great deal more respect from the teenagers than their account implies, it has more structure and organization than is suggested, and in certain respects, such as with the alleged 'lack of a membership scheme', they have got matters factually wrong. This, though, is hardly the point. The Harrises reflections on the youth club, and on teenage misconduct more generally, evoke an altogether different notion of 'discipline' than that in operation at the club; suggesting a strong desire for the village's youngsters to be engaged in activities that are more regulated than either the youth club, or the street. In this the Harrises yearnings are undoubtedly supported by many in the village; and the gulf between these sentiments and the views of the young people we spoke to is sufficiently cavernous to allow inter-generational tension, or at least misunderstanding, to be placed foremost among the village's social divisions. The aforementioned youth worker described the situation thus:

The young people are really fed up of being accused of doing this that and the other, and the old people are fed up seeing young people hanging around the shops, going in churchyards, leaving their condoms and their spliff-ends and everything else in the churchyard and the graffiti being put up everywhere. There's definitely barriers there and they need to be addressed.

The young people we spoke to were 'fed up', in particular, with the fact that adult residents appear to resent their presence in what the teenagers regard as being *their* village as well. As one 16-year-old girl put it: 'I think they expect us to just sit at home and watch telly and do our homework.' On some occasions this adult hostility is even alleged to have boiled over into outright aggression:

> I was on the fence and this man came out of [the off-licence], this really posh guy, and he got into his Jag, and he said, 'If I find any scratches on this car in the morning, I'm going to come down here, find you and break your kneecaps.' It was threatening, the way he said it.

In the main, however, Prestbury's young are merely required to live under the weight of adult expectation that their teenage fun will not in any way besmirch the village's good name; expectations that run counter to young people's rather different sense of the place in which they live: 'All the old people think it's really posh and everything. We should be all dead goody goody, [but] all the younger people are just the same as any other young people.'

Worries about drugs: the village has 'gone to pot'

Foremost among the reasons why Prestbury's adult citizens worry so intensely about congregations of local youths is drugs. The presence of unsupervised teenagers hanging around the village is widely seen as providing what one resident called a 'breeding ground' for drugs; both an obvious target for dealers, and ample opportunities for consumption. As such, drugs are viewed both as contributing to the problems outlined above, and as a troubling concern in their own right. As one retired businessman put it: 'The noise comes from the girls as well as the boys, I must say. But I think they're all a little bit high on something, we don't know what it is, but we've got our own private thoughts.'

The whole question of drugs was viewed with some trepidation by our adult respondents, with stories of drugs being rife among local teenagers seemingly circulating widely round the village – Arthur Harris reported being told that 'practically every child in the village has experimented at some time with cannabis'; a local shop assistant we spoke to described Prestbury as 'an upper-class Moss Side'. Such concerns prompted the Parish Council – following representations from villagers – to request that Macclesfield police address them on the scale of the problem and on what action might be taken. At the ensuing meeting (observed by us), a Macclesfield police officer informed councillors (having spoken to the local beat constable) that Prestbury didn't have a particularly pronounced problem with drugs. This – for the councillors – smacked somewhat of complacency, and in our subsequent focus group they reacted to the police visit thus:

Cllr Adams:	The police told us didn't they, that we haven't really got a drugs problem here.
Cllr Potts:	Of course that was their opinion, or his opinion.
Cllr Adams:	Yes, his opinion, yes.
IL:	Was that an opinion that you shared?
Cllr Garret:	Well it's all relative of course and one doesn't really know what the cities are like, I mean compared with maybe Stockport, I don't know or Manchester. Probably there isn't a drug problem in Prestbury that justifies substantial manpower being put onto that as opposed to the other activities the police get involved in.

Of these contrasting assessments it is that which sets out to distance (and thereby dismiss) the officer's opinion (as 'his', rather than the institution's, 'views') which intersects most closely with villagers' sentiments about the impact of drugs on the village. Many of these worries stem from people's felt lack of knowledge about the prevalence of drugs, their sources and effects, and their seeming incapacity to act in order to protect the village and/or their children.

It is in this climate of anxious uncertainty that drugs become the ready subject of rumour, gossip and story-telling in the village, as residents seek out and invest meaning in what they take to be the signs of drugs. Many such stories surround the supposedly numerous discoveries of the detritus of consumption. Thus it has become commonplace in the village to assert that: 'when the cricket pavilion was burned down a few years ago … the firemen discovered it was full of hypodermic syringes underneath' (the police officer attributed this – when asked by councillors about 'needles being found' – to 'just one incident'). We had recounted to us similar stories about the church caretaker 'sweeping up syringes on a daily basis, dozens and dozens of injection needles'. And even those who doubt the reliability of these 'finds', have their own tales to tell about – in this instance – cannabis litter:

Jill:	You know when the pavilion went down, they had the syringes and stuff in there.
Mary:	How do we get back to their parents?
Jane:	I did the litter on playing fields right through August, and I never saw any syringes, all I saw were tattered cigarettes, with all the tobacco pulled out of it, and all the cigarette papers, where they'd obviously rolled them up with something else to smoke, and matches galore. I couldn't believe it.

(Women's Institute members)

Residents are no less alert to the signs of drugs being bought and sold in the village. On one occasion, a Parish Council official reported to us having witnessed what she took to be drug-dealing on the village high street; she had seen 'teenagers going into the bank to get money' before, 'being passed a bag [ostensibly] containing a "doughnut" brought in Prestbury's [bakers]', an incident she reported to the police. These suspicions intersect with a story – which was circulating widely within the village at the time of the research – about a 'drugs-car' that it was said descends upon Prestbury 'twice a week' from Manchester (or, more particularly, Moss Side), in order to sell drugs to local teenagers.

The young people we spoke to derived much amusement from this tale, taking it as a sign of how gullible and ill-informed local adults are ('the only reason they say that story is because they haven't got a clue, they make something up'), and attributing its source to a 'one-sided' article that had appeared about them in the *Macclesfield Express Advertiser*. Yet few dispute that cannabis (at least) is to be found in the village, and that it *is* consumed by at least some of Prestbury's teenagers (in this respect, these adult tales can be regarded – in part – as attempts to make sense of the fact that such drugs must have come from *somewhere*). The youth worker, for instance, believes that 'the drug problem in Prestbury is far worse than on Upton Priory, far worse', and that 'cannabis is being dealt left, right and centre'. He then complicated matters by recounting the following incident:

Matt: The other night actually, I went outside for a chat with a group of young men and a car pulled up, quite an expensive car, and inside were three quite respectable looking men, I wouldn't say young men, I would say men, ages 27, 28. They went into the car park, wheel spun, came around, a man got out, he looked quite respectably dressed, just like you or me really. He came up to the group of young men that I was talking to and he spoke to one of the young men and he said 'Is anybody selling?'; so the young person looked at me in kind of shock horror. So I just said to this bloke who had come into the car park, I said, 'Excuse me, but I happen to be the youth worker here at Prestbury and nobody does any dealing here', so he says, 'Oh, I'm after some trainers.'

IL: Did you get the impression that the young people knew who this young person was?

Matt: Yes, yes, I think what's happening is, I don't like putting … . The older people in Prestbury, the 20- to 30-year-old people are actually buying drugs off the younger people.

The young people we spoke to also acknowledged the ready availability and use of cannabis in the village (one 14-year-old spoke of it – only half jokingly – as the 'best thing' about Prestbury). They also sought to defend its use, either by making claims about cognate adult drug-use ('There's plenty of adults in Prestbury that do that; they've got money as well'), or by comparing cannabis favourably with alcohol. In each case, Prestbury's young seek to 'condemn the condemners' (Sykes and Matza 1957) by pointing to what they see as the hypocrisy of local adults:

IL:	One of the things they say, the older people that live here, is that they think that you're all smoking drugs …
Chris:	It's true, but not all of us. I don't.
Tony:	It's the older ones, isn't it?
James:	They think it's bad. I think they're hypocrites really, because alcohol is worse.
IL:	Do you think it's harmless and people should not worry about it?
All:	Yes.
Tony:	How many more people have died of alcohol than they have of weed? […]
Chris:	If you think about it, drinking makes you hyper, but if you're stoned all you want to do is sit down and chill out and talk.
Andy:	There's more crimes with drink than there is with …
IL:	Why do you think adults worry about it so much then?
Andy:	It's the older ones, they can't remember when they were young.
Sarah:	Because it's illegal.
Tara:	My dad, he's never taken drugs or anything like that.
IL:	Do you think they just don't know enough about it?
James:	Yes. They're worried that we're going to go on to heavier drugs.
Chris:	That's not true though.
Tony:	They're worried about themselves. If Prestbury gets a bad name so do they, and that's all they're worried about.

(14- to 15-year-old teenagers)

This knowing, confident assurance contrasts starkly with the outlook of Prestbury's adults. For them the youths hanging around in the village represent a tangible and vulnerable target (now deemed in need of protection) from dealers who descend on Prestbury from elsewhere, knowing that the local young have money to spend. (For one resident – who described the teenagers as 'a soft target for drug traders to come in from Wythenshawe' – this constituted reason enough for clearing the streets and 'keeping kids in'.) In these respects drugs come to be viewed in a similar frame to that other travelling crime, burglary (albeit that this one is more troubling and difficult to insure against); a sign that some of the most unsettling aspects of the world beyond are coming to Prestbury:

I didn't say it was any worse than anywhere else. What I'm trying to say is that it's become more and more obvious that this is happening in this little postcard village where everything is in equilibrium, has never been disturbed, and all of a sudden the outside world is creeping in. A lot of the boys that are presumably doing this drug peddling don't even live in Prestbury. They come in from Knutsford areas, and Moss Side in Manchester, because they know that the children round here will have a lot of money in their back pockets. They can afford to buy the drugs.

(primary school parent)

Prestbury residents for the most part view the problems of travelling crime, teenage incivilities and drugs as relatively speaking 'small scale' (indeed they remain proud that this is so, and would recoil from the suggestion that it is otherwise). Local manifestations of these problems stand out, however, 'because' – as Arthur Harris put it – 'the rest of the pattern of village life is so agreeable'; or, in other words, because a place imagined as a protective cocoon from the troubles that afflict English society elsewhere has been violated. Pivotal to the cultural value of this 'English village' is that it is seen to offer a shelter of tranquillity, order and stability which contrasts starkly with the violence, disorder and insecurity of the city (and the wider 'risk profiles' of late modernity). No matter that Prestbury is thoroughly permeated by larger 'social systems and organizations' (Giddens 1991: 184); nor that many of its inhabitants are powerful players in the globalizing, risk-generating corporate world of late modernity. To buy into Prestbury is to purchase a pleasurable, exclusive retreat, a place of rest and recreation, a 'safe haven' for oneself, one's family and one's children, an environment bracketed off from the troubles of the outside world. This is something that many of its residents have taken on hefty – often anxiety-inducing, success-dependent – financial commitments in order to enjoy. Hence the intensely felt feelings of disquiet, disappointment and anger that attach to locally occurring instances of crime and disorder; a reaction not only to the objective harm that these problems cause, but also to the apparent withering of the order and security in which people have invested so much economic and emotional capital:

Terry: When they [our teenage children] do get free time we try and keep them away from Prestbury, and that shouldn't be, that should not be.
Pam: No, the whole point of being in the village …
Terry: We're paying a healthy premium to live in Prestbury to start with. We're paying £50,000 or £60,000 more to live in a house in this area than we would if we lived in another area, so why should we be penalized?
                                                                (primary school parents)

The incomplete village: or, where's 'our bobby' gone?

Discussing the question of young people hanging around the village, one Prestbury resident made the following observation:

> I think the thing that's changed is all the problems that we're experiencing at the weekends from teenagers in the village. The lack of presence of policing. Rob Johnson, the village policeman was taken away from Prestbury, and since they moved the village policeman it seems to have gone totally to pot. There's not even patrols, he's not the village policeman.
>   (primary school parent)

Much of the talk about policing found among adult citizens of Prestbury concerned the fate – or what they saw as the disappearance – of the 'village bobby'. A serving police officer for some twenty-eight years, Rob Johnson had (as of 1995) spent sixteen years as Prestbury's beat officer. For much of that period he resided in the village, working his beat from the police house/station located in front of the primary school. He became, it seems, a well-known and much respected figure; Mary Baker described him as 'kindness itself', someone who has 'done untold good for people living here'. However, in the early 1990s, the police house in Prestbury was closed and Johnson relocated to Macclesfield, from where he has since patrolled his now more extensive beat by car. For the residents, it is as if part of the village architecture has been removed, an essential part of village life gone, a valued institution taken away:

Laura: The other thing that's happened, is of course we haven't a police station here, we used to have.
Kim: We don't have a local bobby anymore.
Liz: They have to come from Macclesfield, so the very quickest they could come is maybe quarter of an hour before they get here.
Jill: They are pretty good though.
Kim: They are very good.
Gay: They are good, but you don't have the same confidence.

(Women's Institute members)

Many of our respondents' felt dissatisfactions with the police are connected with what Arthur Harris called 'this retrograde step' (the closure of the police house was a recurrent feature of our focus group discussions). Two attendant kinds of disquiet are noteworthy here. The first concerns people's sense that a figure once so centrally identified with the village (indeed, as 'belonging' to it) has now become remote from its quotidian life. Part of this is to do with 'our bobby' being placed elsewhere (and by extension shared with others); but it is also, more diffusely, a worry about him being subsumed into larger bureaucratic entities to which people feel little attachment, and which seem at some remove from *local* troubles and difficulties. As one retired businessman put it: 'The very fact that bobbies lived here, I think that meant that they were around. [Now we have] the general concentration, first of all initially in Macclesfield, Congleton, and now it seems in Chester.' More prosaically, people's disquiet about remoteness takes the form of an oft-repeated bemoaning of the apparent absence of Rob Johnson (and the police more generally) from the village. As Joan and Arthur Harris put it:

Joan: We've still got him, but he's thinly stretched isn't he, Rob?
Arthur: Yes, but he doesn't live in the village, and you don't, although he says he's never away, you go down at any time in the evening and you never see him.

A second set of concerns surround what many adult residents see as the inability or unwillingness of the police to tackle the 'problem of youth'.[12] Among some, the behaviour of local teenagers is seen at a direct result of the police's 'abandonment' of the village; the *absence* of an authority figure who 'knows the children' and who 'might pop out at any time' both facilitating the *presence* of young people in the village, and enabling them – as one respondent put it – 'to get away with murder'. Others see the police as failing to take sufficiently seriously the problems young people cause in the village (recall the police's dismissal of Prestbury's 'drug problem'). One Church official thought the police had 'wiped their hands of the whole issue', while the shopkeeper who saw himself facing the brunt of youthful incivilities accused them of being 'extremely complacent' and of being unwilling to act for fear of 'upsetting the "big-wigs" in the village'. He is also evidently a source of local rumour about police inactivity:

> I am told, this is second hand this, the chap in the [aforementioned] shop told me that he had called the police on occasions, and the police, their attitude to them is they live in the village, these youngsters, it's their village, and there's nothing they can do about it, so bad luck.
>
> (home watch coordinator)

The young people concerned do not generally share the views of adult residents about the absence of the police from Prestbury; as routine users of the village's spaces the young are the most likely of its residents to experience contact with the police (cf. Loader 1996). However, despite some grumbles about being 'picked on' or 'moved on' merely 'because we're young', Prestbury teenagers' gripes about their treatment in the village did not revolve centrally around the police. This is partly due to what they viewed as the police's fair-mindedness towards the question of drugs. As one 15-year-old boy explained: 'They don't really do anything unless it's a large dose. Unless it's like dealing or anything like that, they don't do anything.' But it also stems – contrary to local adult opinion – from the fact that the young people both knew and to some degree respected Prestbury's beat officer. Hence the following reaction from our focus group with 14- and 15-year-olds: 'I seriously reckon that Johnson is alright', 'The Prestbury dibble is alright', and 'Rob Johnson is a fair policeman; the rest of them don't know what they're on about.' Prestbury's young people did not, however, believe the village to be under-policed:

IL: One thing the adults say if you talk to them about these issues is that Prestbury needs more police officers to patrol the place.
James: No, they don't, do they? It's not that bad. I don't think it is *[all shouting]*.
IL: One at a time.
James: They've got to concentrate on bigger places like Macc.
IL: Do you agree?
Sarah: Yes. No dibbles here please. We'd all be down the cop shop.
Chris: Why don't they go to a big place?

(14- to 15-year-old teenagers)

A yearning for 'the return' of the 'village bobby' – that compelling figure who combines what one resident called 'legal authority with community spirit' – is without doubt the central demand Prestbury's adult residents have to make of the police. The fact that they are demanding (as they see it), not the reinvention of some (fictional) character from a bygone age, but the return of a figure still fresh in local memory, makes their sense of grievance even more powerfully felt. Thus:

Kim: We just want a resident policeman.
Liz: There are two big points, less traffic and more police.

(Women's Institute member)

I think we have a genuine case for the reinstatement of the village bobby, as quickly as possible.

(primary school parent)

If there's anything I would vote for at the present time more than anything else, it's for the, it's for him to come back again and live in the community.

(Arthur Harris)

What one is seeing amply demonstrated here is the evident attraction people feel to the service and guardianship roles traditionally attributed to English policing (a point we develop in the next chapter). In the case of Prestbury, such attraction is given added weight by the strong association that is generally made between those two powerful icons of English culture – 'the village' and 'the bobby on the beat'. Given this, it is perhaps easy to see how Prestbury's citizens come to view (at least some of) the threats facing *their* 'village' as having to do with 'the removal' of *their* 'bobby'. For not only has an important cultural bond been broken, but its breaking has – so it appears – served to undermine the 'live-ability' of that small piece of the English landscape which they cherish. As Arthur Harris says of his desire to see the 'village bobby' reinstalled:

It's not to prevent burglars, who I suppose can cope quite easily with a policeman who lived in the village. It's really to give you the sense that things are rather more under control than they are at the present time.

6 Policing and demands for order

The concerns expressed in the previous chapter about the fate of the 'village bobby' are by no means unique to Prestbury (albeit that they take a particular form in *that* place). Residents of Macclesfield too often speak of the police as if referring to an old – though perhaps no longer quite so reliable – friend. In the main, our (adult) discussants evinced high levels of attachment to the police as the principal source of local social order and possessed often great expectations as to the kind and level of service that they ought properly to receive. Yet their talk is also emotionally charged with dismay, frustration and disenchantment at the service that is actually delivered, and – among many – with sentiments of loss regarding what in the post-war period has happened to 'our police'. The upshot is that demands for order are frequently couched in terms of desiring a 'return to' (as one established Weston resident put it) the 'old type' of police officer, the person who:

> Wandered around the estate, and the kids knew him, and people knew him, he walked past and he said 'hiyah' and good morning to people that were gardening, or a good afternoon, evening, whatever it were. He was the local bobby.

This chapter is concerned with these sensibilities towards policing; with how different constituencies in Macclesfield think, feel and talk about the police. How do the police figure in the crime- and place-talk of the town's residents? What do people expect of the local police and how do they rate the service they receive? How do their accounts of policing connect with their outlook on various forms of social and cultural change (as this impinges both locally and in more global ways)? In addressing these questions, we proceed as follows. First, we consider the kinds of demands adult residents make of the police and assess their anxieties regarding what they perceive as the police's increasing remoteness from local social relations. We then examine the competing ways in which young people, police officers and adult residents experience and make sense of the police role in regulating young people's occupancy of various public spaces across the town. Finally, we bring into sharper relief both some prevailing (middle-class) sensibilities towards crime, and (their) feelings of 'ownership' towards the police, by considering the response of people who in the main think of themselves as the recipients of police services to one of the few occasions when policing is directed at them – as motorists.

Remote policing: narratives of attachment and loss

Without doubt the pivotal expectation that Macclesfield's adult population has of the police is for them to provide a (more) visible presence on the street. Time and again in our discussions, high levels of general support for the police (manifest in depictions of them as 'marvellous', or 'helpful and sympathetic', or 'first-class') translated into demands for an identifiable police officer to patrol (more or less permanently) the local streets. This was echoed in Cheshire County Council's (1996c) 'Quality of Life' survey which found that 'putting more police on the beat' was the most common solution to the crime problem proffered by Macclesfield Borough residents; 48 per cent accorded it top priority, 71 per cent made it one of their 'top three'.

This powerful attachment to the idea of the 'local bobby' was apparent across Macclesfield (cutting across lines of both class and gender), and *his* absence (and people generally refer to such a figure as 'he')[1] constituted – here as in Prestbury – the principal source of disquiet and complaint. The following discussion among residents of Hurdsfield estate illustrates this well:

Don: I think we've got less [crime and anti-social behaviour] here than they have on the Moss and Victoria Park, and Upton Priory.
IL: Why do you think that is?
Joy: Good parenting *[all laugh]*.
            [...]
Don: I'll tell you what it isn't, it's not policing up here, because we never see any.
Joy: No we haven't, have we? I've been looking out for him.
Don: They've been saying we have for two years, and we never see him. They say, 'Oh, well, he comes when you're not around'. Well I think 'Well hang on a minute, I'm in and out all hours of the day and night and I've never seen him', and I don't think anybody else has.

Our discussants evinced two main kinds of response to this perceived absence of what Cheshire Police's promotional literature calls a 'benevolent blue presence'. The first largely exempts the police from criticism, preferring instead to direct the blame elsewhere. Here the police are characterized as being deprived by government of the resources needed to maintain an adequate patrol presence, 'let down' by the apparent leniency of the courts, or otherwise burdened by bureaucratic constraints imposed on them from the outside. As a retired businessman from Prestbury put it:

In all fairness to the police, I think our Home Office has burdened them with far too much paperwork. It seems a terrible shame that a young and active man, who wants to be a policeman, has to spend all his time filling in damn forms.

The resulting climate of constraint is seen not only to limit the number of officers available on the street, but also as inhibiting the police from carrying out their proper task:

Dave: I would guess that the reason most bobbies don't lift somebody now is because if they do they spend their next three hours in the station doing paperwork.

Jim: That's right.

Jean: And then they take them to court and nothing much happens.

Paul: It's then that the prisoner, as he's called, claims that the bobby has hit him, or touched him in any way untoward, and he's then got to spend the next three hours writing out statements. Now I'm not saying that that doesn't go on, I mean there's the Police Complaints Authority, but it's getting to the point where, to be honest, the bobby is actually scared of doing his job.

(Upton Priory residents)

A second strand of thought and feeling is rather less charitable towards the police, believing them to have become a distant bureaucracy, unresponsive to demands that are both sensible and popular. The discrete complaints paraded under this banner concerned such matters as slow response times, a lack of information about reported incidents, and the disproportionate amount of time the police seemingly devote to the regulation of motorists. Mobilizing the vocabulary of consumerism to express his concerns, one Zeneca manager living in Broken Cross encapsulated this mood of disquiet thus:

The police are reacting. They wait for us to ring 999 and ask for the police, and then they go out, reacting. They need to be proactive in terms of looking to prevent the problem before it happens. The only way they'll do that is to combine with Joe Public who comes in in droves and talks to the police. In the same way as people running a business, you listen to your customers. I think the police need to listen to customers to find out what Joe Public wants.

Underpinning these various frustrations and complaints are two connected concerns. First, that the police are (especially in the face of chronic if low-level noise, nuisance and disorder) becoming increasingly and improperly remote from everyday life. For some, these developments are encapsulated symbolically in a new telecommunications system (introduced in 1994), which means that people can only contact Macclesfield police station by first ringing police headquarters at Chester – what one retired Prestbury resident described as 'being lumped all together as Cheshire'. They take on a more concrete form when people realize just how many other people they share 'their' bobby with, as when this officer explains to horrified Weston residents the precise extent of his beat:

PC Harris: If you imagine coming from Bond Street at the traffic lights. I do Bond Street to Park Lane, up Park Lane, the traffic lights at the Flower Pot [public house], turn left, down as far as Pennington's Lane. Theoretically then the line straight up to Gawsworth Road, along Gawsworth Road to Broken Cross roundabout, down Chester Road, keep going across Chester Road to the bottom end, until we get to roughly a line level with Bond Street again there, and that's my patch.

Sue: On your own?

PC Harris: On my own.

Sue: It's disgusting.

It is clear, second, that people feel the police are answering to priorities that are either obscure to the public or actively disputed by them; and that their idea of what policing ought properly to be about *jars* with many of the police's current preoccupations. This was particularly in evidence at various public meetings we attended during our research, where these anxieties surfaced in often fractious disputes between police representatives and members of the public. In general terms, these disputes revolved around the level and type of patrolling, during which senior officers would often endeavour to 'educate' residents as to the competing demands on police resources and the limits of beat patrols (one police manager was, for instance, at pains to insist that what he called 'modern officers' were quite reasonably unwilling to be either permanently on call, or tied for long periods of their career to one neighbourhood). More specifically, arguments focused upon whether calls concerning noise, nuisance and other troubling (albeit not necessarily criminal) incivilities were (or ought to be) treated by the police as an 'emergency'. Residents from Upton Priory reflected on one such meeting thus:

Jean: All you get told when you ask about the beat bobby: 'Well do you want us to get less burglaries, less car crimes, or do you want them to always be on your estate and have problems with you.' It's sort of prioritize and all this, we just get nowhere. You saw what happened at that meeting.

Dave: There's cutbacks.

Jean: I know they need more money, they need more police, but surely somewhere they can do something about it. ... I don't think they realize how worried people are by what's going on. I don't think they realize how it affects people's lives.

In bemoaning the absence of visible policing, our discussants (mainly, though by no means exclusively, the older ones) would often make wistful reference to a 'better' policing past; a time (located – if at all – in the immediate post-war period) in which officers were to be found – as one Moss Rose resident put it – 'walking around, flashing the torch in gardens'.[2] In making sense of this yearning for order, questions of historical accuracy are not of the utmost importance (Loader 1997a). For while these 'social memories' (Fentress and Wickham 1992) ostensibly make reference to 'how things used to be' (and thus raise claims that can in principle be investigated and found more or less wanting), they are mobilized and put to rhetorical use in the present and need to be judged in that light.

As such, two aspects of these narratives of loss are instructive. First, people seek by means of such stories to communicate the disappearance of an identifiable authority figure, known by, and belonging to, the community. In our discussions people would frequently refer to the police in terms that denote *ownership*, and a resort to the past is in part a means of registering such ownership and mourning its subsequent demise. As one resident of the Upton Priory estate put it: 'They used to live in the community that they policed. That don't happen now. They're divorced from the community they're policing. They're just a figure in a uniform.' Among some – such as these middle-class women living in Broken Cross – the loss of control over the police is couched in terms of a more widespread process of change in the social and moral order of the town:

IL: Has that process of incomers coming to the town had an effect in terms of crime?

Bron: Oh yes.

IL: In what respect?

Bron: I think it does, because you don't know everybody. At one time you tended to know everybody. People went into town a lot more. Lots of people lived in the centre of town, so if you didn't know them you knew somebody's cousin, and you tended to know this. As a result people couldn't get away with it. And of course, if you went home you tended to get what for. If they [the police] brought you home you were for it. Nowadays this doesn't happen.

Mary: I suppose we can say the police and their standing in the community
          ...

Bron: And it was a local police force, which made a difference.

Mary: Of course it did.

Bron: We had our own Chief Constable.

IL: For Macclesfield?

Bron: Yes.

Mary: But I think the way that policing is now being done on this softly, softly approach, whereby they aren't allowed to do what you and I would have expected, a clip round the ear from a police sergeant. ... Well those days unfortunately have now gone, haven't they?

This brings us to a second theme. What matters for many about this remem-bered *integration* of the police into the quotidian life of neighbourhoods was that it meant an authoritative presence was keeping a watchful eye over the local 'community'. Here the subsequent 'withdrawal' of the police is understood as a coming apart of the 'glue' that once held a neighbourhood together and guaran-teed its now fondly remembered quality of life. As such, the figure of the police officer functions, not merely as a vehicle though which people are able to recall and speak about a more cohesive, orderly past; but also as a powerful 'condensing' symbol (Turner 1974) of what is so troubling about the present. A 'community' no longer watched over by the 'local bobby' is not, for many, a fit place to grow up in:

> My heart and soul was in the Moss estate. I loved my childhood growing up on the Moss. And when I came back I weren't unhappy about it because I really felt as if I was were going home. … But now I wouldn't like to think that my grandchildren, great-grandchildren, put it that way, would grow up on the Moss estate at the moment. We are desperately in need of, Renee put her finger on it, really they want a policeman on the beat, don't they?

The crime-talk of Macclesfield residents bespeaks then a powerful attachment, not so much to crime-fighting and its attendant performance indicators, but to the service and guardianship roles traditionally attributed to the English police – in the current jargon of criminal justice to 'problem-oriented' policing (Goldstein 1990). Their desire is for a reliable and visible patrolling presence on their streets, provided by a known figure who is integrated into the social life of local communities, and thus able to exercise pastoral care over it. Nowhere is the perceived loss of this figure more keenly felt – or currently disputed – than in respect of the regulation of the young.

Policing the young: competing local constructions

We saw in Chapter 4 that the activities of the young stand high among the crime-related anxieties of Macclesfield's adult populace, and that disputes between generations regarding the appropriate use of various public spaces across the town constitute a significant cleavage in local social relations. In the midst of these tensions the police are a key player. Teenage incivilities account for a sizeable minority of the demands made on the police by the town's adult residents (see Table 6.1). Of the 3,121 calls made to Macclesfield police station in April and May 1995 from the town's six beats, some 14 per cent concerned youths acting suspiciously or creating a nuisance; this ranging from 7 per cent of calls from beat covering the town centre west/'old town', to one in five of those emanating from Moss Rose/High Street (cf. Waddington 1993). But what do people expect of the police in response to such calls? How does this issue figure in residents' talk? And how do police officers and young people themselves experience and make sense of the policing of the young in public places? Let us consider each player in turn.

The young people[3]

It is evident from young people's narratives of policing that they are, generally speaking, the section of the Macclesfield populace to whom the police appear least invisible or remote. The prevailing disposition (especially among those – of both sexes, and from different areas of the town – who make regular use of local public places) was that the police tend towards omnipresence, and that – if anything – they see rather too much of them. As one 19-year-old male from Hurdsfield succinctly put it: 'We stand at the shops and we get a riot van that comes and parks on the fucking car park and watches us for hours on end.'

Some among our teenage respondents believed this attention to be directed towards them as individuals, the result of their being identified as 'trouble-makers'. A number of the probation and youth workers we spoke to felt that Macclesfield's size and relatively modest crime problem resulted in young people being processed through the system for offences that would be 'just irrelevant in a big city', and that criminal reputations were easily acquired. One youth worker put the point thus: 'The level of offending in this town is minute compared to say like Stockport or Manchester. ... If you do anything of any serious note in this town you stick out like a sore thumb'.[4] This certainly resonates with the experience of one member of our focus group with young men on probation:

> They give you a name. Say something happens, a type of crime has happened, sometimes the police will just come to you straightaway, pull you in for nothing, wasting your time, labelling you. I don't know, I can't explain it, but you know what I mean anyway.

Table 6.1   Recorded offences and demands for policing (1995)

Beat	Areas covered	Recorded offences 1995	Calls to the police April–May 1995	Calls concerning 'nuisance /suspicious youths'* (April–May 1995)
1	Upton Priory/ Kennedy Ave	700	492	64 (13% of total calls)
2	Tytherington/ Hurdsfield	605	542	72 (13%)
3	Moss Rose/ High Street	819	868	176 (20%)
4	Weston	789	513	69 (13%)
5	Town centre (east)/Victoria Park	468	373	35 (9%)
6	Town centre (west)/ 'old town'	769	333	24 (7%)
	Total	4,150	3,121	440 (14%)

Note:
* Authors' category. Includes calls reporting youths causing annoyance or behaving suspiciously.

The dominant theme of young people's talk about policing, however, concerned the police's routine involvement in regulating their use of – and behaviour in – local streets, parks and other meeting places. Two connected reasons for this attention were pinpointed. It is viewed, first, as resulting from the fact that young people *collectively* travel through and congregate in local public spaces. As one 14-year-old boy from the High Street area put it: 'If you walk around with your mates and the police see you, you get stopped. ... Because they see a big group, they have to stop us'. It is recognized, second, that the police are often having to respond to the demands of local residents (cf. Loader 1996: ch. 4). Here young people's reactions ranged from sympathy with the residents' plight (and admissions that they often were noisy); to angry condemnation ('narrow-minded evil little people', as one Hurdsfield youth termed those who resort to the police); to some obvious complicity in the events leading up to the police being called:

IL: Do the residents ever call the police?
Debbie: Yes, all the time.
Tina: When we were walking up through the Moss, this woman opened the
            door, we were like making a bit of noise. She just said eff off and she
            was going to call the police. So we started laughing again, and she
            went mad at us. Everyone was shouting, 'Oh yes, go on, call the
            police, dead scared.'
IL: And what did the police do? Did they come?
Tina: They come round and said would we move on, that was it.
                                        (14- to 15-year-olds, Moss Rose/High Street)

Despite this experience, there is little evidence from our discussions and observations to suggest that Macclesfield's young are in any blanket sense anti-police. While our teenage discussants often voiced irritation and bewilderment at what they see as a disproportionate amount of police attention, many were also keen to draw distinctions between 'good' and 'bad' officers, or else identify instances of 'good' policing (cf. Loader 1996: ch. 6). Some of the sixth formers we spoke to, for instance, wanted *more* police attention directed at the 'scallies' who routinely bothered them; while a 15-year-old girl from Moss Rose posited a vision of pastoral policing not so far removed from that longed for by many older residents of the town: 'If I was a policewoman I would go round, but I'd be checking that everyone is alright. I wouldn't be arresting them.'

Young people did, however, see the police attention directed at them as both – sometimes bafflingly – futile ('The police are going round telling all these kids to move on and you're just going round in circles', as one 14-year-old girl put it), and counter-productive in terms of police–youth relations: 'If the police came less there's got to be more respect, but they're round all the time so you just treat them like teachers sort of thing' (15-year-old boy, Broken Cross). Above all, they seemed somewhat resigned to a mode of regulation that, while mostly entailing no more than being routinely dispersed by the police, runs the ever-present risk of somebody pushing their luck once too often and things getting serious:

> It's not our fucking fault we've got nowhere to go, is it? They move us on, right. They move us on from the shops and we'll go to the park right, and they'll come down the park: 'Come on you're making too much noise.' We'll go [elsewhere] and they'll say, 'Come on, move on'; and in the end someone gets pissed off and says something and you get nicked.
>
> (19-year-old male, Hurdsfield)

The police

Macclesfield police, for the most part, have no particular relish for this task; what one officer described as 'the game' of moving young people from 'point A' to 'point B' to 'point C'. While they recognize the tensions caused (on both council-built estates and in more affluent parts of the town) by teenagers hanging around, and realize that 'youths causing annoyance' have in the main to be moved on, the dominant feeling among officers is that such work is a largely futile activity; 'a waste of our resources' from which 'you're never going to get job satisfaction'. One officer termed it, 'the biggest bug we have to bear'. Others felt that the police were being called upon to solve problems that were more appropriately dealt with elsewhere – by parents, by local 'mini-markets' (who – one officer suggested – employ 'young girls who can't deal with these kids' and rely on the police to deal with the consequences), or by the now defunct park-keeper: 'Park wardens used to deal with them [kids] didn't they? You don't need much expertise to chase kids off parks.'

A number of strands to police thought and feeling on this issue can be identified. It was noted, first, that residents often feel threatened merely by the presence of young people hanging around (irrespective of what they are doing), and thus (rather too readily some felt) turn to the police as the one agency capable of making an authoritative intervention. As one officer put it: 'Congregating in large numbers tends to intimidate people and they get the wrong idea; so straight away they're on the phone to the police.' The following account encapsulates this outlook nicely:

PC Smith: We are the answer to everyone's problems as far as they are concerned. Something's happening, call the police. Whether it's our responsibility or not, it doesn't matter, phone the police.

IL: For what reasons do they telephone, because it's the easy solution or … ?

PC Smith: They won't confront them [groups of youths], will they? They don't come out and confront them because they fear they're going to be victimized. They know where they live, they're standing on the corner of the street. They're not going to come out, they're going to call the police.

A second line of thought couples this sentiment with a degree of tolerance towards young people's situation, and an attendant unhappiness about the police being employed as the instrument of local adult opinion. As one officer put it: 'We're just pushing the problem away. We sympathize with them, they haven't got anywhere to go. There's bugger all for them to do. But they can't stay there.' Here many officers were keen to draw a distinction between what they saw as the majority of 'good kids' and a small minority who 'cause mayhem', and they numbered many of those they are called upon to deal with on the streets among the former. One senior officer we interviewed was especially keen to correct what he saw as common adult misperceptions of Macclesfield's young:

> You've been at meetings that I've been to. I never miss the opportunity to say, 'Look, when you're talking about youth today, then they have more pressures on them than we ever had, and 90 per cent of them are absolutely great kids.' … The older generation thinks that every kid who walks the street, because he might have long hair and a pair of jeans, is a trouble-maker, and it's so far from the truth.

A third strand of police opinion centres upon what is construed as public ignorance of policing. In part this has to do with people seemingly not realizing how limited police powers are in respect of noisy or otherwise troublesome youths who are not necessarily committing a criminal offence. But it also connects with a broader sentiment regarding what officers believe are unrealistic popular expectations of what the police can feasibly contribute to local social order. For some, these expectations are simply contradictory: 'People say how nice it is to see you walking around', one officer remarked, 'but then they ring 999 and want you there in a second.' Others framed the problem in terms of people wanting 'the police to be their policeman':

IL: Is there any way this [the question of teenage incivilities] can be resolved?

PC Smith: I think each household would like its own personal policeman.

WPC Lock: Yes, to stand on their front doorstep and keep people away.

Thus it is that the police conceive of their task in respect of regulating the young not merely in terms of satisfying public demands for order. It is also seen as a matter of tempering certain expectations (not least – as one police manager put it – with regard to people wanting 'our policeman back in houses so that we can knock on his door at any time of day or night'); and of seeking to shape local opinion that is often considered both wide of the mark and not easily satiated. One senior officer put the matter thus: 'You could increase the establishment by 100 police officers in Macclesfield, but that still wouldn't be enough, because people's perception of what a police officer can do and the time he's go to do it is totally invalid. They just do not have a clue.' This he saw as creating some difficult issues, both in terms of allocating resources,[5] and when it comes to striking a

balance between the provision of accurate information and the perceived need
to reassure Macclesfield's residents:

> People's perception of that man stood on a street corner, that he's doing
> such a wonderful thing, is totally flawed. But it's the feel-good factor. To get
> a man out of his panda car when there's nothing doing on a quiet afternoon
> and get him to walk round the block will do tremendous things for that. Sod
> all for reducing crime, but, and it's something I've said many, many times,
> quality of life is important. And there's a balance to how much truth I
> should tell people, because I could have terrified them. You could stop and
> ask somebody, 'How many policemen do you think there are in
> Macclesfield?' and they'd say, '100'. '100!' In reality there was half a dozen.

The (adult) residents

Some among our adult respondents shared the police's weary sense of futility
towards their role in regulating the young ('Where will they go?', one Weston
resident asked, 'They'll only move them on to somebody else'); or else concurred
that the police are being called upon unduly to solve problems that are really the
responsibility of 'the community'. As one resident of Upton Priory put it: 'If
people said, "What can I do to prevent it? How can I help?", then you wouldn't
need as many police. The police could manage on the resources they've got if
people just got more involved.' Others – such as this young male professional
living around Kennedy Avenue – spoke in related terms of residents making
unreasonable requests of the local police: 'They're not going to start patrolling
the streets because somebody of 16 looks like they might have had one cider too
many. There's far more important things to deal with in Macclesfield than things
like that.'

   These, however, represented minority outlooks among our respondents. The
prevalent view voiced during our discussions is that the police have become
increasingly unwilling or unable to take proper action to deal with teenage incivilities. In the face of what is perceived as a decline in the capacity of 'the
community' to regulate the behaviour of the young (and people's evident reluctance to intervene themselves), the demand for order – and concerns about
police remoteness – finds its most vehement expression in respect of young
people hanging around. We repeatedly encountered tales concerning incidents
where the police had either failed to respond promptly to calls about teenage
incivilities, or else had taken what were viewed as insufficient measures upon
their eventual arrival. Among some, this apparent inaction aroused the suspicion
that the police no longer take seriously people's worries about teenage disorder.
As one established resident of the High Street area put it:

> I think the police have sat in their panda cars and divorced themselves from
> this type of problem. Okay, so it's not petty in our lives and your lives, but it
> is petty crime, and I think they've been focused on the sort of more typical

crime, burglaries, other things like this, because, presumably, they can't do anything to the kids, they can't run them in and stick them in the cells, then they find their hands are tied, they're powerless. ... I don't think the police look at it as serious, it must be a minimal crime to them, it must be nothing at all, but it really is worrying.

These concerns take various forms. In general terms, the problem is seen as arising from the progressive withering of respect for (police) authority among the young (noted in Chapter 4). Here – once again – a comparison is often drawn between a somehow more civil, disciplined past in which the young were kept in check by a police officer who was both present and feared, and a present in which the *presence* of the youths stands in stark and telling contrast to the *absence* of the police. On occasions, this takes the form of personal recollections about being 'frog-marched' home by the 'local bobby'; on others, more culturally familiar tropes are used to bemoan developments in police practice and disposition:

IL: Would it make any difference if there were any more police officers on the estate?
Jim: Yes it would.
Dave: Not if they were riding around in a car. If they were walking, then the kids will get to know them, and they will get to respect them. I used to respect a copper. They'd give you a clip round the ear.
Sally: There's no respect, exactly, there's no respect.
Bet: They're too friendly with them as well I think, so they don't respect them. Too friendly.

(Weston residents)

Residents' more specific worries were twofold. They concern, first, the seeming inability (or reluctance) of the police to respond promptly to calls about noisy or nuisance youths. This in part is a (further) means of registering the police's remoteness, for it is that which requires them to be *called* at all. But it also has to do with the police's failure to treat such calls with what residents feel is the appropriate sense of urgency, something that featured especially prominently among the grumbles of those living around the High Street: 'They were kicking the flat door in, just further up. They phoned the police for that; three quarters of an hour it took the police to come.'[6] For some residents of the area, this was interpreted as the police lacking the quantity and quality of personnel that the task – re-imposing order – properly requires:

IL: What do the police do? What's their perception of this issue?
Margaret: Slow response. Very often a youngster, in his early twenties, and he's got young girls, never mind the boys, effing and blinding at him something chronic. And they just end up walking out of the way, they can't cope with it. They really cannot cope with it.

Tom: Because they're under-powered and under-staffed. You can't expect one young PC to deal with twenty or thirty kids shouting verbal abuse. I know they're trained to do it, but they can only take so much and then they either lose their temper and do something they'll regret, or walk away. And they tend to walk away.

A second – related – concern surrounds the apparent reluctance of the police to take what residents consider to be the necessary steps to deal with teenage disorder. Among some, this is not so much a criticism of the police as of the constraints placed upon them by (malign) others, and residents often evince considerable sympathy for what one woman from Moss Rose called the 'heart-breaking job [of] being a policeman these days'. Here officers are viewed as having been hamstrung – and thus demotivated – by either a climate of liberal, 'do-gooding' opinion (to use the characteristic trope); or, relatedly, by the seeming inability of the courts to deal adequately with (persistent) young offenders.[7] As one home watch coordinator from Tytherington put it: 'I feel sorry for the police. All this hard work, and they go to court and the magistrate says: "Go away, don't do it again."' The police officer who was invited by residents to our focus group on the Weston estate was in no mood to dispel this sentiment:

Jim: You as a constable, when you get a case and you go up before the magistrate, you have to stay up, go in your own time to court, stand up there and give your evidence, and then the magistrate pats them on the head and says, 'We'll have a probation report, or a social worker's report on this'; and then when it's all been done, they pat him on the head and they say: 'Go on, don't do it again.' … Don't you think there's too much of these do-gooders?

PC Harris: Unfortunately, I'm not in a position to comment on politics or otherwise. Suffice to say there are a lot of police officers that feel frustrated.

Jim: I can see that, they must be.

Residents' talk about police inaction can, however, adopt a more critical tone, with many believing that – notwithstanding the constraints under which the police operate – more could and should be done. One powerfully voiced bone of contention here arises from the seeming reluctance of the police to involve parents, and impress on *them* the seriousness and consequences of their children's behaviour. This was articulated by some – such as this female participant in one of our High Street focus groups – as a nostalgic, wistful reference to the value of combining legal and parental authority:

I know it was a long time ago, if you did something wrong, the village bobby, if you were caught, you'd get frog-marched back home and he'd go and tell your parents what you'd been up to. Then your parents had a chance to deal with it. But they've no chance to deal with it if they don't know what's going on.

For others, the failure to involve parents serves to crystallize many current anxieties about how the police deal with troublesome local teenagers:

IL: If you call the police in these situations what kind of response would you like?
Dave: Try and get there as soon as possible.
Dot: By the time they get there you're hoping like mad that they'll kill them when they get there, strangle them!
Renee: I'd like to think that if the children that the police are coming to time and time and again, that eventually they will do something about it rather than just keep coming and telling them off.
IL: What would you want them to do?
Renee: To go to the parents and threaten the parents, say if they don't control their child then they'll charge them with their misbehaviour.

(Moss Rose residents)

It is thus clear that feelings of disenchantment and dismay loom large in the police-talk of Macclesfield's (adult) residents – whether they live on council-built estates, or in more affluent locations within the town. That such sensibilities are found among those who think of themselves as recipients of policing services, and who display high levels of *general* support for the police, may occasion some surprise. It should not. For people's frustrations do not arise merely from an apparent police failure to take seriously people's worries and concerns in respect of teenage incivilities, and provide the kind and level of service that these are deemed to warrant. They are also in large measure to do with the great expectations such general (and often sentimental) identification with the police generates. This – as we have seen – revolves largely around the idea that policing ought properly to be concerned with the exercise of routine 'guardianship' over local public space. People, for the most part, wish to see a known and visible figure provide some kind of semi-permanent, pastoral watch over their 'community'. They want to live in a place that is 'looked after' by its own police officer; a respected (and, for some, male) presence whose authority can help bind the young to the moral and legal order of the local community, and thus assist in the maintenance of order, discipline and civility.

That such a figure appears to have been consigned to history (and local memory) is for many the source of considerable disquiet. Their fear is that – notwithstanding the calming utterances of local police managers, and the fact that Cheshire Constabulary has as one of its six stated priorities 'maintaining a community presence through foot and cycle patrols' – the provision of a 'local bobby' runs increasingly counter to the direction in which the police appear to be headed – even in a place like Macclesfield. They worry that the police are becoming a distant and introspective bureaucracy obsessed with performance targets, auditing systems and management-speak (with all its baffling nomenclatures such as 'crime manager') that render policing not only remote from the quotidian life of neighbourhoods (and beyond local influence), but also ever more arcane and mysterious (wasting time on all those 'damn forms'). Their complaint is not merely that the police are failing to do what most local residents want; but that people are less and less sure what it is they do. The police no longer seem to be *their* police.

Why aren't *our* police catching *real* criminals? The policing of motorists

Traffic policing – the mode of policing directed most routinely at those who think of themselves as law-abiding recipients of police services – was not something we made a point of enquiring about in the course of our research. This did little, however, to prevent the subject being raised (in the main, by middle-class residents of Macclesfield and Prestbury), and numerous asides, observations and grumbles were uttered by our focus group participants about the policing of motorists. The following remark – proffered by a female manager living in the town centre during one of our discussions at Zeneca – was fairly typical:

> I'm forever getting parking tickets. The police are great at that, whenever I want to park illegally they're there. If I get my handbag stolen, then I seem to be powerless.

What is striking about the manner in which our respondents spoke about traffic regulation is how much this aspect of their talk about policing resembles – in both substance and tone – that of teenagers; replete as it is with lurking resentment about the police's apparent omnipresence ('You'll get caught if you're doing 34 miles an hour in a 30 miles limit', as one publican put it), and baffled irritation over what are taken to be misplaced police priorities. So let us conclude this chapter with a brief look at this discourse and its meanings; something that will, it is hoped, help us make further sense of how crime and policing are situated and understood within the mentalities and sensibilities of Macclesfield and Prestbury's (middle-class) residents.

This is not to say that irritation was the only response to the policing of motorists evinced during our discussions. Concerns about the speed of traffic (and calls for the police to attend to the issue) also surfaced during our Macclesfield focus groups, and these clearly shape people's sense of the liveability of both the town centre and their immediate locality. In Prestbury too (as we have seen) traffic is a live issue, with the speed and volume of vehicles passing through the village, congestion caused by parents dropping off and picking up their children from school, and parking in the village centre, standing high among local concerns (albeit that demands for remedial action are directed more at Macclesfield Borough Council than the police). During the course of our focus groups in Prestbury, these issues generated often heated debate, not least

when one home watch coordinator objected to what he saw as the rather lax attitude taken by some local residents towards illegal parking in the village. Chief
among his worries was the possible effects of such an outlook on Prestbury's
(already troublesome) young:

> You cannot be selective in the laws that you are going to observe. They are
> there, they should be there to be observed and not openly transgressed. I'm
> just saying that that gives a bad example to the children, who can say, 'Well
> my dad doesn't care a damn about the law because he can park on the pave-
> ment.'

Mostly, however, people raised the issue of traffic policing in tones of bewilderment and annoyance. Some spoke in terms which suggested there is something
slightly underhand about the police treatment of motorists, such as when a
retired businessman from Prestbury referred to officers: 'sneaking along at the
side of the road trying to catch people exceeding 30 miles an hour'. Others –
such as this Zeneca manager – felt that the police approach the whole task with
an inappropriate relish: 'They seem to enjoy sitting there catching people who
are speeding.' What is apparent about these complaints is how pronounced they
are among those who would otherwise provide the police with a rich reservoir of
affection and support:

Miriam:	I never see a policeman. Where do you see a policeman?
Audrey:	There's one or two walk down the close, they've started walking down at eight o'clock at night, down our close going towards the shops, yes. Not every night, and I think they vary the time they come.
Jimmy:	I think it would be better if they concentrated more on police work in the real sense of the word rather than persecuting motorists for parking offences and damn things like that.
Audrey:	But I think if you want help or anything like that, they're very, very good.
Jimmy:	There's a certain amount of bitterness there that makes you regard them as bloody tax collectors, but having said that I agree with the lady over here, they're absolutely marvellous.

(Kennedy Avenue residents)

A number of connected strands go to make up this sentiment, many of which
can be discerned from the small literature that exists on this topic (Hood 1972:
ch. 5; Cressey 1974; Gusfield 1981). It is notable, first, that the vast bulk of
motoring offences are not coded as 'real crime'. This perhaps is now less clearly
so in the case of driving dangerously or under the influence of (excess) alcohol.
But the routine contravention of most laws relating to parking and speeding
strips these offences of much of their capacity to dramatize moral failing – they
become a 'normal lapse from perfect driving' (Gusfield 1981: 130) rather than
actions to which social stigma (or a criminal record) is seen to attach. As one

Prestbury resident remarked of the relative importance of the problem of illegal parking in the village:

> I've never seen a single policeman walk through the village. They all come through in patrol cars. I don't think even then they stop, except to do a few people for parking on the pavement, which is not a crime, it's an irritation.

It follows, second, that those who transgress traffic laws are not for the most part thought of as 'real offenders'; this categorization being prevented, not only by the apparent triviality of many such offences, but also because the culprits generally lack the Otherness that the label 'criminal' so often evokes among those who consider themselves law-abiding (there is, in addition, something about the ubiquity of many traffic infringements that makes police action against any *single* 'offender' seem capricious). The benign imagery (of innocent, victimized motorists) employed by our respondents to characterize the targets of traffic policing offers a nice illustration of this:

> *IL:* What kind of service do you think you get from them, the local police?
> *Emma:* The only time I ever see a police car, it's either parked on the Silk Road waiting …
> *Daniel:* Waiting for the poor motorist.
>
> (Zeneca managers)

> They [the police] will be standing out there with the ray gun catching some lady coming down the hill at 40 miles an hour, speeding. Really. We'd rather they did something about what's going on in the village than catching ladies down the hill.
>
> (retired businessman, Prestbury)

Thus it is that traffic regulation comes to be thought of, not as an arena where the police serve as 'the champions of goodness against public indecency' (Gusfield 1981: 130), but, rather, as an improper object of police work. Some here thought traffic duty – like 'paperwork' – was a chronic misuse of that most valuable of police assets – the police officer:

> It's a waste of training somebody, to put him in a car. You could do it, I could do it, anybody could book someone. Say he's doing over 70 miles an hour, I've got a gun here, a radar gun, and it registers. I can book his number plate. Anybody. It doesn't need police training to do it.
>
> (male resident, Weston)

More commonly, the policing of motorists was mobilized as a means of registering disenchantment with the performance of the police elsewhere; with a mental association being made between the presence of the police at the scene of motoring infringements and their apparent inability to deal with more pressing and serious problems. As one resident of The Villas put it: 'I'd like to see a few more walking round. Not just sitting waiting to stop cars going too fast.' The following exchange – which ensued from a discussion of what might have prompted a group of Weston residents to mount a 'vigilante attack' on a suspected teenage car-thief (Girling *et al.* 1998) – well illustrates the passions this issue can generate:

Mark: I think it's a failure of policing, and I think what would get up my nose ... I understand what you said about the people there with the guns, radar guns. I've been past there quite a few times and this guy has jumped out, and I've thought, it's a classic saying: 'Why aren't they off catching criminals?'

Mandy: Exactly.

Barry: You are criminals, [you're] speeding.

Mark: I think it's that that gets up the majority of people's noses.

Barry: You mean tackling crimes that are acceptable rather than ones that ...

Mark: There are degrees. There are no black and white absolutes.

Barry: It's the law, isn't it? It's like a middle-class crime, isn't it? Speeding is okay because we're middle-class people, it's okay for us to drive at 50 miles an hour. If you kill somebody in a 30 mile zone that's tough as well. You have to be very clear I think about crime. Are any crimes acceptable? The police, at the end of the day, are doing something that probably prevents one person being killed.

Mark: The cynics amongst us say that it's a lot easier to get your crime stats right by stopping a couple of dozen motorists than actually trying to solve crimes.

(Zeneca managers, Prestbury)

Back in 1992, in the pages of *Police Review* (Butler 1992: 1361), the then Conservative Home Secretary, Kenneth Clarke, warned the police of 'the dangers of alienating middle-class support by an over-enforcement of the traffic laws'. There is something about Mark's 'cynicism' which suggests that Clarke's strictures are not without foundation. But why should this be so? And what does this anguished talk about traffic regulation signify about middle-class sensibilities towards policing and the police?

One possibility of course is that this discourse arises from a considered assessment of how police resources ought properly to be allocated. For when set against what is perceived as the police's inability to respond adequately to some troubling problems of neighbourhood disorder, and the prevalence of what are considered 'real' offences (such as car theft), the devotion of scarce police resources to traffic management might well appear remiss. Surveys of public opinion – such as that carried out by the three police staff associations in 1990, which found 'controlling and supervising road traffic' to rank lowest among public priorities (Joint Consultative Committee 1990) – consistently lend support to this interpretation.

Yet the tone and vehemence of much of this talk about the policing of motorists indicates that more is at stake here than a mere reasoned complaint about misplaced police priorities. This may have to do with the fact that traffic laws – almost alone among criminal sanctions – 'bestow their curse on rich and poor alike' (Gusfield 1981: 119); a 'fact' that contravenes what appear to be some deeply embedded and powerfully felt expectations about what the police are for. The accounts we have documented in this chapter suggest that traffic policing is unsettling because it offends against many (middle-class) people's sense of themselves as the proper recipients of police services, and jars unpleasantly with the sentiments of attachment and ownership they feel towards the police. The regulation of motorists serves, it seems, to undermine the received (middle-class) idea that the English police belong to '*us*', to be directed at '*them*'.

7 Some meanings and futures of security

During one of our group discussions with residents living around the old High Street, a male professional in his mid-twenties made the following observation:

> Attitudes have changed now. Police today have got so much to do. They've got to like sort out not just theft, but drug problems, violence, domestic violence. They've got such a wide range. Police twenty, thirty years ago, they would have to deal with theft, but now they have to cover a whole range. They'll have to change, and perhaps the community will have to change. Perhaps we'll have to do our policing ourselves, in a minor way, we may have to patrol.

This may turn out to be a prescient assessment of the contemporary policing scene. For not only does it reference the difficulties the police currently face in meeting the demands made of them by their anxious and expectant 'customers' – something we saw amply demonstrated in the last chapter. But it also resonates closely with much of the prevailing official rhetoric and practice around crime control. This has endeavoured of late – the excitement apparent in some quarters for 'zero tolerance' policing notwithstanding (Dennis 1997) – to decentre the police from the hitherto prominent place they have occupied as guarantors of local social order, and insist that they alone cannot carry the burden of tackling crime. This has been accompanied by concerted efforts to encourage individuals, communities, local authorities and private businesses to become more fully involved in crime prevention activity (Garland 1996; Crawford 1997). We have witnessed a proliferation of multi-agency partnerships against crime. Local authorities have come to play a more prominent role in the funding and delivery of both security technology (such as CCTV) and patrolling (I'Anson and Wiles 1995). The private security industry has continued to expand (Loader 1997b; Jones and Newburn 1998). And individual citizens have been exhorted to become 'Partners Against Crime' (Home Office 1994), either by taking prudent steps to protect their own person and property (by purchasing alarms, locks, lights and so forth), or by participating in neighbourhood or – latterly, and more patchily – street watch. The result has been increasing fragmentation, unevenness and commodification in the provision of crime prevention, with the idea of the sovereign state taking universal measures to ensure the safety of its citizens being 'displaced by a variety of different ways of imagining security, each of which mobilizes a particular sense of community' (Rose 1996: 335).

This chapter is concerned with how different constituencies within Macclesfield and Prestbury make sense of, and respond to, these unfolding landscapes of protection. How are these various forms of security provision interpreted, deployed or resisted by the town's residents? Which do they envisage embracing?, which do they recoil from? and why? We begin by discussing some of the forms of defence and avoidance that Macclesfield people rely upon to protect their person, property or community against criminal threats. We then assess – taking as our point of departure the prospect of CCTV being installed in Macclesfield town centre – the kinds of responses people make to the contemporary proliferation of camera surveillance. We conclude with an analysis of how Macclesfield and Prestbury residents react to the possibility of commercial firms providing the visible patrolling presence that the public police currently appear unable to deliver.

Our aim in taking up these issues is twofold. Part of our purpose is to examine how some of the distinctions that generally pervade debates about security (notably, those between state-, market- and citizen-initiated activity, and between protective hardware and services) figure within people's talk about protection and inform their sensibilities towards different kinds of provision. But we are also interested in how the meanings that people attach to various crime control practices, technologies and services depend, not only on their assessment of whether these might impact beneficially upon problems of crime and disorder, but also on the capacity of these possible 'solutions' to connect with – and condense – residents' hopes and fears about the future liveability of both 'their town' and the world beyond. More of this in due course. Let us turn first to the ways in which security-seeking activity presently pervades the lives – and talk – of Macclesfield residents.

Partners against crime? Seeking security in everyday life

The protection of person and property is seldom merely a matter of purchasing locks, bolts and bars; nor is it limited to the other products and activities that are conventionally coded as 'crime prevention'. There are a range of other decisions that people take that are motivated by reasons other than safety, but which can nonetheless be shot through with – or at least informed by – the quest for security. We noted in Chapter 2, for example, that some Macclesfield (and Prestbury) residents were attracted to the town in part due to security considerations. We saw also that many Macclesfield people's fondness for 'their town' flows from its apparent success in avoiding some of the worst excesses of contemporary English society (drugs, racial tensions and so forth) as these are experienced elsewhere, and, in particular, from its moderate crime levels when set against major conurbations such as Liverpool and Manchester. The reflections of a male computer manager now living around High Street on his move from the middle-class suburb of Didsbury in south Manchester capture this well:

I lived in Didsbury temporarily for six months, which is 5 miles outside the city centre, and I got broken into, cars were always getting broken into. When I moved back, the difference in the premiums for insuring my car for example, it was two-thirds of what it cost in Manchester, there was an enormous difference. I felt a palpable sense of risk in Didsbury compared to Macclesfield.

Cognate considerations apply to Macclesfield's internal boundaries. Though we have seen (in Chapter 3) that crime doesn't figure prominently in residents' talk as a marker of local class divisions (most people believing that property crime travels to Macclesfield from outside), it is nevertheless the case that people's cognitive maps of the town are in part characterized by distinctions between places they will happily visit (or live in) and those they associate with crime-related danger. With respect to the latter, Victoria Park flats was a recurring 'landscape of fear' (Tuan 1979), as was the town centre on Friday and Saturday nights. In terms of the former, consider the association this male resident of The Villas makes between his sense of security and finding – and being prepared to pay for – a neighbourhood inhabited by like-minded people:

Every house that I've bought, I've always looked at the community. If you're going to live, and you want to be safe, you want neighbours that are like yourself, that are conscious, safety conscious, and you feel comfortable with. If you wanted a cheap house, you could buy a cheap house. I'd be rich, I could drive a big car. But by golly, I'd be scared every night.

These remarks serve as a useful corrective to a narrow, 'nuts-and-bolts' view of security seeking. As we hope to have demonstrated throughout this book, crime and efforts to avoid it permeate local social relations in a whole host of ways; ranging from the formation of various habits and routines (such as taking preferred routes through the town's spaces), to decisions about where or where not to live (and purchase property), what school to send one's children to, where to let them play, with whom and so on. Now, however, we want to concentrate on those activities and purchases that *are* more usually herded together under the banner of crime prevention, those motivated solely or principally by the desire to stave off criminal threats.

Home security: habits and technologies of protection

How do Macclesfield and Prestbury residents seek to protect their own property? What routines and technologies do they *individually* deploy to this end? Our focus group discussions elicited numerous examples of security-oriented practices that have come to be embedded in the daily routines of individuals and families. (These surfaced mainly among our middle-class respondents, who were both more likely to speak of their properties as potential targets of burglary, and more explicitly attuned to matters of home security, than those we spoke to on

Macclesfield's council-built estates.) Considered by our participants as sensible precautions against (opportunist) crime, these practices ranged from locking the back door when upstairs or in the garden and parking the car on the drive while away, to (more unusually) keeping 'a baseball bat in the bedroom' (male resident, High Street) and jotting down the registration numbers of unfamiliar/suspicious cars 'just in case' (male resident, Kennedy Avenue). Often, they appeared to entail attempts by some family members to encourage others ('She hardly ever locks the car up, never, ever', as one Prestbury resident remarked of his wife) to raise their levels of everyday security consciousness. The appropriate level of security was even suggested by some – such as this Women's Institute member from Prestbury – to be a source of domestic conflict:

> I'm very conscious. If I'm in my back garden sunbathing, even the backdoor is locked and the key is in my pocket, because I know of other areas where you've sat in the back garden and they've gone in through doors, you fall asleep, or you're gardening. The children hate it, they all say it's like Fort Knox.

Significant as these habits appear to be, Macclesfield and Prestbury residents were nonetheless aware that the lack of occupation of most homes during working hours (coupled, in Prestbury, by the sheer distance between many of the houses) rendered forms of informal or natural surveillance – including those organized under the rubric of home watch – of limited utility (see, further, Hope 1998). A significant proportion of our discussants had thus also purchased various forms of physical protection for their property. These commonly included 'security locks on all the windows and all the doors' (female resident, Upton Priory), but also encompassed 'a fence [with] a bit of barbed-wire across the top of it' (male resident, The Villas); numerous instances of dogs and double glazing being referred to as crime prevention devices; and – mainly among our middle-class respondents in Macclesfield and Prestbury – security lights and house alarms (Cheshire County Council's (1996c) 'quality of life' survey found that 21 per cent of households in Macclesfield Borough had burglar alarms, and some 37 per cent security lights).[1] This retired Prestbury businessman illustrates not only the range of products that may be deployed, but also the tendency of some of the men we spoke to attribute these measures to the anxieties of their wives:

> I think a good dog is probably the best burglar alarm. Even on our small cottage we've got an expensive burglar alarm, and outside lights come on. Even warning bells on the UV [ultra violet] lights, so if anybody even comes in the garden we know, day or night. And window locks, and double glazing. That's only because my wife insists on it all.

One of the most striking things about all this security hardware is just how little discourse, let alone controversy, it prompted (especially compared with

CCTV and private patrols). The issue of home security was rarely, for example, connected in people's talk with the invisibility or failures of the police; nor did it meet with many principled objections about having to resort to the market for protection. This no doubt arises in large measure from the fact that these forms of security relate to the protection of individual properties rather than public spaces and locations; something that for reasons of both prudence (keeping intruders out, responding to the incentives and stipulations of insurance companies)[2] and culture ('An Englishman's home is his castle') means that taking steps to secure one's property has come to be accepted as the proper responsibility of individual homeowners. As one female member of our Broken Cross focus group put it: 'It's up to you to protect yourself as much as you possibly can' – a sentiment that Macclesfield residents rarely extend to the supervision of public space.

Thus it is that people's talk about security hardware (and especially car and house alarms) centred principally upon questions of effectiveness. In the main, residents of Macclesfield were motivated to install alarms by considerations of deterrence, hoping that it would either dissuade offenders from selecting their property, or else make a noise 'deafening enough' (as one Prestbury resident put it) to interrupt a burglary in progress. Here two themes are apparent. It was felt, first, that while such technology might fend off 'amateurs' and 'opportunists', there was little that householders could do to keep out what one Moss Rose resident called 'the determined burglar'. As one Weston resident put it: 'Your average professional burglar doesn't have any trouble at all with a burglar alarm.' The result is conversations about home security pervaded by an often uneasy mix of hope and resignation:

Audrey: We've got an alarm on the car. There's an alarm on the house but it doesn't work, but it's like a deterrent. We lock all the doors, they can't unlock the bedroom door from inside the bedroom if they come in the bedroom.
Miriam: All our windows are lockable, upstairs and down. We've got a mortice lock on the front door, and locks on the back door. We're just hoping with the double glazing and everything, we're okay.
Jenny: They'll get in if they want to.

(Kennedy Avenue residents)

A second, related worry surrounds the seeming inability of intruder alarms to activate (from either neighbours or bystanders) the kinds of informal social control whose absence has rendered such alarms necessary in the eyes of many homeowners.[3] This flows in part from the banal pervasiveness that house and car alarms have acquired in recent years (not least in middle-class areas of Macclesfield) and the resulting tendency of people to 'just ignore them' (female resident, Weston) if they go off. As one Broken Cross resident put it: 'Burglar alarms are a waste of time. Everybody has got them. Nobody listens to them.'

But it also has to do with the incapacity of alarm technology to overcome people's reservations about involving themselves personally in crime control:

> One tends to wake up in the middle of the night and you hear a burglar alarm going, you tend to shrug it off. The last thing I want to do is go in and play the little hero seeing if anybody is in, because if they are disturbed and on their way out, they've probably got a cosh in one hand, or a brick in the other, or something like that.
>
> (retired businessman, Prestbury)

The following account both nicely illustrates these limitations and couples them with some more fundamental objections to the contemporary proliferation of alarms:

> I wouldn't dream of phoning the police if somebody's alarm went off. Not unless it was a next door neighbour and I knew for a fact that they were out. Of course, I would do it then. I am so used to hearing them go off, and I detest them. I think they are a social menace. I think they have been sold by car alarm companies on the basis of fear and all the rest of it.
>
> (male resident, High Street)

This was one of the few occasions that the issue of alarms prompted among our discussants a commentary that transcended the question of effectiveness. But it was not the only one. For both incomers and established residents among our respondents made reference to the uneven take-up of alarms across Macclesfield, and, in particular, to the prevalence of such hardware on the new housing that has gone up in recent years. Having expressed surprise that their new homes had not come with burglar alarms fitted as standard, residents of one such housing scheme – The Villas – remarked on the town's emerging landscape as follows:

John: Newer property has more [alarms] than the older property. If you go down the old roads in the centre of the town, I don't think you see as many there as you would on the new estates.

Rob: It's still very expensive to fit a burglar alarm, one that covers your windows and your doors, access areas. It's quite lucrative. I have colleagues at work, I have moved into a brand new house and fitted a burglar alarm, they say, 'Oh I couldn't afford that.' In a way, I think it's still a big investment.

Ewan: You can't afford not to, I don't think.

Thus it is that the technology some Macclesfield residents deploy in an effort to secure their homes against intruders, serves to signify something about the recent trajectory and possible futures of the town; representing – and in some respects cementing – some of its emergent social divisions. For the most part, however, these unfolding inequalities are met with indifference by Macclesfield's poorer and (ostensibly) less protected residents. Lacking the material resources that might render such technology a thinkable option, and being generally more troubled by disorder than by burglary, those we spoke to on the town's council-built estates either shared some widespread suspicions about the (in)effectiveness of house alarms; or else – as with this Weston resident – looked on with wry bemusement at the security-seeking activities of some of Macclesfield's more affluent citizens: 'I think to some people it's a status symbol to have a burglar alarm. I'm not quite sure what they're trying to protect.'

A defensible place? Walls, watching and 'walking with a purpose'

While Macclesfield's residents take various measures to ensure the physical protection of their person and property, the foregoing observations hardly amount – even in Prestbury – to what in the southern Californian context Mike Davis (1990) has called the voracious consumption of defensive hardware. This disparity is even more marked in respect of security measures taken to protect whole neighbourhoods. Granted, a number of the housing developments built across Macclesfield in recent years are enclosed behind walls (though not – at present – gates) and that this forms part of their appeal for some purchasers – as a resident of one such development bluntly put it: 'I like The Villas because it's got a fence around it'.[4] Granted also, that some of our respondents – such as this publican – saw current trends heading in the direction of a fortress society:

> Ten years from now everybody will have steel roller shutters on the down-stairs windows on their houses, everybody will have them. The seed has been sown, everybody will have them, because they will be frightened of going upstairs to bed and leaving vulnerable areas of property open to crim-inal activities.

And let us not forget that Victoria Park flats are now enclosed behind a controlled-access, camera surveillance, security system.

Yet for the most part residents of Macclesfield and Prestbury not only evinced little interest in, but expressly recoiled from, the idea of the defended neighbour-hood; a reluctance that flows both from their impression of the town as having a currently modest, containable crime problem, and, significantly, from their sense of the kind of place they wish to live in. Thus while Prestbury residents take often extensive steps to protect their own property (the larger houses are walled *and* gated), it is important to them that the surrounding space retains its English pastoral appearance – a sentiment no doubt made possible by the fact that Prestbury's boundaries (and the exclusion of 'undesirables') are secured through the operation of the housing market (cf. Hope 1998). Responding to the sugges-tion that the local off-licence might secure itself with window shutters, one retired businessman articulated this feeling thus:

It would be a retrograde step if they had to do that. It would be the same as like Moss Side with all those shutters. You go through there at night, it's terrible. One of the attractions of the village is that it does look like a village day and night.

So too in Macclesfield itself, where the local Civic Society labours energetically (by monitoring planning applications, running talks on various aspects of the town, and handing out awards to what it views as good, 'in keeping' development) to retain the appearance of Macclesfield as an 'old silk town', and where the Borough Council continues to resist – on aesthetic grounds – the use of external shutters by town centre retailers. There are, it seems, some powerful cultural sensibilities (and interests) standing in the path of urban fortification: a defensible place is not necessarily considered an attractive or liveable one.

Thus it is that most of the measures Macclesfield residents *collectively* deploy to protect their homes or neighbourhood from criminal threat are of a more unobtrusive kind. These mostly take the form of informal arrangements with (immediate) neighbours to share in the guardianship of each other's property – the deployment of what one Villas resident called 'community spirit' (though as one woman living in Upton Priory was at pains to point out, such arrangements are of little use if one suspects that the burglars *are* your neighbours). It was, of course, as we saw in Chapter 4, a recurring refrain among our respondents that such spirit is now largely absent from local social relations, having atrophied significantly in the last few decades. This may be so. Yet we came across various examples of often extremely localized networks that offer mutual – though, importantly for the participants, relatively unonerous – assistance in the defence of people's homes and property. Thus:

> Within our end of the close we keep an eye on each other's houses when people are away for any length of time. We have their keys and their burglar alarm numbers, things like this, so you don't have alarms going off all day. Check around houses if the alarm is going off. That works pretty well.
>
> (male resident, Prestbury)

> We live in like a square and we all watch for everybody. It's three sides, and then there's a garage wall at one side. Believe me, a stranger or somebody acting even remotely suspicious sticks out like a sore thumb.
>
> (male resident, Upton Priory)

In some (though by no means all) of Macclesfield's more affluent areas, these informal arrangements had either crystallized into, or been fostered by, formal home watch schemes (according to Cheshire County Council's (1996c) survey, 28 per cent of households in Macclesfield Borough belong to such a scheme; though at the time of our research none operated on any of the town's council-built estates). Since its inception in 1982, home – or neighbourhood – watch has mushroomed across England and Wales, albeit that the take-up remains uneven (schemes are generally more prevalent in middle-class areas with relatively modest crime levels), and that its success in reducing crime and fear has often not lived up to the official claims made on its behalf (Bennett 1990; Hope 1997b). These difficulties found echoes among a number of our respondents who admitted to 'membership' that amounted to little beyond 'putting a sticker in the window'; spoke of schemes 'starting well' and then 'fizzling out' (male resident, High Street); and ventured that the normalization of home watch schemes had rendered them 'not as effective as they used to be a few years ago' (Zeneca manager, Prestbury).

This stood in some contrast to the views expressed in our two focus groups with home watch coordinators, where the dominant mood – as indicated by this Tytherington coordinator – was one of modest success: 'I find that home watch as far as the area I control is fine. People now know one another, they're kept posted when there's somebody moving house and somebody coming in. We've all got the names and telephone numbers.' The coordinators were, however, only too aware of the difficulties involved in sustaining people's interest over time, especially once the police – who are instrumental in helping most schemes get off the ground – adopt a more background role. Some were clearly frustrated by these problems, finding particular cause for annoyance in the actions of those 'thoughtless' (male coordinator, Prestbury) individuals who either neglected to provide information on their movements, or who appeared to take insufficient care in the protection of their property:

June: We've only got thirteen, it's a very small cul-de-sac. Everybody knows everybody in it. We all moved in from new, so everybody knows the new neighbours and who they are. But I just cannot understand Tom, who's another neighbour, who leaves the kitchen window open. It's only by about an inch, they think nobody can get in.

Emily: They only need to put a screwdriver in and it's open. But they would be the sort of people that once they've been broken into, 'We're in a home watch area, why haven't you been watching my house?' They would be the sort of people, and it would be me that would get it in the neck.

(home watch coordinators, Tytherington)

These frustrations (and the tensions they reveal between 'responsible' and supposedly 'irresponsible' homeowners) are tempered, however, by two further, and related, dispositions found among the coordinators we spoke to. First, an acute desire to avoid being labelled a 'nosey neighbour' (and a notable reluctance to use neighbourhood watch as a vehicle for trying to recreate some lost 'community', cf. Sasson and Nelson 1996); and, second, a realistic assessment of what can and cannot be expected of 'members', something that surfaced repeatedly in refrains about 'not overdoing it' and 'keeping things low key'. This potted history of one Tytherington scheme nicely encapsulates the problem of maintaining informal surveillance among (largely) commuting, professional people, residing in areas where there is often precious little to watch:

Our group was set up ten years ago when we had a number of burglaries in the area. The first coordinator was actually someone who was burgled and felt strongly about it and started the group. He then moved away after about a year and I said I would coordinate it. I found that progressively people became less concerned because we hadn't had a burglary in the immediate vicinity for quite some time. There were problems with children, I had my car broken into, and that's probably all that's happened in the last five years. So people have stopped telling me now when they go on holiday. Just a couple of residents out of the twelve will actually bother to tell me now when they go away. People are relaxed about it now.

The various modes of security seeking considered thus far (neighbourhood watch included) have in common a desire to defend the home, a desire that is extended to the street only insofar as it allows potentially malign strangers access to private property (it is noteworthy that home watch was never mentioned by our respondents as a means of regulating teenage nuisance and disorder). Indeed, when asked about the idea of participating in 'street watch' (a scheme designed to extend informal surveillance to local public space[5]), people responded with, if not outright hostility, then at least considerable unease. Many of their objections were of a practical kind, with people speaking of Prestbury as 'too dark' to make it workable (it has, you recall, no street lights), or of themselves as being either too old or too busy to participate in such activity. As one male manager said: 'I've got far too much to do with my time than to go wandering around Prestbury.'

But more fundamental questions were also raised, mainly in respect of the dangers that were seen as attending this mode of crime prevention. Some immediately thought here of the threat of lawlessness posed by the kinds of people who might be attracted to such patrolling – as one Weston resident remarked (in response to being asked 'if he would consider joining something like street watch?'): 'Vigilantes you mean? Sort of walking around the street with sticks in your hand and that sort of thing'.[6] Others, however, were more concerned that those who volunteered would be taking on burdens and risks that shouldn't really be placed upon the shoulders of individual citizens. First, the possibility of being blamed should things go wrong: 'A lot is expected of you I think, because that one person patrolling, if something did happen, they'll say, "Where were you at this time?"' (home watch coordinator, Prestbury). And, second, the chance that volunteers might themselves be victimized:

> I'm not sure how safe it is for the people who do it. Presumably they're not going to be allowed to be armed in any way, shape or form. Surely they're putting themselves at a great deal of risk. I'm afraid that I think I feel that's what the police force is being paid to do.
>
> (Zeneca manager, Prestbury)

It seems, then, that while Macclesfield residents are willing (time and resources permitting) to make purchases, and engage in activities of various kinds, to protect their own and their neighbours' property, they are much more reticent about participating in surveillance of the wider locality. In part – as this Prestbury resident demonstrates, and as we shall see further below – this has to do with people's sense that the regulation of public space is the proper province of the state. But it also suggests that people's idea of what counts as a legitimate response to crime is conditioned both by their assessment of the threat posed (which, in Macclesfield, is generally taken to be manageable) and by the associations people make between certain modes of protection and particular kinds of places, a cultural sensibility that can act as an important check on what people are willing to do to defend their home or neighbourhood. As one Tytherington home watch coordinator said of street watch (conjuring up an image of inner-city Liverpool): 'Not where I live. I can't speak for the Toxteth area. I can't answer for that, but certainly not where I live. It's not necessary.'

A price worth paying? The seductions and repulsions of CCTV

At the time of our research, Macclesfield Borough Council were, in collaboration with Cheshire Police, in the process of trying to secure funds to extend closed-circuit camera surveillance in the town centre beyond the car parks, where it was already in operation. Having agreed to part-finance the scheme, the Council sought the remainder of the required capital from town centre retailers, the response of whom was – to say the least – patchy. As the manager of one retail outlet explained to us:

> I think it's a good idea. But they wanted us to pay for it. I pay £33,000 per year in rates, and they wanted £3,000 off me to pay for CCTV. I phoned up [headquarters] to ask them if they'd ever contributed to this sort of thing before. They said they had donated £200 or £250 on occasions. They said forget it.

Due to insufficient funds, and the marked unwillingness of the contributors to allow non-contributing retailers to free ride on the scheme, the idea collapsed. A senior police officer reflected on the process thus:

> That is one of my failures, I've got to declare that as a failure. ... I thought it would be great. I think it would be great. It might come one day but people's, the problem was, it wasn't that they didn't want the scheme. The argument you could have is Big Brother and all that, but that never really raised its head quite honestly. It was the funding of it.

It is not our purpose here to account for this failure of multi-agency cooperation (cameras have now, subsequent to the period of our research, been installed along Chestergate, and overlooking the late night 'hot-spot' of Water's Green).

Nor do we wish to dwell on questions of effectiveness (Fyfe and Bannister 1996), consider how categories of suspicion are constructed by CCTV operators (Norris and Armstrong 1997) or discuss the more general sociological issues raised by 'surveillance society' (Lyon 1994). Instead, we want to use the Borough Council's proposed scheme as a basis from which to analyse the cultural reception of CCTV. How did Macclesfield and Prestbury residents respond to this initiative? What sensibilities towards CCTV are disclosed by their talk? To what extent, and for what reasons, are people either drawn towards or repulsed by this possible crime control future?

Our respondents generally evinced support for the introduction of CCTV to the centre of Macclesfield, albeit that this was articulated with varying degrees of force. Among some, the embrace of CCTV appeared to be of a rather pragmatic, even experimental, kind, best encapsulated in the phrase, 'It's worth a try.' People here either pronounced themselves as having 'personally no objections' (female Civic Society member) to CCTV, or, in a more positive vein, expressed the hope that as it had worked elsewhere (and it was often taken as read that CCTV *had* worked elsewhere) there is no reason for it not to improve things in Macclesfield town centre (especially in relation to alcohol-related violence), thereby making people feel 'more comfortable' (female resident, The Villas). As one male Kennedy Avenue resident put it (recalling the security camera image of toddler James Bulger's abduction by two 10-year-old boys from a Liverpool shopping centre in 1993): 'I think it's got to be better than nothing.'

Others, however, were much more passionate and wholehearted in their enthusiasm for CCTV, not only welcoming the town centre scheme as 'a brilliant idea' (female resident, Broken Cross), but also expressing next to no qualms about extending camera surveillance more widely. As one retired female resident of The Villas put it: 'I'm all for it. You can have as many as you want, where you want. ... It wouldn't worry me where you put them.' Some even voiced support for extending CCTV surveillance to residential areas, including their own. A Women's Institute member described as 'wonderful' the suggestion that cameras be installed across Prestbury. A Prestbury home watch coordinator recounted how residents of her street had planned to install *their own* CCTV system, a scheme that foundered only because, 'no one would have the thing plugged into their electricity'. And this Villas resident – a few reservations aside – is clearly enticed by the prospect of their enclave obtaining CCTV protection:

> If there were [cameras] in our area, I'd have a concern that we would become like a community that was being spied on. If you overcome that, I think it would definitely make it a very secure area, and very attractive. It would probably put the price of the property up.

What is striking about this vein of robust enthusiasm for CCTV is that it is couched, not so much in terms of the positive benefits of camera surveillance (which are generally taken to be self-evident), but as an attack on those who oppose CCTV on the grounds that it represents an unwarranted infringement of individual freedom. Hence the baffled anger of one home watch coordinator from Tytherington: 'Their freedom! What about my freedom? I cannot walk down the street. An elderly person cannot go out at night. Whose freedom does it [CCTV] interfere with?' Hence also the sentiments expressed by this female resident of Moss Rose: 'I've no time for these people that say it's Big Brother tactics. If you're doing nothing wrong you've nothing to worry about. If it's going to catch the criminal element, then yes, by all means. Stick them on every street corner, every shop doorway for me.' And then there are these:

> If you're doing things that are wrong, that's the only time you've got to worry about things like that.
>
> (female resident, High Street)

> Well I think if you're not up to dirty tricks, then it doesn't bother you.
>
> (female resident, Upton Priory)

> If you're not out of order, you've nothing to fear from a camera, have you?
>
> (male resident, Upton Priory)

> The only people that have got to fear are them that are doing it.
>
> (male resident, Moss Rose)

> If you're a law-abiding citizen, then you don't need to worry.
>
> (female resident, Kennedy Avenue)

> It's like ID [identity] cards. If you're not doing anything wrong, then why should it worry you to carry some identification?
>
> (female resident, Broken Cross)

> The only people who fear cameras are the ones that are guilty.
>
> (male resident, Broken Cross)

> I think if you've got nothing to hide there's no problem.
>
> (female resident, The Villas)

> To hell with the civil liberties lot. I think it's great.
>
> (retired businessman, Prestbury)

These utterances draw upon and reproduce a powerful (and insufficiently under-stood) strand of English popular orthodoxy about crime and justice which holds that 'law-abiding citizens' have no legitimate cause for worrying about, or objecting to, measures (presumably *any* of the measures) that are taken in the name of crime control. They acknowledge that – in this case – CCTV is a matter of cultural contest (hence the references to Big Brother) only to close the contest with the suggestion that dissent is confined to particular kinds of people:

criminals, and that small, unrepresentative lobby preoccupied with civil liberties. These tropes thus operate within people's crime-talk as 'trumps', for to offer a contrary response is necessarily to locate oneself in one or other of these apparently dubious categories.

We nonetheless did encounter people among our respondents who risked such categorization by failing to share an unbridled enthusiasm for the onset of CCTV. Many of these raised doubts of a generally instrumental kind, concerned either that CCTV would fail to deliver the hoped for reductions in crime and disorder, or that it was taking attention and resources away from other, potentially more fruitful, crime prevention measures. People thus predicted that the cameras would 'get vandalized' (male resident, Upton Priory) or stolen ('Frankly, I don't think they'd be there a week', one Moss Rose resident glumly remarked); raised some familiar criminological problems to do with displacement ('They'll just do it somewhere else won't they?', observed one Hurdsfield teenager); or else wondered why such faith was being placed in a device that so obviously deals in symptoms rather than causes:

> You're just creating criminals all the time. You have the cameras and then you start criminalizing, making people criminals. What are you going to do with them when you've seen them on this camera? Why not say what are they doing here, why do they need to come in here, get drunk and fight?
>
> (male resident, High Street)

For some, a more pressing anxiety attached to the suspicion that CCTV is emerging as a remote, invisible (and for these reasons second-best) replacement for their preferred mode of protection – 'more policemen out walking the streets':

> I think why spend … . What annoys me … I think everybody thinks, 'Oh high-tech solution, Oh marvellous.' Why can't they spend it on people and policemen, human beings, who will talk, know what's going on, who will talk to the kids, who will build up a relationship with the community, rather than going to something high-tech like a flipping camera. I fail to understand that.
>
> (female resident, High Street)

Yet people's worries about CCTV were not solely concerned with whether or not it will 'work'; some among our discussants also raised matters of principle. These commonly included objections to what one resident of the High Street (who was otherwise preoccupied with worry about teenage disorder and vociferously pro-police) called 'the Big Brother syndrome'. But they also encompassed those who associated CCTV with other seemingly impending and undesirable developments in social control (notably identity cards), and who viewed these as a potential 'invasion' of another valued – if, in this context, legally unprotected – facet of English society and culture – an individual's right to privacy. This made, in one or two of our focus groups, for some sharp exchanges of view:

EG:	You may have heard of plans Macclesfield Borough Council has to put CCTV in the town centre. What do you think of that?
Joanne:	Big Brother is back.
Dan:	It's becoming like America.
Simone:	It doesn't worry me.
Joanne:	It's the next stage to ID cards and God knows what.
Simone:	What have you got against ID cards? I come from a country [Switzerland] where everybody is supposed to have them, it's natural.
Joanne:	I think it's a very Germanic thing. I know a lot of European countries have it, but for me, it goes completely against all my principles. I don't accept this argument that if you've got nothing to hide, you don't care. I just know the sort of information they can get on you. I know because I've been a member of Amnesty [International]. I will be on a government file and things, and if I have an ID card, especially when they check on me, Christ knows what they're going to pass on.

(High Street residents)

Joanne's anxieties bring us to a third set of responses to the proliferation of CCTV (both in Macclesfield and the wider world), one best summed up by the term *ambivalence*. Though this ambivalence can take various forms, it generally couples a grudging acceptance of the 'need' for video surveillance, with a range of (often diffuse) worries about how CCTV might come to be used, and about the kind of world it signifies.

One variant of this combines a demand that CCTV is regulated by proper safeguards (a particular concern being to prevent what one Broken Cross resident described as 'councils selling the tapes to be used on television programmes'), with a call for some judiciousness regarding where, for what purpose and against whom, CCTV cameras are deployed. Here, it seems, people's sense of the appropriateness or otherwise of CCTV is mediated in important ways by their sense of place. For while people were relatively accepting of the need for CCTV to be used in specific locations (notably, parts of the town centre) against particular groups of people (what one Hurdsfield teenager called 'beer monsters'), they tended to recoil from the suggestion that camera surveillance be extended any further across the local townscape:

I'd say outside some of the main pubs. Things like that. The car parks, fair enough. But there's no need for them all over Macclesfield, no need for them. Just outside a couple of pubs. I wouldn't like them down the street or anything like that, looking into me window or something like that. It's not on.

(20-year-old male, on probation)

As this suggests, particular resistance is apparent to the possibility of CCTV being deployed in residential settings (a prospect one Kennedy Avenue resident described as 'excessive'), either because 'nothing happens' in 'our streets', or because the provision of surveillance technology in such locations seems un-fathomably inappropriate and 'out of place':

> I find it difficult to … all these cameras. I can't imagine a big tower down our street with cameras on. But if you live in Victoria [Park] flats, maybe that would be quite helpful.
>
> (male resident, Kennedy Avenue)

A second type of ambivalence is less obviously grounded in these local distinctions, referring instead to what are viewed as some unsettling aspects of the wider world. Among some – such as this male resident of High Street – this worry is directed towards the apparent preponderance of crime and violence that permeates English society at large, a problem troubling enough to engender a cautious acceptance of CCTV:

> I was a bit wary about CCTV, until I saw this programme on Channel 4 some months ago. Some of the footage they caught, and some of the things that I saw people do to other people, it appalled me. I thought well I don't want this to go on in society, I don't want that to happen, so CCTV in towns might actually be a small price to pay to reduce that kind of crime.

For others, however, the more urgent concern is whether that price (and both these accounts assume that CCTV exacts some kind of – unspecified – social cost) is too high. While CCTV may not be something to protest about, it can still generate a considerable degree of disquiet:

Jim:	It concerns me, this sort of constant Big Brother is watching you kind of thing. I don't feel entirely comfortable about that. I sometimes wonder just where it's going to go …
EG:	What would you say if there was going to be CCTV in your street rather than the town centre?
Jim:	I feel happy enough without one. I don't suppose I would consciously make any sort of fuss to stop it from happening. But on the other hand I wouldn't campaign to have one. I feel reasonably comfortable without it. I think eventually it will be smart cards that you have to carry about. The police don't have to ask you questions, they just slip it through this thing. They're infringing more and more on your ability to move about freely. Whether it's the price we pay for a total stoppage of crime. I'm not quite sure whether that price is worth actually paying.

(male resident, Weston)

This ambivalence towards CCTV arises, then, from a sense people have that the 'condition of England' (if not perhaps Macclesfield) has become such as to render camera surveillance 'necessary' (what we have come to know as 'fear of crime'), coupled with an anxiety about where contemporary trends in social control (of which CCTV is but one) might possibly be headed (what we might call, rhetorically, 'fear of crime control'). The following discussion illustrates this well, with Angela voicing both a concern about crime (together – in the situational context of this focus group – with a determination not to come across as 'soft') and a desire that something be done about it, with some difficult-to-articulate but nonetheless unsettling feelings about what is happening to the world under the guise of crime control. It seems an appropriate way to bring our discussion of CCTV to a close:

Angela: I'm not really in favour of it [CCTV]. My gut feeling is that I'm against it.

RS: What's your gut telling you?

Angela: Just surveillance really, it's taking things too far, unnecessarily far. Who's going to have access to what's filmed, and for what purposes, those kind of questions. It's the same with all of these things, like 'walking with a purpose' and private police, all those kind of things. I would say no to all of those, and then I would have to think about exactly why am I saying that.

Mike: You feel it's perhaps a little bit Big Brother state?

Angela: Yes.

RS: Would it make a difference to you who is watching the camera then? Is that an issue?

Angela: I suppose that's part of it, who's going to have access to it, what other purposes might it be put to, all those kind of questions, civil liberties type stuff. Though I can see that it's a deterrent for some particular kinds of violent crime and so on. Obviously, I don't want to have any more violent crime that anybody else, or threats of it. I'm just wary about all of that.

(Kennedy Avenue residents)

Freedom without security? Some concerns about private policing

In his book *Freedom*, Zygmunt Bauman argues that consumer choice (and this, he suggests, is what freedom has largely come to mean in contemporary market societies) has provided 'a space for human freedom larger than any other human society, past or present' (1988: 57). Not only does consumption offer freedom without the risks of 'elimination' (bankruptcy, job loss and so on) associated with production; it also enables individuals to exercise responsible choice without (for it is part of the function of advertising to prevent this) undermining their self-assurance. As Bauman puts it: 'The world of consumption appears to have cured freedom from … insecurity. In its consumer version, individual freedom may be exercised without sacrificing that certainty that lies at the bottom of spiritual security' (Bauman 1988: 57).

In the face of the competing demands now made on the police, and their apparent inability to deliver the service that 'consumers' want, it is becoming increasingly plausible to imagine a policing future in which individuals and even entire communities 'exit' (to borrow Hirschman's (1970) term) from public provision and resort to the market in an effort to secure the patrolling presence they desire (see further, Jones and Newburn 1998; Loader 1999). How, though, do Macclesfield and Prestbury residents respond to this prospect? What do they make of the choices that might be available to them in the coming period? Will commercially provided patrols satisfy their demands for protection?[7]

While our respondents commonly voiced the view that the situation in Macclesfield was 'not that bad' (Women's Institute member, Prestbury) or 'had not reached that stage yet' (male resident, Kennedy Avenue), some did imagine thresholds beyond which such options might become attractive. A man in one of our Kennedy Avenue focus groups believed such a point might already have been reached in the inner-city ('where you are in fear of going out of your house'), while others believed that a continued shortfall in police funding might force them to act. These Prestbury home watch coordinators were confident that, in such circumstances, the 'village' would be able to extract from the market a quality service:

Colin: If they [the police] continue to be under-resourced, then I think we're going to be driven to these security firms. I would rather have a security firm than no presence at all. At present we get very little presence where we are.

Rob: If I was in Salford I would probably say yes.

Neil: You'd get a high-class firm.

Tim: In Salford, it's mayhem there.

Neil: In Salford you buy a low-class company. We'd buy a high-class company here.

Much of the interest people expressed here surrounded the question of whether the qualities they prized in the police might be obtainable by alternative means. Some displayed enthusiasm in this regard for the provision of 'more special constables' (male resident, Moss Rose), or for what one High Street resident called 'cheaper officers' of a 'different grade' (cf. Morgan and Newburn 1997: 164–73). Others felt that while police officers had obvious advantages in terms of knowledge and experience ('authority is an important difference between being a policeman and being a private security person', as one Prestbury resident put it), these qualities might over time be acquired by others. The following exchange illustrates this well:

June: The uniform makes a difference, doesn't it?

Terry: I disagree.

Geoff: It commands respect.

Terry: I take the point about the village bobby, because then it becomes a part of the community. Now to me, it doesn't matter whether that person originated in the police force or originated somewhere else, but if they become a community figure with the same responsibilities as the police. They would do, after three or four years as a village whatever, whether you call him the village bobby or the village community officer, whatever. To me … it doesn't matter whether they come from the official police force or not, but they would do the same job in the spirit of the village bobby.

RS: So you're saying that someone who is privately employed wouldn't have the same authority?

Terry: What I'm saying is, I don't think, pick a firm, Blue Star Security Services: 'We're sending Joe Bloggs down one night, Fred Dee the next'. That's neither use nor ornament. It's got to be somebody who's built up a rapport.

(primary school parents, Prestbury)

What is striking about residents' responses to the prospect of private police patrols is that their talk never discloses the kinds of passionate enthusiasm that characterizes much of what people have to say about both the police and CCTV. This qualified support for non-police patrols (found almost exclusively among our Prestbury respondents) nevertheless raises the possibility that private policing might appeal as an act of positional consumption (Bourdieu 1984), something that individuals purchase in order to signify the social distance between them and those forced to depend upon an unresponsive, cash-strapped public service. While the police may not currently 'receive a low grading in the hierarchy of positional symbols' (Bauman 1988: 70), especially when compared with some other forms of public provision (such as care in old age), the disquiet about the increasing remoteness of police patrols documented in Chapter 6 suggests this prospect cannot be entirely ruled out.

Yet, for the most part, members of our focus groups expressed varying degrees of anger and dismay towards the idea that visible patrols might be provided by commercial operators. They do so, first, because they remain attached to the idea of *public* policing, believing that visible protection should be provided by the police and the police alone. One aspect of this amounts to an objection to paying further for what people believe they have already contributed to through general taxation, a sentiment evident in remarks such as: 'We pay enough taxes and where's the bobby on the beat?' (female manager, Zeneca) and 'You're actually encouraging the government to decrease the amount of money that's given to the police' (male clerical worker, Zeneca). A cognate theme holds that there are 'matters of principle' (female resident, Broken Cross) at stake here, with many holding the view that patrolling ought properly to be 'the duty of the police' (female resident, High Street). As one High Street resident exclaimed: 'No! You don't want bobbies like that. Why aren't the police allowed to police, that's their job, they should do that.' Some even articulated this point as a more general objection to the commodification of policing:

I'm not so sure that people should be making money out of fear. I think that's the bottom line. To me, that's the ultimate in market force. You've got a situation where people are frightened, and you get some entrepreneur charging a fiver for relieving your fear.

(male resident, Upton Priory)

A second (connected) set of worries concerned the wider (and uncertain) consequences of private patrols. Among some, these concerns revolved principally around the lack of trust they felt in the companies that (might) operate in this market, with discussants echoing a now familiar litany of allegations about low rates of pay, the employment of 'ex-crooks' and 'companies run by rough-necks' (male resident, Weston). As one security manager working at Zeneca put it: 'I think they just sort of drag whoever they can off the streets and pay them a couple of pounds an hour. If you pay peanuts you end up with monkeys.' Against this backdrop, people would seem to require some reassuring guarantees about quality before taking such a precarious step:

If it was Marks and Spencers, then I would say yes. If it was a small company it would be definitely no. I think criminals set up protection rackets. I think it's a slippery slope. The price will go up, it's a captive market, and if you don't pay you will be the one that's burgled. You can't guarantee that 100 per cent will pay. How do you know that they aren't a front. What I'm saying is, I would object strongly, because I believe the police are there for that. The only alternative, it would be something of quality, a national company of the standing of Marks and Spencers, or that type of company.

(male resident, The Villas)

Intimately bound up with the question of trust is the more nebulous feeling that a market in policing would entail some risky and potentially unpleasant consequences. The seemingly fuzzy border between non-police patrolling and 'vigilantism' attracted frequent comment here, as did the spectre of 'private armies' (male resident, Weston), and the possibility of the unscrupulous running what one publican we spoke to called 'protection rackets'. People's concern, it seems, is that private policing might unleash social problems more troubling than those it purports to deal with, an unease apparent in the remarks of two Prestbury residents about private policing 'not sounding right' and 'going against the grain'. It also, relatedly, offends against people's sense of the kind of place – street, neighbourhood, town, nation – they wish to live in, a powerful manifestation of which is the belief that private patrols are somehow 'un-English', an aspect of the 'American way of life' that 'we' ought to resist:

I would want to know a lot about them before I would consider any action like that. It's like a protection racket in a sense. I don't know whether it's a good thing at all. It's a bit unhealthy in my view, at least in England. It sounds too American to me.

(male resident, Kennedy Avenue)

We don't want to become like the 52nd state of America, because it is becoming like that. Each year you seem to get one step closer to America, we seem to be arming ourselves, we seem to be making our homes like fortresses. ... I can see it eventually where people start carrying guns, and we don't want to become like that, a nation that carries guns.

(male resident, High Street)

Macclesfield residents, then, display a marked reluctance to embrace a privatized policing future. Despite their evident dissatisfaction with the levels and visibility of public police patrols, and their worries about (especially) teenage disorder, they recoil from the prospect of exercising consumer choice in order to secure the protection they would like. We have, of course, seen that residents of Macclesfield and Prestbury are prepared – resources permitting – to resort to the market in a bid to protect their homes and property. But we find little evidence to suppose that this willingness is extended to the commercial provision of those patrol and guardianship functions traditionally attributed to the English police – this notwithstanding Bauman's (1988) claim that consumption offers freedom cured of insecurity. The dispositions documented here suggest that policing might even represent a limit case of Bauman's contentions; an example of the risks of consumption exceeding its attendant pleasures, of freedom exercised at security's expense.

This largely has to do with the low levels of trust people possess in the firms that operate in this market (something that contrasts interestingly with CCTV, where questions of trust figured less prominently in people's talk). This is no doubt a product of the weak regime of legal regulation that currently governs private security (Jones and Newburn 1996), and the (resulting) aura of murky illicitness that surrounds much of the 'protection' industry. But it also flows from the fact that private policing (like street watch and to some extent CCTV) is thought of by many residents as the kind of crime control measure that is 'out of place' in a town like Macclesfield, something they associate with other, more dangerous, inner-city locations.

Far from alleviating their anxieties and making them feel secure, people generally resist – even resent – the idea of a market in policing, with its implied suggestion that responsibility for the supervision of public space should fall upon the shoulders of individual citizens. They take issue, not merely with the 'choices' on offer, but, more profoundly, with being forced to choose at all some-thing they feel the state ought properly to provide, and for which they believe they have already paid with their taxes. People thus have to feel desperately worried about and unprotected from crime, or else – as with some of our Prestbury discussants – possess a robust consumer confidence in their capacity to enlist a 'high-class' firm, before entertaining such a prospect. The residents of

Macclesfield do not, in the main, feel either that anxious about crime, or that certain of their market position. Private patrols offer no compelling response to their demands for order.

8 Conclusions

From east Cheshire to the wider world

We have in this book been concerned to understand the place that crime occupies in the social relations of one medium-sized town in north-west England – a location that intrigued us both because it lay in that realm beyond the (inner-city) metropolis that has so rarely attracted criminological enquiry and because it has over the last several decades been experiencing economic and social changes whose effects on its residents seemed likely to include a certain quotient of crime-related uncertainties and anxieties. Our aim has been to document the worries about, and responses to, crime and disorder found among citizens of this town, and, in so doing, to contribute to a grounded sociology of public sensibilities towards crime and its control. We have therefore taken some pains to document and make sense of the ways in which people's crime-talk intersects with their sense, both of *the place* in which they live, and of *their place* within a wider world of prospects and insecurities.

But how exactly does this approach inform our understanding of that wider world? How can our efforts to discern and understand the responses to crime found among people living in just one English town connect in any significant way with the 'big' issues – to do with fear and insecurity, order and disorder, crime and its control – that trouble people at the turn of the millennium? To address these matters let us return to the imaginary sceptics we introduced in Chapter 1, for in their contrasting ways they are each concerned with some or other aspect of this broader canvas. They were, you recall, the academic, the administrator, and what we might now combine as the political adviser/citizen. They have now had a chance to read the foregoing chapters. They may even have found them of some interest. But it is unlikely that their doubts will have been completely assuaged and they must be given the opportunity to pose their questions afresh. We think they might reformulate them along the following lines:

The academic   Having always had a fondness for local colour, I found some of this quite illuminating. I have learned much about the feelings and concerns of the people of this town. But I still feel the big and significant questions lie elsewhere, and have – I repeat – to do with globalization, the emergence of a risk society, the fates of modernity. What, at a time when western crime control systems are being reconfigured in some fundamental ways, is the value of this kind of research?

The administrator

Of course there are items of interest here, but the more I read the more despondent – and irritated – I became. Not only have you abandoned measurement in favour of interpretation, you also seem no longer to have any real interest in the 'fear of crime' as I understand it. But people worry about crime. These worries can have a devastating effect on their lives. And it remains my job to assess the scale of this problem, and to develop – and sell to ministers – policies that might reduce people's fears. What can you say that will help me?

The political adviser/citizen

It is clear reading your book that questions of order, and disputes about teenage incivilities in particular, loom large in this town (nothing surprising there!). And you have convinced me that people respond to these problems in ways that are both varied and complicated. But what has all this to do with the contemporary politics of what has come to be called 'crime and disorder'. Surely, having done all this research, you have something to say that might help make our communities safer, or give us reason to believe that the future of crime control looks brighter. You do, don't you?

As we indicated at the outset, these questions are also *our* questions, and we take them very seriously. So let us, by way of summary and conclusion, try to address them. Though our answers will overlap and inform one another, we must at least begin with the academic.

Global and local responses to crime

In raising a query about the intellectual value of a detailed, local study to our times, our academic sceptic is able to draw support from a number of recent strands of research and reflection, both in social theory and from within criminology. One such strand – which we discussed at some length in Chapter 1 – focuses attention on how global flows of capital and culture (Lash and Urry 1994), or the emergence of what Manuel Castells (1996) calls 'the network society', lift social relations out of localities, stretch them out across time and space, and in so doing denude 'place' of its importance as a prime source of value, meaning and security in people's lives (see also, Giddens 1991; Bauman 1998). This, no doubt, is a powerful and in many respects cogent assessment of the fate of territorial communities in late modernity. But, as we emphasized in Chapter 1, and hope to have shown in the intervening pages, there remain significant ways in which place continues to matter to people, even, and perhaps precisely, under the global conditions that now obtain. People continue to live *somewhere*, go about much of their routine daily lives *somewhere* and – within markedly differing contexts of freedom and constraint – persist in acquiring and developing material and emotive attachments to particular places, whether that be their home, street, neighbourhood, town or nation. We also believe we have demonstrated that crime and order figure in some powerful if uneven ways in how these places are experienced, imagined and defended – but more of that later.

Our sceptic, however, is first and foremost interested, not in those experiential questions, but in the changing configurations of crime and justice and their relations to contemporary techniques of governance and regulation. S/he consequently draws attention to a further set of global developments (and theory) about which more needs to be said. Two issues in particular are considered germane here. S/he is concerned to point out, first, that we are currently living through some potentially far-reaching transformations in the philosophy, organization, policies and practices of criminal justice systems, both in Britain and throughout western liberal democracies. In the field of punishment, not only are incarceration rates on the rise internationally (Christie 1993), but – perhaps more fundamentally – there is also unfolding a 'new penology' whose focal concerns lie not with the reform of individual offenders, nor with the just allocation of retributive penalties, but in the efficient classification and supervision of risky populations (Feeley and Simon 1992). Ericson and Haggerty (1997) make some cognate observations with respect to policing, emphasizing how in a risk society police officers have become 'knowledge workers', generating and disseminating information that assists external agencies (insurance companies, health authorities and so forth) in the calculation and management of risk. Beyond the state, we are witnessing both the escalation of private policing (Shearing and Stenning 1983; Jones and Newburn 1998), and the development of cities suffused with electronic and camera surveillance systems and fortified by ever more robust hardware and sophisticated gadgetry (M. Davis 1990; Ellin 1997). And this seems but part of a process which is seeing the state relinquish its claim to be the sovereign agent of security and crime control – both 'downwards' to 'responsibilized' businesses, consumers and communities (O'Malley 1992; Garland 1996), and 'upwards' to supra-national networks and institutions (Sheptycki 1995).

Second, our sceptic says, these mutations appear to be happening with either the (active or implicit) support of 'public opinion', or in ways that by-pass such opinion altogether, rendering it redundant. Admittedly, there are aspects of these developments – such as the 'new penology' – that haven't (so far) been able to construct a coherent and saleable cultural account of themselves, as Simon and Feeley (1995) have recently acknowledged. Yet these trends are for the most part being determined by political and criminal justice elites operating in techno-bureaucratic arenas far removed from sites of public will-formation – something that has been well documented both at transnational (Anderson *et al.* 1996) and at local levels (Crawford 1997). Or else they are proceeding in alignment with the active and vocal support of a popular punitivism, which, whether for reasons of direct experience of victimization, media-inspired panic or more general anxiety stemming from the collapse of social democratic support systems, seems all too ready to countenance increased coercion and penal regulation. One only has to look at the public receptions accorded recently to 'zero tolerance' policing (Dennis 1997) and 'three strikes and you're out' (Shichor and Sechrest 1996) to realize that.

This schematic account necessarily condenses a range of attempts to grasp and explain the 'master patterns' (Cohen 1985) that are currently unfolding in criminal justice and penal systems across the late modern world, and it clearly does scant justice to what is often historically informed, closely observed and acutely theorized research (Simon 1993). No matter. This summary will suffice for present purposes, and is in no way intended to disparage or misrepresent a body of work towards which we feel much affinity and with whose main contours we have little fundamental disagreement. We do, however, believe that such work suffers from a number of shortcomings, two of which are pertinent here.

The first of these one might describe as *an insensitivity to place*, a 'weakness' that can all too easily attend attempts to map institutional and social change on a grand scale, but one nonetheless for which there is a price to be paid. In part this has to do with the relative lack of attention such an outlook evinces towards the contrasting ways in which crime and responses to it are constituted within the national political cultures and local 'structures of feeling' of different societies – something that recent (comparative) work has nicely and importantly documented (Nelken 1994; Pavarini 1997; Lacey and Zedner 1998; Ruggiero *et al.* 1998). But it also more pivotally concerns the tendency to *presume* that certain reconfigurations of criminal justice have global prevalence under late modern conditions, rather than to investigate how these mutations are received, resisted or altered in specific institutional and political settings, with all the *unevenness* that such enquiry is likely to reveal.

Our second reservation concerns the *theoretical deficit* that arises from the way in which this literature views – or, perhaps one should say, disregards – 'lay' responses to crime. This disregard either presents 'public opinion' as, in practical terms, superfluous to contemporary trends in crime control, or else depicts 'the public' merely as a reactionary force for greater punitivism and repression. Now, as we have seen, good reasons and a fair bit of evidence can be marshalled in support of both these propositions, and – in an Anglo-American context especially – it is certainly tempting to subscribe to them. Yet such a conclusion is, we think, premature, for there are various ways in which it severely limits our capacity to understand contemporary cultures of crime, justice and punishment. It tends to assign a homogeneous punitiveness to popular responses to crime that may not in fact obtain (cf. Hough 1996). It pays insufficient regard to the economic, social and cultural conditions under which particular demands for order and justice may – or may not – arise (Melossi 1994; Tyler and Boeckmann 1997; cf. Christie 1977, 1980). And it sets to one side any proper examination of how the institutional practices (and direction) of criminal justice agencies intersect with the cultural mentalities and sensibilities that infuse particular social formations at particular points in time (cf. Garland 1990; Loader 1997a).

We have thus in this book tried to put in a word for another (albeit complementary) way of making sense of crime and its regulation – one that tries to address these imbalances by investigating somewhat more strenuously certain local sensibilities towards crime, and their sources, supports and effects. We have wanted to demonstrate, in particular, that many of the conflicts that pervade contemporary debates about crime and its control – over justice and welfare, inclusion and exclusion, state and market and so forth – get played out in specific places to particular and not entirely predictable conclusions. And, in the face of some homogenizing global tendencies in societal responses to crime, we have tried to indicate the persistence of *local* resources that project alternative crime control possibilities to those that currently prevail, and which may yet contribute to making our late modern world otherwise. Let us recall, and reflect upon, two illustrations of how this might be the case.

Public (and private) policing

In Chapter 6 we documented the prevalence of disenchantment and dismay towards the drift of contemporary policing found, not so much among those sections of the population whose relations with the police have been historically tense, such as young people (although the teenagers we spoke to had their grumbles), as among those who think of themselves as recipients of police services and who display high levels of *general* support for the police. This has in large measure, we suggested, to do with the great expectations such general (and often sentimental) identification generates; and, more specifically, with an apparent police failure to take seriously people's worries and concerns (not least in respect of teenage incivilities) and provide the kind and level of service that they are deemed to warrant. The result, we found, is an often vehemently voiced desire to see the 'return' of a known and visible authority figure who can provide a semi-permanent, pastoral watch over the local community.

These demands – as much recent work in the sociology of policing has attested – run increasingly counter to the direction in which the public police appear to be headed, both nationally and globally (Sheptycki 1995; Francis *et al.* 1997). In respect of the former, they run up against the fiscal constraints placed upon the police and the priority setting this inevitably entails; and they are giving way to measures that are fast becoming accepted among police elites as the most (cost-) effective ways of allocating scarce resources, such as targeted patrolling and intelligence-led policing (Home Office 1998: ch. 6). More broadly, against the backdrop of the information-creating and disseminating policing sketched by Ericson and Haggerty (1997), such local demands for order appear increasingly to 'fall into antique mode' (Douglas 1992: 29), displaying as they do a wistful attachment to the (modern) police project of tackling crime and securing territorial order, a project Ericson and Haggerty argue is in the process of being eclipsed.

Here is not the place for a detailed assessment of these developments; nor for a full review of Ericson and Haggerty's ambitious and challenging (albeit, we suspect, somewhat overstated) thesis. What is pertinent to our concerns, however, are the ways in which the (global) developments Ericson and Haggerty highlight *jar* with the kinds of (local) sensibilities towards – and expectations of – policing documented in this book. Ericson and Haggerty, of course, are not much concerned with these tensions; the issue of how policing debates and developments are mediated through political culture falling outside of what – to use an old-fashioned term – we might call their 'problematic'. Yet this feature of their account provides a nice example of how a *theoretical* deficit with respect to public sensibilities renders one unable to grasp the *legitimation* deficits that flow from the police coming to be seen as a distant, introspective and arcane bureaucracy preoccupied with performance targets, auditing systems and the other assorted trappings of managerialism. For these deficits arise precisely out of the *relationship* between the national/global changes in policing that *are* undoubtedly unfolding, and the anger and frustration felt by those 'excluded, but attentive' publics (Atkinson and Coleman 1992) whose experiences and concerns seem to fall outside the remit of this emergent police service. The result, as we have seen, is the development of a paternalistic, almost adult–child, relationship between the police and their 'customers'. On the one hand, police managers, feeling both strapped for cash and unable to fashion a coherent, compelling account of what is really going on, and how they are really allocating their resources, continue to pay lip service to demands for more 'bobbies', and strive to manage impressions in such a way as to assuage public anxiety (we mustn't frighten the children!) and keep frustrations in check. The 'public', meanwhile, remain largely unconvinced, and worry and grumble and generally feel estranged from an institution that no longer seems to 'belong' to them or be responsive to their demands. It is as if an old, trusted friend has let them down.

Yet we have seen also that these dissatisfied customers remain reluctant to look elsewhere in search of the patrolling presence they desire. For all the burgeoning of private markets in security hardware and services, and notwithstanding Bauman's (1988) claim that consumption offers freedom cured of insecurity, we find little evidence that the privatization of the patrol and guardianship functions of the English police exercises much positive appeal (although some among our Prestbury respondents indicated that circumstances could arise that would make the consumption of private policing services plausible for them). In part this is because levels of worry about crime and disorder in Macclesfield and Prestbury are not acute enough to provoke such an unprecedented and unpredictable step. It has also to do with people's evident lack of trust in the firms who (might) operate in this market. But it arises mainly, our research suggests, from the persistent affective attachment people feel towards *the police* as a social institution, and from their sense that *public* policing is – and should be – central to the production and maintenance of local social order. Despite recent attempts to render them another 'mundane institution of government' (Reiner 1992: 270), the police continue to retain traces of a 'sacred' quality within popular sensibilities.

It seems, however, that the era of 'The Police' as providers of a universal, routine presence in the everyday life of communities is drawing to a close, and that, as the police become 'disembedded' (Giddens 1990) from local social relations, responsibility for the guardianship of urban space is rendered ever more diffuse and fragmented. Consequently, various possibilities present themselves. It may be that commercial operators come to dominate a diverse and thinly regulated market for patrolling and security services. It may be, alternatively, that the police assume a prominent role as regulators of the private security industry. Or it may be – as is currently the case in a number of English councils – that local authorities become either the purchasers of (private) policing, or the direct providers of 'community patrols' and Dutch-style 'civic guards' (I'Anson and Wiles 1995; Hauber *et al.* 1996). We clearly inhabit a moment of flux:

> Modern democratic countries like the United States, Britain and Canada have reached a watershed in the evolution of their systems of crime control and law enforcement. Future generations will look back on our era as a time when one system of policing ended and another took its place.
>
> (Bayley and Shearing 1996: 585)

Against this backdrop, it seems probable that the untutored sensibilities we have documented in this book, with their 'archaic', emotional attachment to certain residualized modes of policing, will come to be treated as irrelevant to contemporary debates, perhaps even as an impediment to 'rational' decision-making. For such sensibilities saddle the police with expectations they cannot hope to meet, create a seemingly 'insatiable' demand for their services and make it difficult to generate informed public deliberation about what the police can and cannot contribute to personal and community safety (Independent Committee 1996; Loader 1997a, 1997b). They are also, as we have seen, often deeply nostalgic, imbued with memories of a policing past that people have come to associate with cohesive, disciplined communities, a hierarchical and unquestioned generational order, and a certain – now culturally contested, less hegemonic – kind of masculine authority (Weinberger 1995: 206). Read thus, the likelihood that police elites will strive to keep such sentiments at bay – while people are 'prepared', step by step, drip by drip, for a new and very different world of plural policing (Blair 1998) – is indeed great. So too will be the smouldering resentment that any such exclusion is liable to reinforce.

Yet another possibility remains open, one that endeavours to bridge the legitimation gaps that our research has highlighted by responding to what we think can be read as the immanent democratic potential of these sensibilities towards policing. For they (also) signify rejection of the idea that respect for human safety

can be privatized, deregulated and generally placed upon the shoulders of individuals. They hold an implicit recognition that there is an 'irreducible "public
interest" in all security transactions' (Walker 1996: 65). And they communicate
support, not only for policing provision committed to the 'traditions' of pastoral
care and guardianship, but also to the value of this provision – in whatever form
it comes to be delivered – being *publicly* accountable, a sentiment that manifests
itself in people eschewing 'exit' in preference for 'voice' (Hirschman 1970). On
this basis, some of the local sensibilities we have documented in this book may
yet serve to prevent English policing in the twenty-first century from travelling
further down the path of commodification.

The local aesthetics of security

This brings us to our second example, which concerns the willingness or otherwise of Macclesfield and Prestbury residents to consume, demand or support
various kinds of crime prevention hardware and technology. Three aspects of
this issue merit brief discussion here, each of which illuminates in some way or
other our central concern – understanding how the global and the local intersect
in shaping contemporary responses to crime.

It is necessary first to concede a little ground to our academic sceptic. We *have*
in the course of this research encountered various cases – both in the field of
crime control and elsewhere – of what can best be characterized as merely local
instances of more pervasive, global trends, about which relatively little appears
to have been gained – theoretically – from seeking to understand them in relation to place. The prevalence of domestic burglar alarms across so many of
Macclesfield's middle-class neighbourhoods seems a clear case in point here
(as we have seen, alarms are a much less common sight on the town's council-
built estates). For while people were moved to grumble about the noise and
irritation occasioned by such alarms, and questioned their effectiveness given
people's apparent reluctance to respond to their activation, the most striking
aspect of our discussions concerns just how little comment, let alone controversy,
was prompted by this and other forms of individual household security. In
Macclesfield as elsewhere, it seems, the burglar alarm has acquired a banal
acceptability. It has become part of the urban furniture, melted into the background of everyday life.[1]

The same cannot so straightforwardly be said, however, of our second illustration – CCTV. In recent years, as is well known, camera surveillance of both
public places and sites of 'mass private property' such as shopping centres
(Shearing and Stenning 1983) has proliferated. This has been encouraged both
by an enthusiastic public/media reception that often appears to conceive of
CCTV as a panacea against crime (an impression fuelled by some widely publi-
cized instances in which offenders have been 'caught' on camera), and by the
provision of central government funds for which local authorities have competed
in order to launch CCTV operations. Aspects of these wider processes have
clearly been evident in our local enquiry. It *was* frequently taken as read by

people that surveillance cameras had successfully reduced crime elsewhere; and many of our respondents argued passionately that CCTV should be deployed in Macclesfield (town centre), and took a dim view of those who harboured doubts about this, especially of a civil liberties kind. Nor must we forget the intensive levels of surveillance found on Victoria Park flats, or the fact that since our research ended Macclesfield has travelled further along the road ventured down by so many British towns and cities in recent years (Fyfe and Bannister 1996; Graham *et al.* 1996), by extending cameras beyond the car parks to two other 'trouble-spots' in the town centre.

Yet we also discovered in this place, not only (at the time of our research) a lack of will among local retailers to (part) fund a wider scheme in the town centre (despite the support of the local authority and the police), but also a bundle of concerns among local people about the introduction of CCTV and what it might signify about 'their town' in general, and its 'crime problem' in particular. Much of this, we suspect, has to do with what might be termed 'a local aesthetics of security'. Two aspects of this are noteworthy here. People evinced, first, a concern that Macclesfield's appearance wasn't spoilt by the intro-duction or proliferation of crime control hardware (notably CCTV and steel shutters on shops), such that the town comes to communicate through its archi-tecture the aura of a place that is bedevilled by crime. This connects, second, with an association people made between particular kinds of responses to crime (such as CCTV) and particular kinds of places (such as, within Macclesfield, Victoria Park flats and, further afield, inner-city Manchester or Liverpool); some-thing which gives rise to a mental map on which one finds terrains – such as the residential streets of a place like Macclesfield – where CCTV is considered inap-propriate and liable to generate not so much a sense of security as feelings of disquiet and unease. Granted, these dispositions are generally of a pre-political kind, and remain unlikely to prompt people to – as one Weston resident put it – 'make any sort of fuss' in the face of CCTV's further expansion. They nonethe-less indicate the existence of local cultural sensibilities which may at the very least inject some judiciousness into what often appears as the pervasive, ill-considered and ratchet-like spread of CCTV across the British urban landscape.[2]

This brings us, third, to the case of Prestbury, discussed at some length in Chapter 5. There are numerous ways in which Prestbury – at first sight – appears merely to embody a global phenomenon that, in the US context, the late Christopher Lasch called 'the revolt of the elites' (Lasch 1995; cf. Wolfe 1998). Lasch employs this term to describe the process whereby economically and socially privileged groups exclude themselves from the public amenities and services that have hitherto connected them – however thinly – to their co-citizens within a democracy; the criminological dimension of which concerns the 'enclavization' of the wealthy behind 'gated communities' (M. Davis 1990). Certainly, we encountered much in Prestbury that might be encompassed under this rubric. Many of Prestbury's residents – fearing that they are the targets of professional burglars – do inhabit highly fortified homes. Some live behind high walls and imposing iron gates. And it was among our Prestbury respondents that we encountered, not only the story of a group of residents actively planning to install a 'private' camera surveillance system on their street, but also the least obviously concerned response to the prospect of private police patrols.

Yet we also found in Prestbury a marked reticence towards certain forms of collective security, especially those of an obtrusive kind; something, we think, that renders our account more than merely another tale of the 'paranoid rich' deploying their material resources in order to defend themselves against outsiders. Despite their often acute worries about teenage disorder in the village and its felt impact upon the quality of local life, Prestbury's residents remained steadfastly reluctant to mobilize their financial and political resources in pursuit of the kinds of protective measures (CCTV, shop shutters, 'gating' and so forth) that might have resolved this problem, or at least displaced it elsewhere. The reasons for this are fairly apparent. In part it flows from these being 'local kids', with all the difficulties this presents for a strategy of exclusion. It also helps that (more serious) 'undesirables' are already kept from Prestbury by the operation of the housing and labour markets. But it has principally to do with the fact that while such measures might make 'the community' more overtly civil and free(r) of disorder, they would do so at the cost of destroying the very thing that Prestbury's citizens are concerned to preserve – the English pastoral appearance of 'their village'.

Two related theoretical points arise from this. It demonstrates, first of all, and yet again, that there exist some obdurate cultural sensibilities that shape the kinds of things that people are willing to countenance in the name of crime control. In this case, such considerations serve to temper people's responses to disorder, with residents who exhibit a high level of what Sampson *et al.* (1997) call 'collective efficacy' opting *not* to use their economic and social capital in an effort to deliver what might easily be within their grasp. Second, it suggests a wider point about the nature of order. For while – like so many among our respondents – Prestbury's adult residents clearly and often angrily articulate a demand for order (directed in their case at both the apparent failures of the local youth club and at the absence of the 'village bobby'), the nature of their demands indicates both that 'order' is accorded different meanings within different communities and that people are prepared to act – or refrain from acting – in certain ways in an effort to create and reproduce their preferred variant of it. This, it seems to us, is a crucial point. It is best developed, however, by trying to address the misgivings of our second sceptic – the administrator.

Placing people's worries

We began this work with an interest in furthering understanding of what had come – sometimes rather unquestioningly – to be called 'fear of crime'. While we shared with others a series of dissatisfactions with the way in which the 'fear of crime debate' was constituted (not least in respect of those unhelpful terms of discussion concerning the 'rationality' or otherwise of people's fears) we were nonetheless concerned to account for the apparent (and certainly oft-noted) 'mismatch' between people's expressed levels of worry about crime and their antecedent levels of 'objective' risk. Yet the longer this project has gone on, and the more we have reflected on the issues raised, the more we have become convinced of the following conclusion: traditions of research that treat 'fear of crime' as a separate and discrete object of social enquiry and policy intervention are exhausted.[3]

This may seem a touch bold, so let us be clear. Plainly, we are not seeking to deny that people worry about crimes and incivilities of various kinds; we have seen that among a good number of our respondents such worries are both intensely felt and capable of taking their toll upon the quality of life. Nor do we wish to neglect entirely the connections that exist between levels of anxiety and those of measurable risk. We *do* want to insist, however, that people's worries and talk about crime are rarely merely a reflection of behavioural change and 'objective' risk (though they represent lay attempts to make sense of such changes and risks), but are also 'bound up in a context of meaning and significance, involving the use of metaphors and narratives about social change' (Sparks 1992b: 131). We have sought in the foregoing pages to demonstrate this by providing a grounded sociological account of how crime works in everyday life as a cultural theme and token of political exchange; of how it serves to condense, and make intelligible, a variety of more difficult-to-grasp troubles and insecurities – something that tends to blur the boundary between worries about crime and other kinds of anxiety and concern. We have attempted to show that in speaking of crime people routinely register its entanglement with other aspects of economic, social and moral life; attribute responsibility and blame; demand accountability and justice, and draw lines of affiliation and distance between 'us' and various categories of 'them'. In short, we have been arguing that 'fear of crime' research is at its most illuminating when it addresses the various sources of in/security that pervade people's lives (and the relationship between them), and when it makes explicit (rather than suppresses) the connections the 'crime-related' anxieties of citizens have with social conflict and division, social justice and solidarity.[4]

In developing and refining this perspective, our more particular concern has been to pursue the idea that people's everyday talk about crime and order (its intensity, the vocabularies used, the imagery mobilized, the associations that are made) both depends upon, and helps to constitute, their sense of place; that it takes the form of stories and anecdotes that fold together elements of personal biography, community career, and perceptions of national change and decline. This, in turn, has enabled us to disclose some of the *specific* kinds of entanglement that are acknowledged, and the *specific* sorts of blaming and boundary-drawing that are engaged in, by the *variously situated* citizens of Macclesfield and Prestbury; and thus to formulate a more nuanced analysis of the objects and felt significance of people's worries, and the kinds of demands and actions they give rise to. Let us consider each of these matters a little further.

'Thick' and 'thin' disorder

We noted earlier (in Chapters 3 to 5) that property crime and teenage incivilities tend to loom largest in the crime-talk of Macclesfield and Prestbury's adult residents (it was principally among Macclesfield's young that crimes of violence surfaced as a concern). If there was one feature of such talk that united the majority of the adults then worries about youth was it. But it also remains the case that the residents of Macclesfield and Prestbury respond to teenage incivilities with *varying* degrees of concern and intensity. We found that people living, not merely in the same town, but in the same street and (even) adjacent houses, can draw very different conclusions from, and attach distinct kinds and levels of significance to, the appearance of the same group of 'problem youths'; and these responses cannot simply be read off from people's levels of 'objective' risk, or their direct or indirect experiences of victimization. The type of identification that individuals make with 'fear of crime discourse' (Hollway and Jefferson 1997) depends also on their place within prevailing social hierarchies and their ensuing relationship to a particular geographical community: to how much time they spend there, the kinds of affective and financial investments they have in it, the strength of their social networks, whether or not they have children, how long ago they arrived, and the extent that they feel able – should the need arise – to up and leave. Teenage disorder, in short, does not impact uniformly on people's lives; nor does it invoke a blanket response. Individuals (and whole communities) remain differently positioned with respect to the gathering of 'disorderly' youths, and vary markedly in how they make sense of and handle the problems such youths appear to cause.[5]

In some instances (and this was most pronounced among some of our professional, middle-class respondents), such disorder seems disconnected from other important and valued aspects of people's lives. This generally occurs where a community of place is neither the only nor the most significant repository of meaning and security for people; where their principal sources of loyalty, support and identification lie beyond the immediate neighbourhood. It is a situation where individuals have a relatively light attachment to the place where they happen to reside (having a short history and, in all probability, little future in it). These are people – those perhaps who Bauman (1998: 92–3) describes as 'tourists' of the global age – whose place in the wider world affords (or forces upon them) a high degree of geographical mobility and a corresponding cosmopolitanism of outlook; both things that enable them to distance themselves, materially and emotionally, from the stresses and troubles that afflict the neighbourhood in which they live, but do not in any deep-rooted sense regard as 'home'. All in all, this adds up to what we might term 'thin' disorder.

'Thick' disorder, by contrast, describes a situation where the 'problem of youth' acquires a heightened material and metaphorical force by being embedded in a web of local ties and affiliations. This we have seen occur in two very different situations. It arises first where people acquire high levels of emotional attachment to their community of place, either because long-standing residence has served to deeply entwine their personal biography with that of their locality (such as in Moss Rose, or among some of our High Street respondents), or because people have come to see their chosen place of residence as the source of great value and meaning in their lives (as we have shown to be the case for many citizens of Prestbury). Second, but conversely, teenage disorder can acquire 'thickness' in situations where people feel either socially or spatially fixed 'in their place', an experience, Bauman (1998: 9) suggests, whose debilitating effects are intensified in a world where, 'mobility has become the most powerful and coveted stratifying factor; the stuff of which the new, increasingly worldwide, social, political, economic and cultural hierarchies are daily built and rebuilt'. For these people ('locals' cast adrift in a global world), the appearance of a group of youths on the neighbourhood streets can be rich indeed in social meaning; serving as a powerful signifier of either all that has 'gone wrong' in one's own life (recall the example of the 'battle-weary' shopkeepers discussed in Chapter 4), or of the daily erosion of the order, civility and respectability that many of our (older) respondents have come to associate with the 'local community'. 'Thick' disorder is all too often disorder as the last straw.

Engulfment, banishment, inclusion

We have demonstrated during the course of this book that a marked level of unevenness can be discerned across Macclesfield with regard to the kinds of order people desire (or wish to preserve, or recreate), and the activities and measures they are prepared to engage in, or lend their support to, in an effort to bring such order about. We earlier remarked on aspects of this in respect of Prestbury, but let us now press the matter a little further. The demand for order is rarely all-of-a-piece. Rather, a diversity of legitimate orders are embedded in people's crime-talk, each of which connects in different ways with considerations of place, the respective obligations of state and citizen, the appropriateness and anticipated efficacy of local and national interventions, and the question of how best to understand and deal with those deemed in breach of the expected requirements of lawfulness, respect and civility.

The first point to recall here is that much of people's crime-talk – as we saw in Chapter 4 – takes the form of rather 'placeless' accounts that make explanatory reference, not so much to the immediate locality, or even to the town or region, but to the 'condition of England' and the wider world. Youth crime, in particular, appeared to prompt discourse (sometimes of an abstract kind, sometimes comprising local instances of such abstractions) concerning such matters as the state of the family, joblessness, the erosion of standards and discipline, the dearth of respect for authority and so forth. Though people would frequently argue about the effects and relative importance of these various economic, social and cultural shifts, there is clearly a shared recognition here that the instances of teenage crime and incivility from which 'our town' no longer seems exempt possess causes and consequences that stretch far beyond the boundaries of Macclesfield, and demand actions and policies that must be formulated and put to work on a broader stage. This is undoubtedly so – there are no *purely* local solutions to the problem of order. But this recognition also seems to bring with it a sense of what Giddens (1991) calls 'engulfment', a term he uses to describe situations where 'an individual feels overwhelmed by a sense of powerlessness in the major domains of his phenomenal world' and 'dominated by encroaching forces from the outside, which he is unable to resist or transcend' (1991: 193). This, we suggest, may account for the punitive and exclusionary forms that this abstracted talk generally takes – forms that resonate closely with, and borrow a great deal of vocabulary from, the 'tough on crime' stances that prevail in much contemporary media and political discourse on 'law and order'. For the realization that the crime question is something pervasive in, and endemic to, English society as such can both undermine any sense people have that these matters are susceptible to effective action taken locally, and accentuate their investment in the need for 'firm' measures at the larger (national) level. Once couched in these terms, nothing else seems to fit the bill.

This is not to say, however, that people's belief in the availability of local resources of security is entirely exhausted; nor is it to argue that a focus on 'the local' necessarily generates responses that are any less punitive in substance or tone. Often, this is simply not the case. Perhaps the most striking illustration of this we have chosen not to write about in these pages, but have discussed at length elsewhere (Girling *et al.* 1998). It concerns the very public detention and subsequent humiliation of a suspected teenage car thief by a group of 'vigilantes' on the Weston estate in June 1993; an episode we sought to account for precisely in terms of people (whose ex-council houses are proving difficult to sell, thus closing down the option of 'flight') mobilizing locally to defend the fragile respectability of their estate from what they saw as the 'out of control' activities of local youths. It is not necessary to elaborate here on either the details of this incident, or on its subsequent appearance in the local (and national) press and the town's 'crime-talk', save to report the evident willingness of many of our respondents to condone (or at least sympathize with) the actions of the vigilantes, and to take it as read that they 'got' the right person. This event does, however, offer a stark reminder (whose lessons cannot easily be shirked), not only of people's capacity, given a certain mix of circumstances, to act locally to preserve the kind of order they desire (and to generate a fair measure of support for doing so); but also, more importantly, of the potential of such actions to buttress an 'order' that banishes those (with violence if necessary) who are deemed to undermine it. There can be few better illustrations of Adam Crawford's claim that:

> Given both the anxieties that crime evokes, and its tendency to bifurcate the criminal from the law abiding, and the 'rough' from the 'respectable', crime may well be the worst social issue around which to construct open, tolerant, and inclusive communities.
>
> (Crawford 1997: 274)

Yet it remains possible to envisage circumstances where a focus on 'the local' prompts demands that are more inclusionary and reintegrative in emphasis and not first and foremost oriented towards criminal justice responses; something that suggests we should qualify Crawford's otherwise sage assessment of the dynamics and prospects of a local politics of crime. We have seen that when residents recognize that the youths hanging around the streets are local kids, and speak about them as such (recall the public meeting – discussed in Chapter 4 – that took place on the very same estate as the vigilante incident), their demands are not simply for 'tough', exclusionary measures that might deepen local cleavages and amplify extant tensions, but that the (unruly) young are reintegrated into 'the community' under the protective, unbending wing of adult rules and prescriptions. It may be (as the youth workers we spoke to suspect) that the kind of 'community' this entails (and the conditions set for young people's admission to it) is untenable, offering little basis from which to establish new forms of intergenerational trust within localities. But such a response at least lends some support to an oft-repeated criminological claim (most famously outlined by Nils Christie (1977) and subsequently developed in work on mediation and family group conferences (Smith *et al.* 1988; Braithwaite and Mugford 1994)) that is all too often effaced in the punitive scripts of dominant media discourse and political rhetoric on youth crime: namely, that people respond in more modulated and complex ways to events and issues in which they are personally implicated than to those of which they are more abstractly aware.

We find then within the sensibilities of citizens living in this single English town an assortment of ways of apprehending and seeking to address the crime question, each of which can be interpreted as 'projecting' a distinct vision of order, a particular conception of what is required (by whom) to bring it about, and a preferred means of responding to those who might threaten it. It is with this in mind that we turn to the question posed by our final sceptic – the political adviser/citizen – who asks: how does your work speak to the contemporary politics of 'crime and disorder'?

The politics of order and the futures of crime control

At the end of the nineteenth century, in his lectures on *Professional Ethics and Civic Morals*, Emile Durkheim proffered the following observation:

> The role of the State is not to express and sum up the unreflective thought of the mass of the people but to superimpose on this unreflective thought a more considered thought, which therefore cannot be other than different. It is and must be a centre of new and original representations which ought to put the society in a position to conduct itself with greater intelligence than when it is swayed merely by the vague sentiments working on it.
>
> (Durkheim 1992 [1957]: 92)

Today, more than a century on, these remarks seem particularly germane. We inhabit times – not least when it comes to questions of crime and justice – where editorialists, pundits and politicians routinely appear to reflect 'the unreflective thought of the mass of the people'. Much of what is said and done under the banner of 'law and order' politics – the campaigning, the drawing-up of manifestos, the formation of policy, the enacting of legislation – purports to respond to the impassioned and untutored sentiments of the voting public. The ability so to do has seemed a prerequisite of success in British politics since at least the mid-1970s, and was certainly a pronounced feature of the Conservative Party's electoral triumphs of the 1980s and early 1990s (Hall *et al.* 1978; Brake and Hale 1992). New Labour's subsequent return to power in 1997 seemed due at least in part to its success in persuading the voters of 'Middle England' – those, perhaps, whose voices have appeared in this book – that it was no longer 'soft on crime', that it understood their anxieties and aspirations *vis-à-vis* 'crime and disorder'.

There is, of course, much in respect of this that is not merely politically prudent, but also politically responsible. There are good reasons why what, in another context, John Keane (1996: 50) has called 'the politics of civility' should preoccupy political attention. The question of how to create urban spaces that *all* citizens are able to use, free of intimidation and harassment, is indeed an urgent one. Yet there remains something troublingly reductive about much party political and media discourse about crime. In part this has to do with the tendency of contemporary politics to translate the questions of in/security that attend living in a global risk society into 'the apparently straightforward issue of "law and order"' (Bauman 1998: 5). But it also arises from the prevailing assumption that 'public opinion' on crime is deeply and ineluctably punitive in outlook and disposition. We regard this notion as unhelpfully sweeping and dismissive. Our enquiries in one small corner of 'Middle England' indicate, we believe, the existence of a more unfinished, complicated and open set of responses to the problem of order than is allowed for in the dominant scripts of media and political discourse. They also suggest the possibility of a politics of crime control that strives to respond in alternative ways to public concerns and sensibilities. So let us conclude by setting out – in a necessarily brief and schematic fashion – two possible scenarios. We think they can both claim some kind of resonance (albeit perhaps of differing strengths) with the sensibilities documented in this book. But they anticipate *very* different futures.[6]

There is no doubt that we have encountered much in this study that seems to lend support to the criminal justice-centred, 'tough on crime' stances that have largely constituted the politics of 'law and order' in recent decades. Even in a town such as Macclesfield, which enjoys a moderate level of prosperity, and relatively modest crime rates, the citizens we spoke to evinced both some pressing concerns about the impact of crime and – especially – disorder on the quality of life, and expressed some often emotionally charged demands for 'something to be done' to protect 'us' from 'them'. Such sensibilities can shape the politics of crime in a number of ways. On the one hand, they operate as a constraint both on those political actors who wish to find a more humane, parsimonious place for criminal justice within the gamut of institutions and policies that contribute to safer societies; and on progressive practitioners and administrators who, faced with resource constraints and aware of the limits of what they can achieve, can thus become sorely tempted to proceed (as we have seen in respect of the police) by shielding their activities from the glare of disapproving public scrutiny. On the other hand, these sensibilities offer a seemingly deep and guaranteed reservoir of support for politicians (especially at the national level where, Scheingold (1991) suggests, crowd-pleasing, symbolic gestures are more easily made) who wish to build a future characterized by such things as: 'three strikes and you're out!', 'boot camps' and the associated ingredients of penal expansion; the proliferation of gates, bars, surveillance cameras and the cognate technologies of a 'fortress society'; two-tier policing which couples private residential patrols for some with 'zero tolerance' crackdowns on others; and, to be sure, the continued – and anxiety-*reinforcing* – display of the criminal justice spectacle across the increasingly diverse outlets of the mass (or, better, niche) media. This is a future where social conflicts and divisions are dealt with by segregation and exclusion, and where only security hardware and the punitive interventions of criminal justice stand between anxious citizens and the dangerous Other.[7] It is hardly a recipe for a safe, cohesive or just society. Yet it remains the future projected by both the dominant motifs of our respondents' crime-talk and by much of the popular culture and politics of crime found within contemporary English society. To the insecure and fretful members of the risk society, it may even seem like a coherent, plausible and attractive outcome.

This isn't, in our view, however the only story that can be compellingly told, nor the only future that can be envisaged or built. For not only have we found among the citizens of Macclesfield and Prestbury a decided ambivalence about certain aspects of this, perhaps the most currently embedded of our two scenarios (such as the blanket deployment of CCTV, or the advent of private policing). But these public sensibilities can also be read as 'projecting' a preference for the meaningful and effective exercise of 'voice' (Hirschman 1970) in relation to criminal justice institutions, and for finding more inclusive, participative means of handling the conflicts (notably those between generations over the use of public space) that bedevil local social relations. They suggest that the prospect of building institutions which enable all citizens to articulate their experiences and concerns *vis-à-vis* crime and justice, and allow for democratic deliberation over community tensions and disputes, remains an immanent rather than utopian one.[8] And they provide reason to think that there is continued political and cultural mileage in seeking to respond to citizens' demands for order in ways that connect with – and speak the language of – equity and social justice. It is not entirely wishful to suggest that this future too remains open for us.

Clearly, there are dangers in travelling down this path. As authors such as Crawford (1997) and Jordan and Arnold (1995) have – with varying degrees of sympathy – pointed out, and as our vigilante example tellingly makes clear, public participation in crime control can take some discriminatory and repressive forms. Yet if the punitive passions (and actions) of citizens are – as we think in part they are – the impotent cries of spectators watching dramas in which they play little part, and for whose outcomes they exercise no responsibility, then keeping such sentiments 'in the shadows' (Durkheim 1992 [1957]: 87) also has its costs. It leaves the (impassioned) demands of citizens undiscussed and unchallenged and does nothing to make good the legitimation deficits suffered by institutions from whose actions attentive, concerned citizens have been excluded. There are – as ever now – no guarantees. Here as elsewhere in contemporary politics we must strive to 'strike an effective balance between opportunity and risk' (Giddens and Pierson 1998: 193). But it is our judgement that an informed, tolerant and inclusive politics of order – 'a greater intelligence', as Durkheim would have it – remains most likely to emerge from a public sphere (supplemented though it must be with protections for 'unpopular' minorities, see Loader 1996: ch. 7; Crawford 1997: ch. 7) that enables citizens to deliberate upon – and search for ways of resolving – the kinds of troubles and conflicts that we have documented in this book. Among the primary challenges now facing criminological thinking, therefore, is that of reconsidering the relations between criminal justice and democratic politics in ways that are institutionally plausible under contemporary conditions.

In the closing stanza of the *Four Quartets* T.S. Eliot observes that the end of exploration is 'to arrive where we started/ And know the place for the first time'. Among the things that we rediscovered in Macclesfield is that every criminological topic, however apparently mundane, is intrinsically political. The antique dilemma between liberty and security arises afresh for each time and in each place that we encounter it.

Glossary of place-names

This glossary lists the various places in both Britain and abroad that were mentioned during our interviews and focus groups. Each entry details the geographical location of the place concerned (where necessary), followed by a summary of the ways it was deployed in discussion.

Alderley Edge prosperous commuter town lying some 6 miles north-west of Macclesfield. *Cited as* a target for travelling criminals; a place whose residents shop in Macclesfield.

Argentina *cited as* a nation whose football stadia resemble Victoria Park flats.

Bedfordshire county in south-east England. *Cited as* a place with a 'lot of foreigners' compared to Macclesfield.

Beirut *cited as* a city resembling Victoria Park flats.

Birmingham England's second largest city lying some 80 miles south of Macclesfield. *Cited as* site of clubbing for Macclesfield's older teenagers and young people; the home of 'pedlars' who sell their (unwanted) wares in Prestbury.

Bollington village on the north-east outskirts of Macclesfield. *Cited as* a place – like Prestbury – with a separate identity from Macclesfield.

Cheadle Hulme prosperous suburb on the southern edges of Greater Manchester. *Cited as* 'rich' in contrast to Macclesfield.

Congleton Cheshire town lying some 8 miles south of Macclesfield. *Cited as* a place whose residents shop in Macclesfield.

Didsbury south Manchester commuter suburb. *Cited as* a place of higher crime risk – and insurance premiums – than Macclesfield.

Disley village lying some 10 miles north of Macclesfield (on the fringes of the police division). *Cited as* a target for travelling criminals.

Esher affluent town in Surrey, south-east England. *Cited as* a place like Prestbury, in the scope and seriousness of its crime problem as in other things.

Fort Knox *cited as* the place children alleged that one Prestbury parent had turned their home into.

Gawsworth village on the southern fringes of Macclesfield. *Cited as* a target for travelling criminals.

Germany *cited as* a nation with more receptive ('continental') attitudes to ID cards, CCTV and the like than England.

Harrogate prosperous town in Yorkshire. *Cited as* the former place of residence for one teenager.

Henley affluent town in Buckinghamshire, south-east England. *Cited as* a place with crime problems akin in scope and seriousness to those of Prestbury.

Holmes Chapel prosperous Cheshire town lying 10 miles south-west of Macclesfield. *Cited as* a motorway access point for Macclesfield's travelling criminals.

Knutsford prosperous Cheshire town lying 10 miles west of Macclesfield. *Cited as* home to those who sell drugs to Prestbury's teenagers; a motorway access point for Macclesfield's travelling criminals.

Langley village on the eastern fringes of Macclesfield. *Cited as* a target for travelling criminals.

Liverpool city some 40 miles north-west of Macclesfield. *Cited as* home of travelling criminals and 'pedlars' who sell their (unwanted) wares in Prestbury; site of abduction of James Bulger in 1993 (captured on CCTV).

Macclesfield *cited as* home 'to a certain extent' to Prestbury's travelling criminals.

Manchester Macclesfield's nearest metropolitan conurbation lying some 15 miles to the north. *Cited as* home of travelling criminals; the most immediate place of origin for Macclesfield and Prestbury's drugs; a place with crime problems five years ahead of those found in Macclesfield; a city with a high ethnic minority population; site of clubbing for Macclesfield's older teenagers and young people.

Midlands industrial region of central England (encompassing cities such as Birmingham, Wolverhampton and Nottingham). *Cited as* a region with a high ethnic minority population; the home of Macclesfield's travelling criminals.

Moss Side deprived area of inner-city Manchester. *Cited as* most immediate place of origin for Macclesfield and Prestbury's drugs (Prestbury described as an 'upper-class Moss Side'); a landscape of fear – full of shutters; a worse estate than any in Macclesfield; more violent than Macclesfield town centre.

New York City *cited as* a place of random violence – felt by one teenager to be akin in this respect to Macclesfield; the former place of residence of one Prestbury teenager.

Nottingham city in the east Midlands some 60 miles south-east of Macclesfield. *Cited as* the home of 'pedlars' who sell their (unwanted) wares in Prestbury.

Oxford *cited as* the place where the son of one Broken Cross woman attends university.

Potteries area around Stoke-on-Trent eponymously renowned for its pottery industry. *Cited as* having a separate identity from Macclesfield.

Poynton small town lying some 6 miles north of Macclesfield. *Cited as* a target for travelling criminals; a place which attracts (some) extra police resources on Friday and Saturday nights.

Prestbury   *cited as* home – viewed from Macclesfield – of drugs and 'serious' criminals; a place whose residents shop in Macclesfield.

Salford   city within Manchester. *Cited as* a location of high crime rates and drugs ('den of thieves', 'mayhem'); worse than any of Macclesfield's estates; home to Macclesfield and Prestbury's travelling criminals; a place where one would need private police protection.

Singapore   *cited as* the previous place of residence of one Macclesfield resident; a nation that has housing properly fortified and designed against crime.

Spaghetti Junction   colloquial name for Britain's largest motorway interchange (on the M6 in the Midlands). *Cited as* aesthetically similar to Victoria Park flats.

Stockport   satellite town on the south-eastern edges of Greater Manchester some 10 miles north of Macclesfield. *Cited as* most immediate place of origin for Macclesfield and Prestbury's drugs; a place with high ethnic minority population; more violent than Macclesfield town centre; site of nights out for Macclesfield's younger teenagers.

Stoke   city lying some 20 miles south of Macclesfield. *Cited as* site of clubbing for Macclesfield's older teenagers and young people; the home of Macclesfield's shoplifters.

Sutton   village on the eastern fringes of Macclesfield. *Cited as* a target for travelling criminals.

Toxteth   deprived area of inner-city Liverpool (also known as 'Liverpool Eight'). *Cited as* a high-crime area. A place (unlike Macclesfield) where street watch would be needed/appropriate.

USA   *cited as* direction in which England and thus Macclesfield is headed, in crime as in other things; an approved source of crime control innovation (curfews); a nation replete with 'un-English' things such as guns, private police and 'fortress' homes and cities.

Warrington   town in north-west Cheshire some 20 miles from Macclesfield. *Cited as* a place for shopping on Macclesfield's 'doorstep'.

Watford Gap   service station on the M1 motorway in Northamptonshire; has served since at least the 1980s as a symbolic marker of the 'North–South divide'. *Cited* in this context.

Wilmslow   prosperous commuter town lying some 8 miles north-west of Macclesfield. *Cited as* having a separate identity from Macclesfield; 'rich' in contrast to Macclesfield; a target for travelling criminals; a declining shopping area; a place whose residents shop in Macclesfield.

Wolverhampton   old industrial city in the Midlands lying some 50 miles south of Macclesfield. *Cited as* site of clubbing for Macclesfield's older teenagers and young people.

Wythenshawe   large council-built estate in south Manchester. *Cited as* the most immediate place of origin for Macclesfield and Prestbury's drugs; home of Macclesfield's travelling criminals.

Notes

Preface and acknowledgements

1 Perhaps it is the cultural fate of towns such as this – in a global age – to become the butt of the metropolitan sneer. Compare this gem, which rounded off a report of the visit by (recently twice relegated) Manchester City football club to (recently twice promoted) Macclesfield Town for a Second Division 'derby': 'It was wet, it was cold, it was Macclesfield, but Manchester City survived with their ego intact' (*Independent on Sunday*, 13 Sept. 1998). City had won the game 1–0.

1 Speaking of crime

1 The term 'Middle England' has become, more or less concurrently with the life-span of our research, a routine trope of journalism and the object of competition between the main British political parties in their claims to represent its values and aspirations. The genealogy of this term remains to be written. However, it is worth noting that it is a usage that expressly conjures its analogue 'Middle America'. The latter term has been regarded by US political scientists since the late 1960s as connoting *both* a certain level of material affluence *and* a characteristic 'cluster of fears'. On the invention of 'Middle America' see variously Hunter (1987), Ehrenreich (1990) and, polemically, Galbraith (1993); a more systematic sociological treatment can be found in Gans (1988). We thus deploy the term 'Middle England' with a hefty dose of ironic caution and, notwithstanding its presence in the book's title, it possesses no great analytical value in what follows. This must especially be so in the present case given that Macclesfield also uneasily cross-cuts that other ideational division of the English social landscape, 'the North–South divide' (see Shields 1991: ch. 4).

2 It also seems to us that a research enterprise like the one we have undertaken incurs obligations to its participants that are even more immediate than those it owes its other potential readers – and neither should have to fight their way through a thicket of impenetrable 'shop' language in order to discover what we are saying to or about them. To have done work of our sort is also to have been somewhere and with particular people, and there are debts of courtesy and hospitality that flow from that. It is, moreover, one condition of adequacy in this kind of work (if only one) that those whose perspectives we report and discuss here should be able to recognize the timbre of their own voices somewhere in these pages, even while the burden of interpretation lies inescapably with us.

3 In principle the term 'discourse' means little more than 'connected speech'. It is a term that attracts much technical discussion and many usages, of varying degrees of precision. For now it is worth remembering that discourse derives from the Latin *discurrere* meaning 'to run around'.

4   We should make it clear at this juncture that our concerns in this book lie (in the main) with those mentalities and sensibilities towards crime that are disclosed in the course of people's *public* talk. Though we conducted a small number of biographical interviews oriented towards eliciting how crime and 'the town' figured in the trajectory of people's lives (interviews in which aspects of those lives that might not have been divulged in a collective setting were sometimes disclosed to us), the bulk of our interviewing effort comprised group discussions with people occupying different 'positions' in the social relations of Macclesfield and Prestbury (see methods discussion for details). This of course has its limitations (as will become apparent as the book unfolds, our chosen methods tended to generate deliberation upon a relatively narrow range of 'conventional' crimes). It struck us, however, that this was a price worth paying in order to pursue a line of enquiry that has been largely neglected in the 'fear of crime' literature (but see, Sasson 1995). It is also worth noting here that our extension of this literature lies in trying to grasp the meanings and contours of the things that people say when they talk about crime, and of the kinds of controversies that arise in such discussions.

5   While Giddens asserts that place has become 'phantasmagoric' (1991: 147), he nonetheless concedes that localities continue to matter, albeit in a transformed, distinctively late modern way:

> Everyone continues to live a local life ... yet the transformations of place, and the intrusion of distance into local activities, combined with the centrality of mediated experience, radically change what 'the world' actually is. ... Localities are thoroughly penetrated by distanciated influences, whether this is regarded as a cause for concern or simply accepted as a routine part of social life. ... No one can easily defend a secure 'local life' set off from larger social systems and organizations.
>
> (Giddens 1991: 184, 188)

6   One might note, for instance, the contentious and sweeping nature of Giddens's claim that places are 'chosen' and its apparent casualness about the dull compulsions of labour and housing markets. The latter issue in a high degree of polarization and segmentation, dynamics which recent criminology has done much to illuminate. This is quite apart from the simple underestimation of how 'local' and embedded a life many people (especially working-class people outside the 'headquarter cities' and intellectual hotbeds) continue to lead, and for whom acquiring a satellite dish is not quite the life-altering transition which sociologists sometimes appear to assume.

   Savage and Warde (1993) attribute to Wirth (1938) a classic mistake in urban sociology, namely to assume that the spread of urban living necessarily ushers in a placeless and generic 'urbanism'. It may be that some versions of current social theory (or at least those theorists of globalization whom Robertson (1995: 25) regards as 'homogenizers') are on the point of committing a similar error. On the other hand, as Robertson further argues, there is little that is 'local' now that does not involve some 'translocal' element (1995: 26).

7   Bauman argues that one of the principal social cleavages opened up by globalization is that concerning fixity and mobility – the freedom (or not) to move around. For Bauman only a limited number of fates are possible under the altered conditions of late (or post-) modernity. One either becomes a 'tourist' (a cosmopolitan moving across borders and time-zones with ease), or a 'vagabond' (uprooted, ejected, exiled, finding no secure home or welcome anywhere), or one is stuck (left behind, washed-up, unable to move). We shall have cause to return to these distinctions later in the book.

8   At the broadest level, what might it mean for the culture and practices of crime and its control to say, following Beck, that we were living in a 'risk society'? Beck gives this

no direct attention. On the other hand, his definition of environmental risks as 'inadvertent consequences of modernity present in unwelcome abundance' (1992: 26) seems deeply redolent of debates on the growth of crime, as do his remarks on the enhanced importance of 'agencies of definition' (1992: 23). So too are his propositions about 'commonalities of anxiety' (1992: 49, 52, 56, 75–6), arguably those about the 'cosmetic nature of prevention activity' (1992: 57), and about 'scapegoating' (1992: 75, *passim*), as well as those on 'the normalization of emergency powers' (1992: 80). The latter two at least (and his views on the stratification of risk positions) are topics on which he has more to learn from criminology than the reverse (cf. Hall *et al.* 1978; Hope 1997b) and where criminology has much to say on *risk* proper (and not just on 'danger'). The boldest attempt yet to follow through a Beck-inspired line of thought on crime/policing/risk regulation is in Ericson and Haggerty (1997).

9   Some readings of such notions as 'globalization', 'detraditionalization' and 'risk society' would appear, at least initially, to license a certain cosmopolitan indifference to questions of place – but this is sharply disputed (see in particular the debates collected in Featherstone *et al.* 1995). On one side stand those perspectives which, in responding to what are in equal measure some of the most exciting and dismaying aspects of 'global modernities', see place as having been more or less evacuated (as 'phantasmagoric' in Giddens's (1991) view). In some versions of this argument the global flows of capital and culture usher in a largely borderless world, and 'hollow out' not merely the nation-state but also the place-specificity of forms of everyday life. On the other are those who view 'globality' rather as a condition of '*divergent* modernization' (Robertson 1995), a process which produces not sameness but rather many new 'particularizations' (and in so doing discloses the recalcitrant survival of many kinds of difference in local culture and identity, albeit in altered and hybridized form) (Featherstone and Lash 1995). All parties see 'place' as having been decisively reconfigured in late modernity – infiltrated and transformed by economic and cultural forces that escape and exceed the traditional constraints of geographical boundaries. Recent European work in comparative criminology supports the latter interpretation and identifies pronounced differences between European countries in social anxiety and preoccupation with 'community' (Lacey and Zedner 1995, 1998), attitudes to violence and support for 'law and order' solutions (Melossi 1994), and the investment of trust in persons and institutions (Nelken 1994). For a more general account of the differing routes through modernity of European nation-states see Therborn (1995).

10 This is plainly true (albeit in a way that is not very place-reflexive) of the classic survey question 'How safe do you feel walking alone around here after dark?' As feminists (notably Stanko 1990a) have made clear this question inherently involves both a gender-specific differential risk of victimization *and* a relation to place. Conversely, the spatial imagery of crime as exterior-threat-to-place may make offences which are 'internal' *both* hard to depict as 'crime' *and yet* especially disturbing. This may contribute to the chequered and contentious histories surrounding the 'domestic' and institutional abuse of women and children. In a quite different way, it poses problems for the public understanding of some kinds of financial crime, especially those involving the computer storage of information and/or issues of intellectual property in which it is not easy for a lay person to grasp what *happened* and *where*.

11 This has been grasped more clearly in relation to crime fiction and film than news and documentary media – and detective fiction is replete with examples of stories and story-sequences whose popularity and success (in some cases over decades) is closely tied to their convincing evocation of *milieu*. This is well understood by Knight (1980), and more dimly by Sparks (1992a: 82–6, 125–30). The more general point is that almost all stories involve some sense of setting and place and that quite commonly the projection of a world (Ricoeur 1981) is as essential to story-telling as are the events of the plot (see also Genette 1982).

12 Raymond Williams's (1964) rich and suggestive phrase 'structures of feeling' cognately captures much of what we take the term 'sensibilities' to signify here, and it might have served equally well in orienting our enquiries and analyses (cf. Pred 1983; Taylor *et al.* 1996). However, given Williams's original use of the term to refer to the cultures of national social formations, and the precise uses that some commentators have argued it should have (Pickering 1997: ch. 2), we have on this occasion at least decided that the latter term more adequately conveys the situated, complex and emotionally laden character of everyday crime-talk.

13 This is not to say that such places have been entirely ignored. Following Mannheim's (1948) example, a number of recent criminological studies have ventured beyond the city, albeit not always in ways that are explicitly grounded in, or theorized in terms of, place (see Shapland and Vagg 1988; Stanko 1990b; Dingwall and Moody forthcoming; a notable US example can be found in Baumgartner 1988). There is little doubt, however, that the criminology of suburbs, small towns and rural areas remains highly and unfortunately undeveloped, as does, by extension, the criminology of the middle-classes (the obvious but specific exception of work on white-collar crime notwithstanding). This seems especially problematic in respect of public sensibilities towards crime, where our levels of interpretative understanding have advanced little beyond the speculation proffered by Jock Young in the late 1980s about the fears and outlooks of 'suburban souls' (though see, Taylor 1995).

For us, this state of affairs has had two main consequences. It has meant, first of all, confronting (methodological) challenges that don't generally arise in criminological work and about which there is little disciplinary experience or reflection. These include developing research relationships with people who are very unused to – and in some cases uncomfortable with – being the subjects of research, and who on occasions could see little value in studying crime in – relatively prosperous, trouble-free – spots like Macclesfield and (especially) Prestbury.

Our second – more significant – challenge arises from the absence within criminology of any established tradition of writing about relatively prosperous communities, and concerns how to formulate and convey an interpretatively adequate account of middle-class experiences, anxieties and opinions *vis-à-vis* crime and social order. One would think here that help would be at hand from within the wider field of sociology. For not only is there to be found there a rich – if somewhat atheoretical – tradition of British and North American 'community studies' upon which to draw (for English instances, see Stacey 1960; Strathern 1981 and the recent overview in Crow and Allen 1994; for the US, see Lynd and Lynd 1929; Gans 1967); but there has in recent years emerged a sociology of the middle classes that is much concerned with matters of place and which appears to share some of our theoretical concerns (Hoggart 1993; Butler and Savage 1995; Cloke *et al.* 1995; and for the US, Gans 1988; Ehrenreich 1990). With the notable exception of Gans, however, this latter body of work has tended to evince little interest in developing a hermeneutically sensitive (let alone empathetic) interpretation of the middle-class lifeworld; displaying a tendency to attribution and judgement that sometimes borders on the impolite and which certainly amounts to a failure of sociological imagination (a quality that is perhaps most needed and illuminating when it is hardest to exercise). All that remains to be said here is that, while the burden of interpretation properly rests with us, and while there will be aspects of what follows with which our respondents might wish to take issue, we will at least strive to do hermeneutic justice to their troubles, concerns and aspirations. It is for readers to judge whether we succeed.

14 At one time we adopted the phrase 'ethnography of anxiety' to describe our research effort (cf. Girling *et al.* 1998). We have ceased to use it (it now strikes as rather grandiose), though it indicates some of the aspirations that we entertained for this work.

15 We take these interpretative stances to attempt that 'creative reconstruction of meaning' which Thompson (1990: ch. 6) calls 'depth hermeneutics'. How informatively we have accomplished this is for readers to judge. One aspect of this which we consider to be particularly fruitful lies in the attempt to distinguish those aspects of crime-talk which are very locally specific (where crime-talk is also place-talk) from those which draw on more generic and placeless representations and vocabularies.

2 About Macclesfield

1 We are of course aware of the perils that attend the kind of – perhaps voyeuristic, potentially reductive – enterprise that follows. For in addition to raising a host of questions that are not easily resolved (who are we describing this place to, for what purpose, and with what degrees of empathy and distance?) we also risk representing Macclesfield as an authentic, aesthetically coherent, bounded entity, akin to the countless 'middletowns' that used to appear – untheorized – in the community studies that once flourished in British and North American sociology (we should have done sufficient in Chapter 1 to convince readers that this is neither our position, nor intention). We nonetheless think these risks are worth taking. Though we remain relative strangers in our chosen research setting, we have come to know its places fairly well, and we feel it important, especially in work that claims to be grounded in a sense of place, that some of that 'sense' is evoked for readers *by us*. We must be clear, however, that the account that follows describes *our* – not our respondents' – impressions of this town.

2 Following the local elections in May 1995, Macclesfield Borough Council comprised thirty-three Conservative councillors, thirteen Liberal Democrats, eleven Labour councillors and three 'Ratepayers'. The town returned three Labour and three Liberal Democrat representatives.

3 Recent years have also seen, in the environs surrounding the town, a proliferation of out-of-town shopping centres, many of which might pose a threat to the economic viability (and future) of Macclesfield's town centre. Prominent among these are the site at Handforth (some 10 miles to the north), home to the first John Lewis store to open outside of London; and the Trafford Centre (reputed to be the biggest shopping mall in Europe) which opened in October 1998, a mere 45 minutes car journey from Macclesfield on the south-western fringes of Greater Manchester.

4 So too has Macclesfield come to be dominated by that other pervasive object of contemporary urban living – the car; something that was registered in the prominent place traffic congestion was accorded when people were asked to select the 'worst thing' about Macclesfield. One notable sign of this was our respondents' fondness for remarking that Macclesfield was the only place they knew where 'they' (the Council) had 'put a by-pass through the middle of the town'; a tale whose resonance is indicated by the fact that it was told to us in relation to no less than three different roads.

5 Shortly after Upton Priory was built, one (Macclesfield-born) social commentator described the estate (though without naming it) as 'some tasteless council houses close to the boundary line' which, he thought, served to warn Prestbury of the encroaching threat posed by 'Greater Macclesfield' (Turner 1967: 31).

6 The textile industry began to contract as a major source of employment in Macclesfield in the 1960s, and this continued throughout the 1970s. In 1960 5,515 people were employed in the industry (47 per cent of total manufacturing and 26 per cent of total employment). By 1971 this number had fallen to 3,098 (24 per cent of the total manufacturing and 13 per cent of total employment). The fate of the textile industry in Macclesfield is in broad terms similar to its decline in other textile towns. However, the town still has a number of much 'leaner and meaner' textile businesses dealing mainly in artificial fibres. It is also still home to one of the largest silk

producers in the country, and locally produced silk is still sold to visitors mainly through the Heritage Centre.

7   A survey of Macclesfield Chamber of Commerce members in 1989 revealed that 78 per cent of the membership were in sectors other than manufacturing, with 40 per cent of businesses to be found in the 'professional services' sector (Jackson 1990). The largest employers in the services sector were financial services, including banking and insurance. The 1991 *Census* records that 15 per cent of Macclesfield district's economically active residents were self-employed.

8   The history of the Hurdsfield industrial estate in the east of the town provides a good example of the local authority's response to what in the immediate post-war period was a local economy in potentially deep decline. The estate was created by the Council in the 1950s (becoming fully operational in the early 1960s) and represented a conscious attempt by the County Planning Authority and Macclesfield Borough Council to diversify. After a period of initial stagnation, the site became very active and the best plots came to be taken by (what was then) ICI, Geigy, Sisis, Johnson of Hendon and the Ace Oil Company. By the late 1960s the estate was almost fully occupied. There are currently six major industrial estates and two business parks within Macclesfield Borough, three of them falling within the town itself – Lyme Green park, the aforementioned Hurdsfield estate and Tytherington business park. Located next to the residential area of Tytherington, the latter has been earmarked as a 'high quality business environment' by Macclesfield Borough Council.

9   According to a number of Zeneca directors interviewed in 1989 (Jackson 1990), Macclesfield's distinctive appeal arose from the following factors; 'clean air ensuring product purity'; proximity to the research centre of Alderley Park; availability of people with a wide range of skills, and good residential facilities that would enable the company to attract and retain high quality senior and professional staff.

10 In December 1998, as we were putting the finishing touches to this book, Zeneca announced a £41 billion merger with its Swedish rival Astra (to create AstraZeneca). The deal was reported to threaten 6,000 jobs world-wide, and a further 1,000 in Britain.

11 Zeneca helped to fund the setting up of the Macclesfield Silk Heritage Centre in 1983, and subsequently (in 1987) provided a manager for the centre on a two-year secondment. CIBA-Geigy have also provided centre managers on this basis.

12 As Philo and Kearns (1993: 3) observe: 'The self promotion of places may be operating as a subtle form of socialisation designed to convince local people, many of whom will be disadvantaged and potentially disaffected that they are important cogs in a successful community and that all sorts of "good things" are really being done on their behalf.'

13 Given this context, we were expecting to encounter a certain antipathy from among local urban managers towards the prospect of researchers carrying out a study of *crime* in the town – crime being prominent among the things capable of denting a place's image (and economic prospects). However, this never in fact materialized and, in some respects, quite the opposite reaction occurred. Our research was the subject of two news reports in the local press, both of which took it as a matter of local pride that Macclesfield had been chosen for such a study ('Town crime under the microscope', *Macclesfield Times* 5 Oct. 1995; 'Town selected for major crime study', *Macclesfield Messenger*, 6 Oct. 1995).

14 It is not our concern in this book to consider in any general sense the impact and meanings that poverty has in the midst of such proximate affluence. A number of things do, however, spring immediately to mind: (i) Macclesfield's overall economic success (and 'affluent' reputation) can clearly make it more difficult for the Council to secure funding for projects on the town's deprived estates; (ii) the local employment market, consisting as it does of predominantly high-skilled, high-tech jobs, has relatively little to offer the town's un- or semi-skilled jobless; and (iii) the national

supermarkets price items in Macclesfield in the second most expensive band (second only to the London band that is). Against this backdrop, there is clearly a danger at present that some of Macclesfield's people and places will be 'left behind' by contemporary processes of economic restructuring. As one Weston resident curtly put it: 'We're suffering because of the money people.'

15 A list of the places referred to by our respondents during our discussions appears in the Glossary, together with a brief description of their geographical location and meanings-in-use.

16 We agonized long and hard over the use of real place-names or pseudonyms in this research. As will by now have become more than apparent we have concluded that work which claims to be grounded in a sense of place cannot credibly pseudonymize place-names without special and compelling reason to do so. The same does not hold, however, for individuals and we have taken all reasonable steps to ensure that the people quoted in the book (whose names have been changed) cannot be identified.

17 This view is echoed in the experience and reflections of another Tytherington home watch coordinator:

> I've found northern people very friendly. Where we came from in Bedfordshire, unfortunately I left family behind, and we go and visit there every so often. We find that there are a lot more ... I'm not prejudiced against ethnic people, but down there there are a lot more foreigners compared to Macclesfield. When we did move up here, and my youngest son started in primary school, the question was asked of him, 'How many black children were in your class down south?' I thought that was a strange question to ask a small child. So he said 'Well about half', to which the teacher in the primary school said 'Well we've only ever had one black child here in the eighteen years that the school has been built.' That to me summed it all [up].

A local head teacher reflected on this situation thus: 'I think in some respects Macclesfield is very disadvantaged because it is very non-multicultural. Very, very typically British isn't it. Typically fairly northern as well.'

3 The common places of crime

1 For crimes of violence and sexual offences, Cheshire Police in 1995 recorded the following figures for Macclesfield's six beats: 2 murders, 1 attempted murder and 7 counts of conspiracy/threat to murder; 4 rapes and 10 indecent assaults (one of a male); 171 woundings, 10 woundings with intent to endanger life, 15 robberies, 3 counts of violent disorder and 18 public order offences.

2 The Vauxhall Conference is the foremost non-professional league in English football, of which Macclesfield Town were members in 1995. They have since been promoted and are now members of the (professional) Football League.

3 In what follows we report people's responses to being asked about crime *in Macclesfield and its constituent neighbourhoods*, a focus which tended to orient the conversations around particular kinds of offences – namely burglary, car crime and low-level nuisance and disorder. Two points are of relevance here, one methodological, the other substantive. In terms of the former, we suspect that the 'etiquette' of discussions about crime conducted between strangers, neighbours, or (workplace) acquaintances in a group setting renders certain kinds of offences (such as 'domestic' violence against women and children) difficult, if not impossible, to discuss – hence they rarely arose in our conversations. In terms of the latter, our foregrounding of 'the town' resulted in an emphasis on those offences which appear to invite comparative discussion over and

above those 'backstage' crimes whose prevalence may not be construed as depending upon questions of locality.

4   It is noteworthy here that the middle-class residents we interviewed from the area around Kennedy Avenue spoke of themselves as living in Upton Priory, a nomenclature that more usually signifies the adjacent council-built estate. 'Kennedy Avenue' is in this regard a creation of ours; it does not operate locally to describe any specific part of the town.

5   Its reality notwithstanding, it is possible to conjecture that 'travelling crime' operates within police discourse as a device for handling failure (and heading off possible criticism); a residual category into which is placed the unsolved and the unsolvable. As one police manager put it:

> Yes, burglary and car crime I would say, yes. You've got your own home-grown idiots who are into a bit. There's a big difference between your town centre burglaries and those were usually committed by your home-grown, whereas burglary in dwellings were coming in from Manchester, in particular Manchester. They were hitting us hard as they always will do at Poynton, Prestbury, and Disley to a lesser degree. *That's just a fact of life and nothing is going to change that.*

6   In 1995, Cheshire Police recorded 268 cases of shoplifting for the two beats covering the town centre.

7   During the course of our research one informant we spoke to remarked that local store detectives made a point of being alert for, and passing on information about, 'shoppers' with Liverpool accents.

8   In 1995 Cheshire Police recorded the following violent offences for the two beats covering the town centre: 43 woundings; 4 woundings with intent to endanger life; 4 robberies; 4 public order offences, and 1 case of violent disorder.

9   This is one of the few instances we came across of women talking explicitly in our focus groups about their safety as women. This is not to say that our female respondents did not have worries about male violence in public places – the oft-mentioned concern about 'avoiding pubs at closing time' has very much to do with the threat posed by drunk and potentially violent men. The relative absence of elaborated conversations about the risks of male violence may in part be due to the dynamics of group discussions involving both men and women – a situation that arose in the majority of our focus groups. However, the issue hardly arose in the interviews and (informal) conversations with women conducted by the female member of the research team. This lends some support to Stanko's (1990a and 1990b) view that women's strategies for managing safety have become such a taken-for-granted aspect of contemporary women's lives as to no longer warrant explicit discussion. The implication of Stanko's point is that women develop expertise in managing their safety *regardless* of locale and the prerequisites of such expertise may not therefore loom large in comparative discussions concerning crime and place.

10   The tapes are kept for a week and if no incidents are reported they are erased. The Borough Council has a policy of seeking to prosecute all 'recorded' offences of damage to (council) property; evidence relating to other criminal offences is passed to the police. The concierges and the police seemed acutely aware here of what they saw as the risk of residents seeking to (ab)use CCTV evidence in furtherance of their own ends, not least in respect of neighbour disputes, and both sought to prevent the system from being embroiled in such conflicts. As one senior officer put it:

> I had been very careful when the concierge system started. Like the tapes for evidence, we would not get involved in neighbour disputes and use the tapes,

unless they came to major blows and it became a serious crime. So I was very prescriptive as to how the tapes would be used in evidence and I also wanted to secure the safety of the concierge people themselves, and ensure that we didn't do anything to damage the relationship that clearly they had to build up with the community in there.

4 Youth, disorder and inter-generational conflicts

1 At the time of the research Macclesfield (and its immediate environs) could boast five general youth clubs (Bollington, Fermayne, Morton Hall, Prestbury and Upton Priory – though the latter temporarily closed during the course of the research), four areas (Weston, Moss Rose, Hurdsfield and Thornton Street) covered by detached youth workers, and three specialist youth projects (a homeless project, motor project and young mothers' group).

2 Aside from public houses, the other town centre outlets that are open in the evening and to which teenagers can gain admission are fast food restaurants. According to the manager of one such outlet:

> It's like moths round a light bulb. We have to ban some people from the store, around a dozen in five years. We've had fights in the restaurant, they defile the tables, throw milkshake around, turn on the taps in the toilet. They still hang round outside.

Among the measures the manager has taken to prevent teenagers spoiling the 'friendly family atmosphere' he is trying to create are a 'minimum bill' and a 'no loitering sign':

> They're used a lot in the US. They're not common here. I put it up when I arrived. We use it to get rid of them. Sometimes you get a group who buy one coke and sit there all night. Saturdays especially is a problem. You get twenty kids with two cokes between them and there's mums and dads and small children who can't get a seat.

Despite these problems, the manager rated fraud among his staff as a far more pressing concern, making him almost alone among our respondents in listing work-place offences at the top of his inventory of crime worries.

3 In articulating these distinctions, young people from across Macclesfield share with adult residents a tendency – noted in Chapter 3 – to portray Victoria Park flats as the town's Other; a dangerous location that is to be both ritually denigrated ('down in the flats, they've got guns down there as well') and avoided ('I wouldn't go round Victoria flats'). In young people's talk this reputation attaches mainly to the 'Flat Rats' who (unlike other groups) are widely felt to 'go round looking for trouble'. As one 17-year-old male from the Weston estate explained: 'The Weston and the Moss collide. Vicky flats, they've got a gang and they'll collide with anybody. Vicky flats, they'll tend to fight with anybody.'

4 Cheshire County Council (1996c) found 61 per cent of parents of schoolchildren in Macclesfield Borough 'agreeing' or 'strongly agreeing' with the statement: 'I worry that my own children may become involved in drugs.' Only 10 per cent of 14- to 18-year-olds expressed 'agreement' (none 'strongly agreed') with the cognate proposition: 'I worry that I may become involved with drugs.'

5 This situation less obviously applies in Hurdsfield which is generally considered to be the 'best' of the town's council-built estates (and which at the time of the research was not a location in which young people routinely congregated), and (for different

reasons) in Victoria Park, where not a single tenant has purchased their flat since the Conservative government introduced the 'Right to Buy' scheme in 1980.

6 According to the Cheshire County Council survey (1996c), 54 per cent of Macclesfield Borough respondents considered that 'family breakdown' was a 'very significant' cause of youth crime. This compared with 26 per cent for 'young people not involved in community activities', and 20 per cent for 'lack of moral teaching/no respect'. All of these are implicated in the 'social breakdown' frame which Sasson (1995) found to predominate among his respondents in Boston, Massachusetts.

7 It was on this estate, some two years earlier, that a suspected teenage car thief was apprehended, stripped and tied to a lamppost by a group of local 'vigilantes' (see, on this, Girling *et al.* 1998).

8 Although, significantly, the category of 'minority troublemaker' continued to permeate residents' talk, shifting itself onto absent Others. Residents found it difficult to entertain the idea that they might in fact be conversing with this 'minority', who only half an hour before had been the butt of their accusations. Once in the room and talking the youths became 'alright' kids; the 'troublemakers' remained elsewhere.

9 Needless to say the youth workers concerned saw matters differently; not least in respect of residents' objections to them delivering the youth service curriculum (one reported that members of his management committee had systematically removed from the walls of the youth club educational posters on 'safe sex' and drugs). One youth worker we interviewed summed up his reasons for (reluctantly) leaving his former post at the local youth club thus:

> Basically, I may as well bang my head against the wall, there was no getting through to them [the management committee]. I mean, I admire them for what they were trying to do and everything, but then they wouldn't give the young people any freedom or respect. I really feel that older people think that respect should just be given, adults basically feel that respect is their God-given right.

5 Anxieties of affluence in Prestbury village

1 This is not the first time Prestbury has had to fend off such accusations, nor its only appearance in the 'lifestyle' sections of the national press. In 1967 an article in the *Observer* 'colour supplement' described Prestbury as 'the poshest village in Britain', prompting two stout defences of the place in that June's issue of *Cheshire Life*. A further journalistic portrait of Prestbury in the 1960s can be found in Turner (1967: chs 2–3).

2 Of the thirty-five people who participated in our five focus groups with adult residents, thirteen had moved to Prestbury from London or the 'Home Counties', eight had moved from the North of England, one from the West Midlands and twelve from elsewhere in Cheshire. One retired participant listed his previous places of residence as 'Austria, Belgium and South America'.

3 This kind of imaginative geography has long been a feature of Prestbury's coverage in the 'lifestyle' press: as far back as 1963 the village was being referred to – this time by *Cheshire Life* – as 'Manchester's Sunningdale'. At one level its appeal is obvious; Prestbury's wealth connects it clearly with 'the South' (which, especially since the early 1980s, has stood for affluence in the English ideational landscape) and places it in some contrast to the less prosperous 'North'. But it may also have something to do with what Weiner (1981) calls the 'Southern metaphor' lying at the heart of partic- ular powerful notions of 'Englishness'; wherein 'the South' stands for the tradition and tranquillity of the nucleated village in contrast to the grim, industrial earthiness of 'the North'. See further on the 'North–South divide', Shields (1991: ch. 4).

4   These include: the Amenity Society, choir, Women's Institute, Conservative Party (which – like the WI – has its own noticeboard in the village), three Probus clubs (for retired *pro*fessional and *bus*iness men), tennis, squash and cricket clubs, and a host of activities organized by the Church.

5   Prestbury is, it seems, largely devoid of the division between 'real villagers' and service-class 'incomers' that has been identified in much of the sociology and anthropology of English villages (Newby 1977; Strathern 1981; Rapport 1993). This is in part due to the (historical) absence of an indigenous agricultural population that (now) feels displaced by demographic change. Prestbury has for a long time been a place of retreat, recreation and retirement rather than paid work, first for the landed gentry (those whom Mary Baker, a 79-year-old born-and-bred Prestbury resident with whom we conducted a life-history interview, fondly and deferentially remembered as 'the upper ten'); and now for the cosmopolitan middle classes, the bulk of whom occupy (or used to occupy) positions in the world of finance and business beyond Prestbury's borders. This is not to deny, however, that its residents inhabit Prestbury in different ways, or that conflicts do not arise between the various 'middle-class lifestyle strategies' identified by Cloke *et al.* (1995: 236–8), all of which can be found in contemporary Prestbury: (i) the 'local gentry'; (ii) 'village regulators' (much concerned to monitor the local planning process); (iii) those who 'move in and join in', and (iv) those who 'move in for self and show', for whom Prestbury provides an aesthetic backdrop to life centred around home and garden. We suggest below that the gathering of local teenagers in the village high street provides one such site of tension.

6   This mode of talk about the village is not new. A *Cheshire Life* piece from October 1963 describes Prestbury as having become 'more suburban and less rural', and as home to the 'vagabonds of business life', 'executives constantly on the move between factories'. The then parish vicar was quoted as saying: 'We are acquiring all the trappings of a modern town. Prestbury is becoming a dormitory village. It has changed rapidly in the last few years.'

7   Conversely, it is noticeable how conscious Prestbury residents are of the reputed dangers of Macclesfield town centre (and especially certain of its pubs) at weekends. They also more readily refer to Macclesfield's council-built estates in terms denoting danger than seems current among Macclesfield residents themselves. As one Prestbury resident put it, with an interesting slip of the tongue: 'I wouldn't wish it on my worst enemy to walk through the centre of Moss Side at nine o'clock on a Saturday, the Moss estate rather, or the Weston.'

8   Within the English popular imagination – as Raymond Williams (1973) has cogently documented – 'village', 'town' and 'city' are thought of as proper settlements, with particular sets of values attached, and part of what the fear of 'suburbanization' amounts to is that these important cultural distinctions are in some way blurred (Matlass 1994: 82). 'Suburb', for instance, evokes a different relationship to place and sense of 'home' than is suggested by the term 'village'. Among suburbanites, 'home' principally denotes 'house and garden' and is often associated with a corresponding withdrawal from surrounding public spaces, whereas in a village 'home' is more easily taken as meaning the whole place (Williams 1973: 281). While many Prestbury residents are no doubt suburban in precisely this sense, the home/ownership connotations implied by the term 'village' are central to Prestbury's imaginative appeal, not to mention its positional 'value'. For a cognate (criminological) discussion of the nearby – and even more implausible – 'village' of Hale in south Manchester, see Taylor (1995).

9   The *Parish Council Newsletter* of spring 1993 informed such parents of the dangers they are causing in the following forthright terms:

Parents leaving and collecting children at school continue to threaten the lives of their own and others' children with their careless and downright selfish parking habits. *PLEASE* take more care – better to walk a few extra yards than be responsible for injury or death.

10 In 1995, Cheshire Police recorded 228 property offences for the beat covering Prestbury, including sixty-eight domestic burglaries, thirty-one non-domestic burglaries, fifty-two thefts from vehicles, and thirteen stolen vehicles. Compared with Macclesfield, three of the town's four residential beats recorded a higher rate of domestic burglary than Prestbury (Tytherington/Hurdsfield being the highest, with ninety), while all four of the town's residential beats recorded higher levels of car crime.

11 In 1995, Cheshire Police recorded twelve incidents of criminal damage for the beat covering Prestbury. No incidents of shoplifting and no public order offences were recorded by the police in that year.

12 In April and May 1995 Prestbury residents made 124 (April) and 156 (May) calls for assistance to Macclesfield police station. It is worth noting that none of the 124 requests made in April and only six of those made in May concerned 'nuisance or suspicious youths', a relatively low figure which may have to do with the lack of residential property surrounding the area in which the teenagers tend to gather.

6 Policing and demands for order

1   This is, of course, partly a (now contested) convention of ordinary language use; but it might also, more critically, be read as revealing an expectation on the part of many that police officers should be men. As one female resident said of the police response to teenagers congregating in and around High Street: 'Sometimes they send women out. It's stupid. What use are they?'

2   That (older) Macclesfield residents speak in these ways about policing should occasion little surprise. As Pearson (1983) has perhaps most famously demonstrated, invocations of 'golden ages' of tranquillity have long permeated popular discourse about crime (see also Weinberger's (1995) interviews with retired police officers, which resonate with fond reminiscences about the lost world of foot patrols). More broadly, Lash and Urry (1994: 246–8) note how 'an appeal to the past' has become a pervasive feature of life in late modernity; while Patrick Wright (1985: 22) similarly suggests that during periods of rapid social change ('where values are in apparent disorder and where social hierarchy has lost its settled nature') people often find solace in imagined, nostalgic versions of the past.

3   We were sorely tempted to entitle this sub-section 'the young residents', not least because many of the teenagers who are party to these disputes about disorder *are* local residents. Our decision to refrain from doing so offers a brief reminder that in both adult crime-talk and media and official discourse about this issue, the term 'resident' is invariably used in ways that preclude it from signifying the young.

4   This process was nicely illustrated during a 'shop watch' meeting we observed in October 1995, the focal point of which was a presentation by a police officer of what he called 'an offender profile' of some 'long-standing shoplifters'. Having apologized for 'only having time for thirteen this time', he proceeded to show a slide of each 'offender' complete with a commentary on their physical characteristics, personality defects and *modus operandi* (this included portrayals such as 'no brainer of the first order' and 'more bent [i.e., gay] than a banana', and advice to shopkeepers only to touch a man rumoured to have hepatitis 'with rubber gloves'). The audience lapped all this up with keen interest, frequent murmurs of recognition and a collective whoop of 'Robbo!' when one notably familiar face appeared on the screen. A cognate instance of such local notoriety – that of suspected car-thief and vigilante victim Mark Cooper – is discussed in Girling *et al.* (1998).

5   Despite the weariness he sometimes displayed (not least when reflecting on police–community consultative committees) towards what he took to be unwarranted public demands for police resources, one senior officer we interviewed remarked that he nonetheless felt obliged to 'fly the flag' in certain locations across the division. He made a point, for example, of periodically sending the only 'public order van' at his disposal to Poynton (a small town some 6 miles north of Macclesfield) on Friday nights, not because he felt their late-night disorder problems justified such an allocation, but – as he put it – 'for political reasons'. The one cold Friday night that two of us spent out with the van in Poynton in February 1996 was indeed without incident.

6   This concern about the policing of young people's mis/behaviour in and around the High Street was framed by one resident in terms of what he saw as the area's (relative) inability (as compared with other more affluent parts of Macclesfield) to influence police practice:

>   I'm sure they must know [about the youths gathering]. It's what they do about it. Are they bothered? I think they're quite happy if they're contained. They don't mind them being in St George's [park] because they know where they are, that's my impression. It's when they start moving out of the area that they get worried. If they're wrecking that then they are not robbing people's houses. That's just the way I figure it. They're happier if they're in one little area, keep them there. But if that little lot went up and stood in the middle of Tytherington, outside some of these big houses, they would be there like a shot, make no mistake about it, and that annoys me.

7   In this regard, discussions about *local* crime and policing (which we in various ways prompted during our focus groups) would on occasions slide into more general, *place-less* conversations about punishment (which, to the irritation of some of our participants, we did not ask about). This latter – sometimes angrily punitive – discourse laid the blame for the crime problem squarely at the door – not of the police – but of the courts and prisons, which were viewed as treating (unknown) offenders with undue leniency (cf. Hough and Roberts 1997). As a member of our publicans' focus group put it:

>   This business of magistrates dishing out sentences. You can get five to fifteen years. I think they should make it mandatory sentences, good ones, for certain crimes. Never mind this 'We'll take into consideration.' If you commit a certain crime you get, bingo, that's it, so many years. But, like I said before, I don't think that's the answer because they go to prison and it's the life of Riley.

7 Some meanings and futures of security

1   Little is known currently about the extent to which people consume domestic security hardware or about the meanings such consumption has for them. However, important collaborative work on citizens' crime prevention behaviour is currently being carried out using data from the 1994 British Crime Survey by Tim Hope (Keele University) and Steve Lab (University of Bowling Green, Ohio) – the survey reports that 62 per cent of respondents had installed window locks, 31 per cent security lights and 18 per cent burglar alarms. A survey of the British private security industry – which includes information on the types of customers that purchase its various services – can be found in Jones and Newburn (1998: ch. 3).

2   One insurance company representative we interviewed said that his firm had for a number of years placed Macclesfield properties (and cars) in the second lowest quintile of risk, and that while discounts of between 5 and 10 per cent were offered for alarms, five-lever door and window locks, and membership of neighbourhood watch,

none of these were preconditions for insurance being offered (see, further, O'Malley 1991).

3   Though it is worth noting that 13 per cent of calls to Macclesfield police station during April and May 1995 were alarm-related; 7 per cent arose from a direct link from the premises to the station; the remaining 6 per cent from calls made by the public.

4   While Villas residents conceded that 'from the outside, to a stranger, its look[s] a secure area', they themselves felt the estate to have been badly designed, with partic-ular attention being drawn to gaps in the encircling wall, a public footpath that runs down one side of the development, and an adjacent children's play area. One resi-dent contrasted The Villas with his previous housing experience thus:

> I lived in Singapore for three years. Where we lived the planners designed it so that nobody could get at us. A very high fence, barbed wire, it was secure, it was designed. Our estate was designed by an idiot, who made places for burglars to hide.

5   Street watch was launched in 1993. According to a Home Office (1994: 12) publicity booklet, street watch members would, in consultation with the local police, 'work out specific routes and regularly walk their chosen area' in order to 'provide a visible public presence to keep an eye out for crime and to deter it'. This was originally referred to by the then Home Secretary Michael Howard as patrolling, a phrase he withdrew following objections from the police, in preference for the more elliptical 'walking with a purpose'. Since its introduction, street watch has largely remained an idea.

6   The spectre of lawlessness also haunted the (otherwise fairly sympathetic) responses our focus group discussants made to one actual vigilantism incident that occurred in Macclesfield in June 1993 (just prior to the start of our research); the forcible deten-tion and very public humiliation of a suspected teenage car thief on the Weston estate. An extended discussion of this event and its meanings can be found in Girling *et al.* (1998).

7   The extracts reported here are taken from discussions in which people were asked how they would respond to a leaflet from a company offering to patrol their street in return for a small annual payment from each resident.

8 Conclusions

1   This is not to deny that an interesting piece of 'biographical' research remains to be done on the house (and car) alarm, seeking to recover the mix of material, crimino-logical and cultural conditions that have enabled this object to become – in the short space of about twenty years – such a pervasive feature of the urban landscape, at least across 'Middle England'. Such work might also benefit from an explicitly comparative dimension, given both the seemingly lower levels of alarm consumption found on mainland Europe, and the mentalities and sensibilities that shape the cultural acceptability (or otherwise) of particular crime prevention measures in different parts of the world (see, for example, Moriyama 1995).

2   A broader comparative point might also be made here. For Britain stands almost alone in the world (although Singapore also springs to mind) in both the use it makes of CCTV for the surveillance of public spaces, and in the levels of media and lay enthusiasm this generally attracts. Even in the US – often considered the market leader in developing and deploying security technology – levels of camera surveil-lance in *public* spaces remain low, perhaps because of that country's deep cultural suspicion towards 'big government' interfering with individual freedoms. It speaks volumes about our times that in England – a nation possessed of a strand of popular

thought and feeling which has long exhibited a distrust towards the state and shown a great historical attachment to the 'rights of the free-born Englishman' (Thompson 1980; Melossi 1998) – civil liberties objections have occupied such a marginal place within the (little) public debate that has taken place over the proliferation of CCTV.

3   This remains the case, in our judgement, even once the term 'fear' is replaced – as has recently become fashionable (e.g. Hough 1995) – with such cognates as 'anxiety', 'worry' or 'concern'. While there is much to be said for deploying these more adequate terms (as we ourselves have done, interchangeably, throughout this book), and for reserving the word 'fear' to describe an individual's response to *immediate* danger (such as a tightening of the stomach), the theoretical issues at stake here demand analytical not merely terminological development. The problems that attend treating 'fear of crime' as a discrete phenomenon have no resolution in the thesaurus.

4   There is no denying that taking this on board at the level of policy is no easy task and one can see why our administrator might recoil from such conclusions and seek solace in more familiar – and politically saleable – simplicities. Yet while no quick policy prescriptions flow from this revised way of seeing, we don't think that our work invites the structurally fatalist conclusion that little can be done about crime (and people's worries about crime) this side of some wholesale social change. At the very least it says to policy-makers: abandon those rather silly (and now formulaic) utterances about people's 'irrational fears' and about 'fear of crime being a worse problem than crime itself'; stop treating 'fear of crime' as a discrete site of policy research and activity, and reposition it as but one aspect of the task of repairing damaged social relations (say, between young and old) and creating more inclusive, tolerant communities.

Among the reasons why this is likely to prove difficult is because it runs counter to what Bauman (1998) has recently diagnosed as the contemporary reduction of diffuse social uncertainties and insecurities to questions of personal safety and 'law and order', something, he suggests, that has the 'political advantage' of shifting attention away from matters governments seem powerless to do a great deal about (such as the operation and effects of global markets) towards 'one containing a lot of electoral potential' (1998: 118).

5   For these reasons we must regard those modes of analysis which posit youth in some generic way as 'metaphors of social change' (J. Davis 1990; Pearson 1994; Loader 1996: 22–9) as only partially illuminating. By alluding to the common signifying capacities possessed by the young, these perspectives can obscure the contrasting – and by no means obvious – meanings that are attached to teenage disorder within particular localities.

6   It is worth noting here that the first major piece of criminal legislation enacted by the New Labour government – the Crime and Disorder Act 1998 – to some extent cuts across the two futures we propose to outline. This seems to be a matter of conscious design. In seeking to transcend the antinomies that have long pervaded debates on crime and justice, the Act seems by turns to be for justice *and* welfare; preventative *and* punitive; to want to assist people *and* come down hard on them; to seek to exile *and* reintegrate offenders; to be potentially democratic *and* technocratic. All this provides a considerable challenge to criminological thinking that we have no intention of taking up here. It also remains an open – and intriguing – question how this uneasy synthesis will unfold in practice over the coming years.

7   For all its nuance, there are aspects of the Crime and Disorder Act which clearly possess the potential to contribute to this kind of future, not least the two measures that stand closest to the issues raised in this book: anti-social behaviour orders (ASBOs) and local child curfew schemes. The danger with these provisions is that they will channel what we have suggested are some diffuse, complex public anxieties about children's and young people's use of public places down some narrow, criminal justice path. While Home Office guidance explicitly envisages that both ASBOs and

curfews lie at the end of a process, something that kicks in only after other solutions have been tried and failed, it seems likely that *the very availability* of these options will pull the rug out from under other local preventative activity, as angry, put-upon residents demand that these novel, emotionally satisfying 'solutions', with their promise of a 'quick fix', are given a try. In certain localities it is easy to imagine a group of residents, noisily supported by the local press, building up a head of steam for these measures that it will take a brave local politician to resist.

8   Though they are seldom articulated in quite this form (and often lost in another, more familiar kind of political rhetoric about crime), there are aspects of New Labour's 'criminology' which might yet prefigure such an alternative future. We are thinking here of the potential for inclusive democratic deliberation contained within 'local community safety partnerships'; the encouraging utterances made in support of reparation and mediation schemes, and the anticipated reshaping of the youth justice system along more restorative, participatory lines (Home Office 1997).

Bibliography

Anderson, M., den Boer, M., Cullen, P., Gilmore, W., Raab, C. and Walker N. (1996) *Policing the European Union: Theory, Law and Practice*, Oxford: Oxford University Press.

Anderson, S., Kinsey, R., Loader, I. and Smith, C. (1994) *Cautionary Tales: Young People, Crime and Policing in Edinburgh*, Aldershot: Avebury.

Appadurai, A. (1996) *Modernity at Large*, Minneapolis: University of Minnesota Press.

Atkinson, M. and Coleman, W. (1992) 'Policy Networks, Policy Communities and the Problems of Governance', *Governance: An International Journal of Policy and Administration* 5, 2: 154–80.

Bagguley, P., Mark-Lawson, J., Shapiro, D., Urry, J., Walby, S. and Warde, A. (1990) *Restructuring: Place, Class and Gender*, London: Sage.

Barke, M. and Turnbull, G.M. (1992) *Meadowell: The Biography of an Estate With Problems*, Aldershot: Avebury.

Bauman, Z. (1988) *Freedom*, Buckingham: Open University Press.

Bauman, Z. (1998) *Globalization: The Human Consequences*, Cambridge: Polity.

Baumgartner, M.P. (1988) *The Moral Order of a Suburb*, New York: Oxford University Press.

Bayley, D. and Shearing, C. (1996) 'The Future of Policing', *Law and Society Review* 30, 3: 585–606.

Beck, U. (1992) *Risk Society: Towards a New Modernity*, London: Sage.

Bennett, T. (1990) *Evaluating Neighbourhood Watch*, Cambridge: Cambridge University Press.

Blair, I. (1998) 'Off-Beat Solution', *Guardian* 17 July.

Bottoms, A.E. and Wiles, P. (1986) 'Housing Tenure and Residential Community Crime Careers', in A. Reiss and M. Tonry (eds) *Communities and Crime*, Chicago: University of Chicago Press.

Bottoms, A.E. and Xanthos, P. (1989) 'A Tale of Two Estates', in D. Downes (ed.) *Crime and the City*, London: Macmillan.

Bourdieu, P. (1984) *Distinction: A Critique of the Social Judgement of Taste*, London: Routledge.

Bourgois, P. (1995) *In Search of Respect: Selling Crack in El Barrio*, Cambridge: Cambridge University Press.

Braithwaite, J. and Mugford, S. (1994) 'Conditions of Successful Reintegration Ceremonies: Dealing with Juvenile Offenders', *British Journal of Criminology* 34, 2: 139–71.

Brake, M. and Hale, C. (1992) *Public Order and Private Lives: The Politics of Law and Order*, London: Routledge.

Brown, S. (1995) 'Adult Pasts and Youthful Presents: "Community Safety", Age and the Politics of Representation', paper presented to the British Criminology Conference, Loughborough, July.

Butler, T. (1992) 'Paying the Service Charge', *Police Review* 24 July:1360–1.

Butler, T. and Savage, M. (eds) (1995) *Social Change and the Middle Classes*, London: University College London Press.

Campbell, B. (1993) *Goliath: Britain's Dangerous Places*, London: Methuen.

Castells, M. (1993) 'European Cities: The Information Society and the Global Economy', *Tijdschrift voor Economische en Sociale Geografie* 84: 247–57.

Castells, M. (1996) *The Information Age: Economy, Society and Culture. Volume 1 – The Rise of the Network Society*, Oxford: Basil Blackwell.

Census of Population, 1991 Office of Population Censuses and Surveys, London: HMSO.

Cheshire County Council (1991) *Areas of Family Stress*, Ellesmere Port: Cheshire County Council Research and Intelligence Unit.

Cheshire County Council (1996a) *Our Cheshire (Volume C – Crime and Concerns about Crime)*, Ellesmere Port: Cheshire County Council Research and Intelligence Unit.

Cheshire County Council (1996b) *Our Cheshire (Volume D – Drugs)*, Ellesmere Port: Cheshire County Council Research and Intelligence Unit.

Cheshire County Council (1996c) *Our Cheshire (Volume J – Geographical Variations)*, Ellesmere Port: Cheshire County Council Research and Intelligence Unit.

Christie, N. (1977) 'Conflicts as Property', *British Journal of Criminology* 17, 1: 1–19.

Christie, N. (1980) *Limits to Pain*, Oslo: Universitetsforlaget.

Christie, N. (1993) *Crime Control as Industry: Towards Gulags Western Style?*, London: Routledge.

Cloke, P., Phillips, M. and Thrift, N. (1995) 'The New Middle Classes and the Social Constructs of Rural Living', in T. Butler and M. Savage (eds) *Social Change and the Middle Classes*, London: University College London Press.

Cohen, S. (1972) *Folk Devils and Moral Panics*, Harmondsworth: Penguin.

Cohen, S. (1985) *Visions of Social Control*, Cambridge: Polity.

Cohen, S. and Young, J. (eds) (1973) *The Manufacture of News*, London: Constable.

Crawford, A. (1997) *The Local Governance of Crime: Appeals to Partnerships and Community*, Oxford: Clarendon.

Cressey, D.R. (1974) 'Law, Order and the Motorist', in R. Hood (ed.) *Crime, Criminology and Public Policy*, London: Heinemann Educational Books.

Crow, G. and Allen, P. (1994) *Community Life: An Introduction to Local Social Relations*, Brighton: Harvester.

Damer, S. (1974) 'Wine Alley: The Sociology of a Dreadful Enclosure', *Sociological Review* 22: 221–48.

Davis, J. (1990) *Youth and the Condition of Britain: Images of Adolescent Conflict*, London: Athlone.

Davis, M. (1990) *City of Quartz: Excavating the Future in Los Angeles*, London: Vintage.

Dennis, N. (ed.) (1997) *Zero Tolerance: Policing a Free Society*, London: Institute of Economic Affairs.

Dingwall, G. and Moody, S. (eds) (forthcoming) *Crime and Conflict in the Countryside*, Cardiff: University of Wales Press.

Donnelly, P.G. (1988) 'Individual and Neighborhood Influences on Fear of Crime', *Sociological Focus* 22: 69–85.

Douglas, M. (1986) *Risk Acceptability According to the Social Sciences*, London: Routledge & Kegan Paul.

Douglas, M. (1992) *Risk and Blame: Essays in Cultural Theory*, London: Routledge.

Dowds, L. and Ahrendt, D. (1996) 'Fear of Crime', in R. Jowell, J. Curtice, A. Park, L. Brook, D. Ahrendt and K. Thomson (eds) *British Social Attitudes 12th Report*, Aldershot: Dartmouth/SCPR.

Durkheim, E. (1992)[1957] *Professional Ethics and Civic Morals*, London: Routledge.

Eck, J. and Weisburd, D. (eds) (1995)*Crime and Place*, Monsey, New York: Criminal Justice Press.

Ehrenreich, B. (1990) *Fear of Falling: The Inner Life of the Middle-Class*, New York: Harper-Perennial.

Ellin, N. (ed.) (1997) *Architecture of Fear*, Princeton, NJ: Princeton Architectural Press.

Empson, W. (1935) *Some Versions of Pastoral*, London: Chatto and Windus.

Ericson, R. and Haggerty, K. (1997) *Policing the Risk Society*, Oxford: Clarendon.

Evans, K., Fraser, P. and Walklate, S. (1996) 'Whom Can You Trust?: The Politics of "Grassing" on an Inner-City Housing Estate', *Sociological Review* 44, 3: 361–80.

Fabian, J. (1983) *Time and the Other: How Anthropology Makes its Object*, New York: Columbia University Press.

Featherstone, M. and Lash, S. (1995) 'Globalization, Modernity and the Spatialization of Social Theory: An Introduction', in M. Featherstone, S. Lash and R. Robertson (eds) *Global Modernities*, London: Sage.

Featherstone, M., Lash, S. and Robertson, R. (eds) (1995) *Global Modernities*, London: Sage.

Feeley, M. and Simon, J. (1992) 'The New Penology: Notes on the Emerging Strategy of Corrections and its Implications', *Criminology* 30, 4: 452–74.

Fentress, J. and Wickham, C. (1992) *Social Memory*, Oxford: Basil Blackwell.

Ferraro, K. and LaGrange, R. (1987) 'The Measurement of Fear of Crime', *Sociological Inquiry* 57: 70–101.

Fielding, T. (1995) 'Migration and Middle-Class Formation in England and Wales 1981–91', in T. Butler and M. Savage (eds) *Social Change and the Middle Classes*, London: University College London Press.

Foster, J. (1990) *Villains: Crime in the Inner City*, London: Routledge.

Francis, P., Davies, P. and Jupp, V. (eds) (1997) *Policing Futures: The Police, Law Enforcement and the Twenty-First Century*, Basingstoke: Macmillan.

Fyfe, N. and Bannister, J. (1996) 'City Watching: Closed Circuit Television Surveillance in Public Spaces', *Area* 28, 1: 37–46.

Galbraith, J.K. (1993) *The Culture of Contentment*, Harmondsworth: Penguin.

Gans, H. (1967) *The Levittowners*, London: Allen Lane.

Gans, H. (1988) *Middle American Individualism*, New York: Free Press.

Gans, H. (1995) 'Urbanism and Suburbanism as Ways of Life: A Reevaluation of Definitions', in P. Kasinitz (ed.) *Metropolis: Center and Symbol of Our Times*, New York: New York University Press.

Garland, D. (1990) *Punishment and Modern Society: A Study in Social Theory*, Oxford: Clarendon.

Garland, D. (1996) 'The Limits of the Sovereign State: Strategies of Crime Control in Contemporary Society', *British Journal of Criminology* 36, 4: 445–71.

Garofalo, J. and Laub, J. (1978) 'The Fear of Crime: Broadening our Perspective', *Victimology* 3: 242–53.

Genette, G. (1982) *Figures of Literary Discourse*, Oxford: Basil Blackwell.

Gerbner, G. and Gross, L. (1976) 'Living with Television: The Violence Profile', *Journal of Communication* 26: 172–99.

Giddens, A. (1990) *The Consequences of Modernity*, Cambridge: Polity.

Giddens, A. (1991) *Modernity and Self Identity: Self and Society in the Late-Modern Age*, Cambridge: Polity.

Giddens, A. and Pierson, C. (1998) *Conversations with Anthony Giddens: Making Sense of Modernity*, Cambridge: Polity.

Gill, O. (1977) *Luke Street*, London: Macmillan.

Girling, E., Loader, I. and Sparks, R. (1998) 'A Telling Tale: A Case of Vigilantism and its Aftermath in an English Town', *British Journal of Sociology* 49, 3: 474–90.

Goldstein, H. (1990) *Problem-Oriented Policing*, New York: McGraw-Hill.

Graham, J. and Bowling, B. (1995) *Young People and Crime* (Research Study 145), London: Home Office.

Graham, S., Brown, J. and Heery, D. (1996) 'Towns on Television: CCTV in British Towns and Cities', *Local Government Studies* 22, 3: 1–27.

Gray, J. (1997) *Endgames: Questions in Late Modern Political Thought*, Cambridge: Polity.

Gusfield, J.R. (1981) *The Culture of Public Problems: Drinking-Driving and the Symbolic Order*, Chicago: Chicago University Press.

Hagan, J. (1994) *Crime and Disrepute*, Thousand Oaks, CA: Pine Forge Press.

Hale, C. (1992) *Fear of Crime: A Review of the Literature*, Canterbury: University of Kent.

Hall, S., Clarke, J., Critcher, C., Jefferson, T. and Roberts, B. (1978) *Policing the Crisis: Mugging, Law and Order and the State*, London: Macmillan.

Hamner, J. and Saunders, S. (1984) *Well-Founded Fear*, London: Hutchinson.

Hartless, J., Ditton, J., Nair, G. and Phillips, S. (1995) 'More Sinned Against than Sinning: A Study of Young Teenagers' Experiences of Crime', *British Journal of Criminology* 35, 1: 114–33.

Harvey, D. (1989) *The Condition of Postmodernity*, Oxford: Basil Blackwell.

Hauber, A., Hofstra, B., Toornvliet, L. and Zandbergen, A. (1996) 'Some New Forms of Functional Social Control in the Netherlands and their Effects', *British Journal of Criminology* 36, 2: 199–219.

Heelas, P., Lash, S. and Morris, P. (eds) (1996) *Detraditionalization: Critical Reflections on Authority and Identity*, Oxford: Basil Blackwell.

Hirschman, A. (1970) *Exit, Voice and Loyalty: Responses to Decline in Firms, Organisations and States*, Cambridge, MA: Harvard University Press.

Hoggart, R. (1993) *Townscape with Figures: Farnham – Portrait of an English Town*, London: Chatto and Windus.

Hollway, W. and Jefferson, T. (1997) 'The Risk Society in an Age of Anxiety: Situating the Fear of Crime', *British Journal of Sociology* 48, 2: 255–66.

Hollway, W. and Jefferson, T. (2000) 'The Role of Anxiety in Fear of Crime', in T. Hope and R. Sparks (eds) *Crime, Risk and Insecurity: Law and Order in Everyday Life and Political Discourse*, London: Routledge.

Home Office (1994) *Partners Against Crime*, London: Home Office.

Home Office (1997) *No More Excuses: A New Approach to Tackling Youth Crime in England and Wales*, London: Home Office.

Home Office (1998) *Reducing Offending: An Assessment of Research Evidence on Ways of Dealing with Offending Behaviour* (Research Study 187), London: Home Office.

Hood, R. (1972) *Sentencing the Motoring Offender*, London: Heinemann Educational Books.

Hope, T. (1997a) 'Inequality and the Future of Community Crime Prevention', in S.P. Lab (ed.) *Crime Prevention at a Crossroads*, Cincinnati, OH: Anderson Publishing.

Hope, T. (1997b) 'Community Crime Prevention', in M. Tonry and D. Farrington (eds) *Building a Safer Society: Strategic Approaches to Crime Prevention* (Crime and Justice, vol. 19), Chicago: University of Chicago Press.

Hope, T. (1998) 'Privatopia on Trial?: Property Guardianship in the Suburbs', in K. Painter and N. Tilley (eds) *Surveillance* (Special issue of Crime Prevention Studies), Monsey, New York: Criminal Justice Press.

Hough, M. (1995) *Anxiety about Crime: Findings from the 1994 British Crime Survey*, London: Home Office.

Hough, M. (1996) 'People Talking about Punishment', *Howard Journal of Criminal Justice* 35, 3: 191–214.

Hough, M. and Mayhew, P. (1983) *The British Crime Survey*, London: Home Office.

Hough, M. and Roberts, J. (1997) *Attitudes to Punishment: Findings from the 1996 British Crime Survey*, London: Home Office.

Hunter, A. (1987) 'The Role of Liberal Political Culture in the Creation of Middle America', *University of Miami Law Review* 42, 1: 93–126.

I'Anson, J. and Wiles, P. (1995) *The Sedgefield Community Force*, Centre for Criminological and Legal Research: University of Sheffield.

Independent Committee (1996) *The Role and Responsibilities of the Police*, London: Police Foundation/Policy Studies Institute.

Jackson, A.R. (1990) 'An Assessment of Industrial Change in Macclesfield', unpublished MA thesis, Manchester Polytechnic.

Jackson, P. (1989) *Maps of Meaning: An Introduction to Cultural Geography*, London: Routledge.

Joint Consultative Committee (1990) *Operational Policing Review*, Surbiton: Joint Consultative Committee.

Jones, T. and Newburn, T. (1996) 'The Regulation and Control of the Private Security Industry', in W. Saulsbury, J. Mott and T. Newburn (eds) *Themes in Contemporary Policing*, London: Policy Studies Institute.

Jones, T. and Newburn, T. (1998) *Private Security and Public Policing*, Oxford: Clarendon.

Jordan, B. and Arnold, J. (1995) 'Democracy and Criminal Justice', *Critical Social Policy* 15, 2: 170–82.

Kasperson, R. (1992) 'The Social Amplification of Risk: Progress in Developing an Integrative Framework', in S. Krimsky and D. Golding (eds) *Social Theories of Risk*, New York: Praeger.

Keane, J. (1996) *Reflections on Violence*, London: Verso.

Killias, M. (1990) 'Vulnerability: Towards a Better Understanding of a Key Variable in the Genesis of Fear of Crime', *Violence and Victims* 5: 97–108.

Knight, S. (1980) *Form and Ideology in Crime Fiction*, Bloomington, IN: Indiana University Press.

Krimsky, S. and Golding, D. (eds) (1992) *Social Theories of Risk*, New York: Praeger.

Lacey, N. and Zedner, L. (1995) 'Discourses of Community in Criminal Justice', *Journal of Law and Society* 22, 3: 301–25.

Lacey, N. and Zedner, L. (1998) 'Community in German Criminal Justice: A Significant Absence?', *Social and Legal Studies* 7, 1: 7–25.

Lasch, C. (1995) *The Revolt of the Elites and the Betrayal of Democracy*, New York: Norton.

Lash, S. and Urry, J. (1994) *Economies of Signs and Space*, London: Sage.

Lewis, D. and Salem, G. (1986) *Fear of Crime: Incivility and the Production of a Social Problem*, New Brunswick: Transaction Books.

Loader, I. (1996) *Youth, Policing and Democracy*, Basingstoke: Macmillan.

Loader, I. (1997a) 'Policing and the Social: Questions of Symbolic Power', *British Journal of Sociology* 48, 1: 1–18.

Loader, I. (1997b) 'Private Security and the Demand for Protection in Contemporary Britain', *Policing and Society* 7: 143–62.

Loader, I. (1999) 'Consumer Culture and the Commodification of Policing and Security', *Sociology* 33, 2: 373-92.

Logan J. and Molotch, H. (1987) *Urban Fortunes: The Political Economy of Place*, Berkeley: University of California Press.

Lynd, R. and Lynd, H. (1929) *Middletown: A Study in Contemporary American Culture*, London: Constable.

Lyon, D. (1994) *The Electronic Eye: The Rise of Surveillance Society*, Cambridge: Polity.

Macclesfield Borough Council (1995) *Planning Department Handbook 1995*, Macclesfield: MBC.

Mannheim, H. (1948) *Juvenile Delinquency in an English Middletown*, London: Routledge & Kegan Paul.

Massey, D. (1984) *Spatial Divisions of Labour*, London: Macmillan.

Massey, D. (1994) *Space, Place and Gender*, Cambridge: Polity.

Matlass, D. (1994) 'Doing the English Village 1945–1990: An Essay in Imaginative Geography', in P. Cloke, M. Doel, D. Matlass, M. Phillips and N. Thrift *Writing the Rural: Five Cultural Geographies*, London: Paul Chapman.

Maxfield, M. (1984) *Fear of Crime in England and Wales*, London: Home Office.

Measham, F., Newcombe, R. and Parker, H. (1994) 'The Normalization of Recreational Drug Use amongst Young People in North-West England', *British Journal of Sociology* 45, 2: 287–312.

Melossi, D. (1993) 'Gazette of Morality and Social Whip', *Social and Legal Studies* 2: 259–79.

Melossi, D. (1994) 'The Economy of Illegalities: Normal Crimes, Elites and Social Control in Comparative Analysis', in D. Nelken (ed.) *The Futures of Criminology*, London: Sage.

Melossi, D. (1998) 'Remarks on Social Control, State Sovereignty and Citizenship in the New Europe', in V. Ruggiero, N. South and I. Taylor (eds) *The New European Criminology: Crime and Social Order in Europe*, London: Routledge.

Merry, S. (1981) *Urban Danger: Life in a Neighborhood of Strangers*, Philadelphia, PA: Temple University Press.

Morgan, R. and Newburn, T. (1997) *The Future of Policing*, Oxford: Oxford University Press.

Moriyama, T. (1995) 'The Possibilities of Situational Crime Prevention in Japan: Can Japan no Longer be a Haven of Safety?', paper presented at the British Criminology Conference, Loughborough University, July.

Nelken, D. (1994) 'Whom can you Trust?: The Future of Comparative Criminology', in D. Nelken (ed.) *The Futures of Criminology*, London: Sage.

Newby, H. (1977) *The Deferential Worker*, London: Allen Lane.

Norris, C. and Armstrong, G. (1997) 'The Unforgiving Eye: The Social Construction of Suspicion and Intervention in CCTV Systems', paper presented to the British Criminology Conference, Belfast, July.

O'Malley, P. (1991) 'Legal Networks and Domestic Security', *Studies in Law, Politics and Society* 11: 171–90.

O'Malley, P. (1992) 'Risk, Power and Crime Prevention', *Economy and Society* 21, 3: 251–68.

Pahl, R. (1970) *Whose City?: And Other Essays on Sociology and Planning*, Harmondsworth: Penguin.

Pahl, R. (1995) *After Success: Fin-de-Siècle Anxiety and Identity*, Cambridge: Polity.

Parker, T. (1983) *The People of Providence*, London: Hutchinson.

Pavarini, M. (1997) 'Controlling Social Panic: Questions and Answers About Security in Italy at the End of the Millennium', in R. Bergalli and C. Sumner (eds) *Social Control and Political Order*, London: Sage.

Pearson, G. (1983) *Hooligan: A History of Respectable Fears*, Basingstoke: Macmillan.

Pearson, G. (1994) 'Youth, Crime and Society', in M. Maguire, R. Morgan and R. Reiner (eds) *The Oxford Handbook of Criminology*, Oxford: Oxford University Press.

Philo, C. and Kearns, G. (1993) 'Culture, History, Capital: A Critical Introduction to the Selling of Places', in G. Kearns and C. Philo (eds) *Selling Places: The City as Cultural Capital, Past and Present*, Oxford: Pergamon Press.

Pickering, M. (1997) *History, Experience and Cultural Studies*, Basingstoke: Macmillan.

Pred, A. (1983) 'Structuration and Place: On the Becoming of Sense of Place and the Structure of Feeling', *Journal of the Theory of Social Behaviour* 13, 1: 45–68.

Rapport, N. (1993) *Diverse World-Views in an English Village*, Edinburgh: Edinburgh University Press.

Reiner, R. (1992) *The Politics of the Police* (2nd edition), Brighton: Harvester.

Ricoeur, P. (1981) *Hermeneutics and the Human Sciences*, Cambridge: Cambridge University Press.

Robertson, R. (1995) 'Glocalization: Time–Space and Homogeneity–Heterogeneity', in M. Featherstone, S. Lash and R. Robertson (eds) *Global Modernities*, London: Sage.

Rose, D. (1984) 'Rethinking Gentrification: Beyond the Uneven Development of Marxist Urban Theory', *Environment and Planning D: Society and Space* 2: 47–74.

Rose, N. (1996) '"The Death of the Social?": Refiguring the Territory of Government', *Economy and Society* 25, 3: 327–56.

Ruggiero, V., South, N. and Taylor, I. (eds) (1998) *The New European Criminology: Crime and Social Order in Europe*, London: Routledge.

Sampson, R. and Wilson, W.J. (1995) 'Towards a Theory of Race, Crime and Urban Inequality', in J. Hagan and R. Peterson (eds) *Crime and Inequality*, Stanford, CA: Stanford University Press.

Sampson, R., Raudenbush, S. and Earls, F. (1997) 'Neighborhoods and Violent Crime: A Multilevel Study of Collective Efficacy', *Science* 277, 15 August: 918–24.

Sasson, T. (1995) *Crime Talk: How Citizens Construct a Social Problem*, New York: Aldine de Gruyter.

Sasson, T. and Nelson, M. (1996) 'Danger, Community and the Meaning of Crime Watch: An Analysis of the Discourses of African American and White Participants', *Journal of Contemporary Ethnography* 25, 2: 171–200.

Savage, M. and Warde, A. (1993) *Urban Sociology, Capitalism and Modernity*, Basingstoke: Macmillan.

Scheingold, S. (1991) *The Politics of Street Crime: Criminal Process and Cultural Obsession*, Philadelphia, PA: Temple University Press.

Shapland, J. and Vagg, J. (1988) *Policing by the Public*, London: Routledge.

Shearing, C. and Stenning, P. (1983) 'Private Security: Implications for Social Control', *Social Problems* 30, 5: 493–506.

Sheptycki, J. (1995) 'Transnational Policing and the Making of a Postmodern State', *British Journal of Criminology* 35, 4: 613–35.

Sherman, L., Gartin, P. and Buerger, M. (1989) 'Hot Spots of Predatory Crime: Routine Activities and the Criminology of Place', *Criminology* 27, 1: 27–55.

Shichor, D. and Sechrest, D.K. (1996) *Three Strikes and You're Out: Vengeance as Public Policy*, Thousand Oaks, CA: Sage.

Shields, R. (1991) *Places on the Margin: Alternative Geographies of Modernity*, London: Routledge.

Shiner, M. and Newburn, T. (1997) 'Definitely Maybe Not? The Normalisation of Recreational Drug Use Amongst Young People', *Sociology* 31, 3: 511–29.

Simon, J. (1993) *Poor Discipline: Parole and the Social Control of the Underclass 1890–1990*, Chicago: University of Chicago Press.

Simon, J. and Feeley, M. (1995) 'True Crime: The New Penology and Public Discourse on Crime', in T. Blomberg and S. Cohen (eds) *Punishment and Social Control*, New York: Aldine de Gruyter.

Skogan, W. (1990) *Disorder and Decline: The Spiral of Decay in American Neighborhoods*, New York: Oxford University Press.

Skogan, W. and Maxfield, M. (1981) *Coping With Crime*, Beverly Hills, CA: Sage.

Smith, D., Blagg, H. and Derricourt, N. (1988) 'Mediation in the Shadow of the Law: The South Yorkshire Experience', in R. Matthews (ed.) *Informal Justice*, London: Sage.

Smith, S. (1986) *Crime, Space and Society*, Cambridge: Cambridge University Press.

Smith, S. (1989) 'Social Relations, Neighbourhood Structure, and the Fear of Crime', in D. Evans and D. Herbert (eds) *The Geography of Crime*, London: Routledge.

Social Exclusion Unit (1998) *Bringing Britain Together: A National Strategy for Neighbourhood Renewal*, London: Stationery Office.

Sparks, R. (1992a) *Television and the Drama of Crime*, Buckingham: Open University Press.

Sparks, R. (1992b) 'Reason and Unreason in Left Realism: Some Problems in the Constitution of the Fear of Crime', in R. Matthews and J. Young (eds) *Issues in Realist Criminology*, London: Sage.

Stacey, M. (1960) *Tradition and Change: A Study of Banbury*, Oxford: Oxford University Press.

Stanko, E. (1990a) 'When Precaution is Normal: A Feminist Critique of Crime Prevention', in L. Gelsthorpe and A. Morris (eds) *Feminist Perspectives in Criminology*, Buckingham: Open University Press.

Stanko, E. (1990b) *Everyday Violence: Women's and Men's Experience of Personal Danger*, London: Pandora.

Strathern, M. (1981) *Kinship at the Core: An Anthropology of Elmdon, a Village in North-West Essex in the Nineteen-Sixties*, Cambridge: Cambridge University Press.

Strathern, M. (1982) 'The Village as an Idea: Constructs of Village-ness in Elmdon, Essex', in A.P. Cohen (ed.) *Belonging: Identity and Social Organisation in British Rural Cultures*, Manchester: Manchester University Press.

Sykes, G. and Matza, D. (1957) 'Techniques of Neutralization: A Theory of Delinquency', *American Sociological Review* 22: 664–70.

Taub, R., Taylor, D. and Dunham, J. (1984) *Paths of Neighborhood Change*, Chicago: University of Chicago Press.

Taylor, D., Taub, R. and Peterson, B. (1986) 'Crime, Community Organization and Causes of Neighborhood Decline' in R. Figlio, S. Hakim and G. Rengert (eds) *Metropolitan Crime Patterns*, Monsey, New York: Criminal Justice Press.

Taylor, I. (1995) 'Private Homes and Public Others: An Analysis of Talk About Crime in Suburban South Manchester in the mid-1990s', *British Journal of Criminology* 35, 2: 263–85.

Taylor, I. and Jamieson, R. (1998) 'Fear of Crime and Fear of Falling: English Anxieties at the Approach of the Millennium', *Archive Européenne Sociologique* 39, 1: 149–75.

Taylor, I., Evans, K. and Fraser, P. (1996) *A Tale of Two Cities: Global Change, Local Feeling and Everyday Life in the North of England – A Study in Manchester and Sheffield*, London: Routledge.

Therborn, G. (1995) *European Modernity and Beyond: The Trajectory of European Societies 1945–2000*, London: Sage.

Thompson, E.P. (1980) *Writing by Candlelight*, London: Merlin.

Thompson, J.B. (1990) *Ideology and Modern Culture*, Cambridge: Polity.

Thompson, J.B. (1996) *The Media and Modernity: A Social Theory of the Media*, Cambridge: Polity.

Tuan, Y. (1979) *Landscapes of Fear*, Oxford: Basil Blackwell.

Turner, G. (1967) *The North Country*, London: Eyre and Spottiswoode.

Turner, V. (1974) *Dramas, Fields and Metaphors: Symbolic Action in Human Society*, Ithaca, NY: Cornell University Press.

Tyler, T. and Boeckmann, R.J. (1997) 'Three Strikes and You're Out, but Why? The Psychology of Public Support for Punishing Rule Breakers', *Law and Society Review* 31, 2: 237–65.

Urry, J. (1995) 'A Middle-Class Countryside?', in T. Butler and M. Savage (eds) *Social Change and the Middle Classes*, London: University College London Press.

Waddington, P.A.J. (1993) *Calling the Police*, Aldershot: Avebury.

Walker, N. (1996) 'Defining Core Police Tasks: The Neglect of the Symbolic Dimension?' *Policing and Society*, 6: 53–71.

Walklate, S. (1997) 'Risk and Criminal Victimization: A Modernist Dilemma?', *British Journal of Criminology* 37, 1: 35–45.

Walklate, S. (1998) 'Excavating the Fear of Crime: Fear, Anxiety or Trust?', *Theoretical Criminology* 2, 4: 403–18.

Watt, P. and Stenson, K. (1997) '"It's a Bit Dodgy Around Here": Safety, Danger, Ethnicity, and Young People's Use of Public Space', in T. Skelton and G. Valentine (eds) *Cool Places: Geographies of Youth Cultures*, London: Routledge.

Weinberger, B. (1995) *The Best Police in the World: An Oral History of English Policing from the 1930s to the 1960s*, Aldershot: Scolar Press.

Weiner, M. (1981) *English Culture and the Decline of the Industrial Spirit*, Harmondsworth: Penguin.

Whyte, W.F. (1943) *Street Corner Society*, Chicago: Chicago University Press.

Williams, R. (1964) *The Long Revolution*, Harmondsworth: Penguin.

Williams, R. (1973) *The Country and the City*, London: Chatto and Windus.

Williams, R. (1981) *Culture*, London: Fontana.

Wilson, J.Q. and Kelling, G. (1982) 'Broken Windows: The Police and Neighbourhood Safety', *Atlantic Monthly* March, 29–38.

Wirth, L. (1938) 'Urbanism as a Way of Life', *American Journal of Sociology* 44: 1–24.

Wolfe, A. (1998) *One Nation, After All*, New York: Viking.

Woodiwiss, A. (1996) 'Searching for Signs of Globalisation', *Sociology* 30, 4: 799–810.

Worpole, K. (1992) *Towns for People: Transforming Urban Life*, Buckingham: Open University Press.

Wright, P. (1985) *On Living in an Old Country: The National Past in Contemporary Britain*, London: Verso.

Wynne, B. (1992) 'Risk and Social Learning: Reification to Engagement', in S. Krimsky and D. Golding (eds) *Social Theories of Risk*, New York: Praeger.

Wynne, B. (1996) 'May the Sheep Safely Graze?: A Reflexive View of the Expert–Lay Knowledge Divide', in S. Lash, B. Szerszynski and B. Wynne (eds) *Risk, Environment and Modernity: Towards a New Ecology*, London: Sage.

Young, J. (1987) 'The Tasks Facing a Realist Criminology', *Contemporary Crises* 11, 2: 337–56.

Young, J. (1998) 'From Inclusive to Exclusive Society: Nightmares in the European Dream', in V. Ruggiero, N. South and I. Taylor (eds) *The New European Criminology: Crime and Social Order in Europe*, London: Routledge.

Zedner, L. (1995) 'In Pursuit of the Vernacular: Comparing Law and Order Discourse in Britain and Germany', *Social and Legal Studies* 4, 4: 517–34.

Index